THE CHEMISTRY OF FIRE

The Chemistry of Fire

Essays by Laurence Gonzales

The University of Arkansas Press
Fayetteville
2020

ISBN: 978-1-68226-151-4
eISBN: 978-1-61075-733-1

Manufactured in the United States of America

24   23   22   21   20   5   4   3   2   1

⊗ The paper used in this publication meets the minimum requirements
of the American National Standard for Permanence of Paper for Printed
Library Materials Z39.48-1984.

Designed by Liz Lester

Cataloging-in-Publication Data on file at the Library of Congress

"Johnny Winter" first appeared in *Playboy* in December 1974; "The Cult of War" first
appeared in *Notre Dame Magazine* in Summer 1989; "Change Redemption" first appeared
in *Men's Journal* in May 1995; "ValuJet Crash" first appeared in *Men's Journal* in September
1996; "Stealing *Titanic*" first appeared in *National Geographic Adventure* in Spring 1999;
"Space Station" first appeared in *National Geographic Adventure* in Fall 1999; "Spring
Opening" first appeared in *Men's Journal* in Fall 1997; "Hill Fever" first appeared in
National Geographic Adventure in October 2004; and "Mount Washington" first appeared
in *National Geographic Adventure* in November 2004.

This book is dedicated to
Debbie, Elena, Simon,
Amelia, Terry, Jonas,
Emmett, Carolyn Claire,
Francis Henry,
and Annelise Carolyn

Your cowardice may keep
You from your assignation with my ghost,
The love you promised me when I was dust,
Not air. And yet I cannot even sleep,
I cannot die, but I will feel my ghost

Driven to find this orchard every year,
This picnic ground, and wait till everyone
Tires of the sundown, turns the headlights on,
To float them off like moths into the dark.
I will stand up to strip my hunger off,
And stare, and mumble, knowing all your love
Is cut beside my name on the white rock,
While you forget the promise and the year.

You sat beside the bed, you took my hands;
And when I lay beyond all speech, you said,
You swore to love me after I was dead,
To meet me in a grove and love me still,
Love the white air, the shadow where it lay.
Dear love, I called your name in air today,
I saw the picnic vanish down the hill,
And waved the moon awake, with empty hands.

—JAMES WRIGHT, "The Assignation"

No one remembers. Even you, my brother,
summer afternoons you look at me as though
you meant to leave,
as though it never happened.
But I killed for you. I see armed firs,
the spires of that gleaming kiln—

Nights I turn to you to hold me
but you are not there.
Am I alone? Spies
hiss in the stillness, Hansel,
we are there still and it is real, real,
that black forest and the fire in earnest.

—LOUISE GLÜCK, "Gretel in Darkness"

CONTENTS

THE CHEMISTRY OF FIRE

· 1 ·

Mount Washington

WHEN MONROE COUPER and Erik Lattey left Harvard Cabin in Huntington Ravine, the weather was not bad, considering that they were on Mount Washington. The temperature was in the teens, and the wind gusts ranged from forty to sixty miles an hour on the summit. The weather was forecast to hold, and since they didn't plan to go to the summit, they weren't worried. They were going to climb a frozen waterfall known as Pinnacle Gully and be back at the cabin before dark. They decided to travel light and leave their larger overnight packs at the cabin.

Climbing magazine had recently published an article about an ascent of Pinnacle Gully, an exciting story of triumph over adversity, which had attracted a lot of climbers to that route. No one knows if Couper and Lattey had read it, but they were enthusiastic novice ice climbers and well may have. The story worried Mountain Rescue Service volunteers who felt that it might encourage people to push on beyond their abilities. Couper and Lattey thought of Pinnacle as an easy climb, a natural next step after the guided trips and climbs the two had completed during previous seasons. They were wrong.

While the two men were hiking up the broad and rugged trail toward Pinnacle, Alain Comeau, a leader with Mountain Rescue Service and a local guide, was taking a group up another trail. He saw fast-moving clouds on the horizon. As he said later, "I've been in the worst weather on Mount Washington." He knew how bad it could be. He started his group back down to seek shelter. Bill Aughton, director of search and rescue at the Appalachian Mountain Club, was also guiding that day. He was so impressed that he photographed the weather before turning his group around.

Comeau had guided Monroe Couper and had taught him ice climbing. "He'd had a bit of experience before that," Comeau told me. "He wanted to learn to lead. He wanted to move off on his own. But the Pinnacle was not the right next step. It's a serious climb in a serious environment. A lot of people aspire to a climb like that. Technically he could have done it, maybe, on a good day in perfect conditions. But Pinnacle is a vertical ice climb and very technical. On a scale of one to five, this is a three plus. They had all brand-new gear, too, which tells you something."

As Couper and Lattey reached the base of the gully, they realized that in their rush to get started, they had forgotten their climbing rope. It was noon by the time they'd returned to Harvard Cabin, retrieved the rope, and left again to make the strenuous hike for the third time. After that, they would have been tired and therefore much more vulnerable to hypothermia. "They definitely would have been sweaty when they started," Comeau said. "And in this environment, it's essential to stay dry."

They could have easily calculated that they no longer had the time to make the climb and descend before dark. They could have seen the weather moving in, as Comeau had. They could have recognized that leaving your rope behind is a sign of mental impairment. And even if all that evidence didn't deter them, they could have read the big yellow signs posted at the trailheads. They say, "Stop." Then in smaller letters, "The area ahead has the worst weather in America." Not some of the worst, but *the worst*. General Electric tested early turbojet engines on top of Mount Washington because of that. The notice continues unequivocally: "Many have died there from exposure, even in the summer. Turn back now if the weather is bad."

Even without the posted warning signs, they could have looked up to see what Comeau and Aughton saw.

Couper and Lattey pressed on.

. . .

The mythology is that anyone can get up Mount Washington, if not to ski, then at least to stand on top and look around. Every year, many people do. But a beautiful day on Mount Washington can turn bitter so fast that most people can't imagine it. They've never seen or felt anything like it, so they don't have that true belief we get from direct experience. Like falling into icy water, it shocks and numbs and defeats people before they have a chance to think clearly. The first person to climb Mount Washington in winter conditions was also the first person to die there. In October 1849, Frederick Strickland, an English gentleman bent on experiencing the outdoors, began his climb.

Ill-informed and ill-prepared, he succumbed to hypothermia, ripped off his clothes, and died short of the summit. Scores of people have died there. But death is only one measure of the hazards. For every body that comes back, dozens more have been injured or have suffered needlessly and have had to be rescued. As on Everest, some dead climbers have never been brought back.

Recently, I hiked up Tuckerman Ravine Trail on the first beautiful warm day of spring to see some of the half-million people who visit there each year. As I slogged up the steep, slippery slush in a dense forest of birch and pine richly floored with blowdown and the damage from ice storms, I was never out of sight of at least a dozen people on the switchbacks. The sun was warm, casting a cathedral light through the trees. I saw octogenarians in long johns and six-year-olds in high-tech, expedition-weight summit gear. There were snowshoes and no shoes and serious-looking people with ice-climbing gear. Everyone was grinning, joking, saying hi to strangers. It seemed utterly unreal that a day like this could turn nightmarish in a whiteout blizzard within a matter of minutes.

After studying accidents for decades, I had come to Tuckerman Ravine with a question in mind: How do smart, capable, even well-prepared people—people such as Monroe Couper, 40, and Erik Lattey, 28—make seemingly stupid mistakes and end up in such serious trouble? There are many happy places with dark secrets—from the beaches of southern Lake Michigan with their deadly rip currents, to Longs Peak in Colorado with its grand slippery slide that sucks people in. And when it comes to death and suffering, those places have one thing in common: people—even experienced people—underestimate the hazards and overestimate their ability to cope with them.

Located within a day's drive of nearly a quarter of the nation's population, Mount Washington is what modern-day search and rescue volunteers call "instant wilderness." (The Potomac River is another such place of high hazard and seemingly bland complexion within easy reach of millions.) We travel from the relatively safe environments of cities and suburbs, where our mistakes are generously forgiven, and we may bring with us the careless ways we've learned there. Worse still, we travel to these danger zones and have a benign experience of them (such as my experience on Mount Washington on that beautiful sunny day). And that gives us a false sense of security and a misplaced confidence.

Mount Washington, the highest peak in the Presidential Range, is only 6,288 feet high. Most people don't take it seriously. "Climbers from out west like to say that they have to dig to get to six thousand feet," Rick Wilcox told me.

He is co-owner of International Mountain Equipment and one of the founders of the specialized Mountain Rescue Service.

Rick Estes, who conceived and headed that service, says, "People come here and say, 'I've climbed K2. I've climbed Annapurna. How bad can Washington be?'"

Three major storm tracks converge on the top of Mount Washington. The jet stream runs across the summit, while the cold Labrador Current and the warm Gulf Stream meet off the coast. A local weather observer told me that this weather system is called "the exhaust pipe" of the continent.

The average wind speed on Mount Washington is 44 miles an hour in winter and 26 miles an hour in summer. Averages can be deceptive. A typical average wind speed in the lowlands is 4 to 8 miles an hour. Corrected for altitude, the wind on Mount Washington is about fifteen times stronger. Winds with the velocity of a hurricane occur on the summit two out of three days from November to April and three out of four days in January, the windiest month.

Wind itself is a deceptive force. A hurricane is defined by a wind going 73 miles an hour or more. But a wind of 100 miles an hour exerts twice the force of that. It's not linear. Nicholas Howe, an authority on accidents in the Presidential Range, wrote in his book, *Not Without Peril*, about one night when the pen went off the recording chart at 162 miles an hour: "Facing the wind made it difficult to exhale, back to the wind made it difficult to get a breath in. Strictly speaking, it was physics, but it felt like drowning in an ocean of air."

Unlike conditions in the lower elevations, where the coldest days are the calmest, Mount Washington's lowest temperatures occur along with its highest winds. Charles F. Brooks of the Mount Washington Observatory wrote, "Temperatures of 30 below zero coupled with winds in excess of 100 mph are not uncommon."

In May alone, 20 to 30 inches of snow can fall. On the summit, 250 inches of snow fall each year on average. But most of the snow that people encounter is blown to lower elevations by the wind. Nothing stays on top for long. "An inch on the summit equals a foot in the ravines," Wilcox says. At times you can see the snow boiling off the summit from miles away. It settles on the eastern side of the mountain. "There is no other mountain that has the same loading on the eastern slopes."

And yet, if Mount Washington is more extreme than other danger zones, it's not entirely exceptional, either. The fact is, most people do not die or even get seriously injured when visiting Mount Washington or other popular places where obvious hazards exist. I make a distinction between hazard and danger. Danger comes when you suspend your awareness of the hazard and refuse to change your plan.

. . .

Wet and tired before they began, Couper and Lattey struggled from the start. At Pinnacle Gully, other climbers watched the two move at an agonizingly slow pace up the first pitch of a mere 150 feet.

"They should have taken a couple of hours on that at most," Wilcox told me, "but it took them close to four hours." That should have made it obvious to Couper and Lattey that it was time to quit. "A simple rappel down to the bottom—two ice screws worth maybe fifty bucks each—what's your life worth?" Wilcox asked. "They would have come back another day."

But by then hypothermia would have had a chance to set in, as each man had to take a turn standing still in the cold to belay the other in sweaty, inadequate clothing. Whatever water they hadn't drunk would certainly have been frozen .

"If you look at the etiology of a lot of these accidents, you find that they are due to dehydration," says Maury McKinney, who is Wilcox's partner at International Mountain Sports and a member of the Mountain Rescue Service. The dehydration sets in motion a physical and mental deterioration that will eventually result in death from exposure. Add exhaustion, and the downward spiral is that much more rapid.

At the top of the first pitch, they faced another five hundred feet of climbing on similar ice. The normal turnaround time is three o'clock at the latest, but Couper and Lattey were seen there, hanging on the wall and not making good progress, at five in the evening.

"The last climbers to pass them were around three thirty–ish," Wilcox said, "and they were still a good distance from the top of the gully, maybe halfway up with four hundred feet to go. Daylight ends at four thirty or five here at that time of year. Couper and Lattey had asked the group that passed them if they'd wait at the top and show them the way down, a walk-off route." But as it grew dark, the group couldn't wait any longer.

Reaching the top, Couper and Lattey found themselves on an exposed slab, in darkness, with temperatures that were rapidly dropping toward minus twenty-five and winds rising to gusts of 108 miles an hour. Comeau said,

"There's no real way down once you get to the top. You're really exposed for a mile of horrendous travel across the Alpine Garden."

At the same time, the other climbers had made it down to Harvard Cabin and began noticing the two packs. No one in the cabin knew whom the packs belonged to. Searchers around town on this Saturday night began to hear their beepers go off.

. . .

In any hazardous situation, there are three zones: the safe zone, the danger zone, and the dead zone. By leaving the safety of the cabin and hiking up Huntington Ravine, Couper and Lattey had passed from relative safety into the danger zone out on the ice. Because of hypothermia, dehydration, and exhaustion, they were unable to process new information. "Their judgment was failing as they got deeper and deeper into trouble," said Wilcox. They had one way out, and they could no longer think clearly enough to take it.

That is the heart of the mystery of why rational people do irrational things: they were no longer making decisions. Their mistakes were all behind them, stretching back for months. Their fate was purely physical by then. Their bodies were simply going up the wall of ice without the aid of reason, following an outdated plan toward an imagined idea of rest and safety that no longer existed.

"It's the repeats that get to you," Wilcox said. We sat talking in his cluttered office at International Mountain Sports, which lies in the shadow of Mount Washington in North Conway, New Hampshire. Wilcox and McKinney can outfit and train you for anything from a day hike to an Everest expedition. (Wilcox made it up Everest himself, while McKinney climbed K2). Since 1972, Wilcox has been on more than five hundred rescue operations. After seeing the same accidents over and over again for thirty years, he said in frustration, "What am I going to do? I sell this stuff to them."

One accident repeatedly occurs on the Lion's Head Trail, the standard hiking route to the summit. It's not technical, but it is snowy. Crampons are a good idea. Up to a hundred people climb it every weekend, and at least one person a month breaks a leg. It's the same every time.

Lion's Head Trail follows a high ridge from east to west on the north headwall of Tuckerman Ravine. Going up it is straightforward but strenuous and rocky. Going down is slick and tricky. It can also be exhausting, and exhaustion always impairs judgment. Just before the trail begins to drop off the ridge back to Tuckerman Ravine Trail, it borders a long, wide, creamy-looking chute of snow that doesn't appear to be too steep. White on white is deceptive. At that point, you're well below the summit, and if you're not tired, you're a cardiovascular giant. You're probably at least a little dehydrated, too, further impairing your judgment. Your body desperately wants to stop walking downhill. And your body almost always gets what it wants. That's why people see this spot and think: I've got a great idea. I'll slide down. Glissading is a conventional mountaineering technique, but like self-arrest, it takes training and a keen eye for conditions. It also requires removing your crampons.

In seconds, you can get to going thirty miles an hour or so, a frighteningly dangerous speed when you're on your butt on a high ridge. Fear adds more stress, which confounds good judgment. With clear thinking completely out of the picture, reflex will take over, and you'll put your feet down to stop yourself. With or without crampons, your own momentum will flip you, and then you'll go cartwheeling a very long way indeed. If you're lucky, this will merely snap one or more of your leg bones. In the pack room in the basement of the Appalachian Mountain Club, a traditional meeting place, I had noticed numerous young people walking around with leg braces on. Now I knew why. Some aren't so lucky as to be walking around in braces. "After a rain, we get fatalities on that route," Wilcox noted.

McKinney had been listening to our conversation. He poked his head into the office and said, "Yeah, if you want gear, go up to the bottom of Lion's Head Trail Monday morning. Lion's Head is definitely the scene of the most accidents."

"What we need is education, respect, and common sense," Wilcox said. He pointed out the window to Cathedral Ledge, which offers great rock-climbing from easy to advanced. He said he could predict the accidents there like clockwork. In fact, some of them are the work of clocks.

"When they change the clocks in the fall, it starts getting dark at five," he explained. And every year several people do the same thing. They start climbing with their heads in the old time, get benighted on top, and decide they can tough it out, because when they began it was sixty-five or seventy degrees. They make it to nine or ten o'clock, when it gets down to about thirty degrees, and start yelling for help—that's how close to civilization they are. The base is a fifty-yard walk from a hotel parking lot. "It's only three hundred feet, two rappels. But we have to go up and get them." He threw his hands up in the air and shouted, "Can't you see the sun going down?"

The top of Cathedral Ledge is in the town of Bartlett, but the bottom is in the town of Conway, and one day when someone fell off and died, the police got into an argument over who had to clean up the mess. One of them finally shouted in frustration, "Well, he was fine when he left Bartlett!"

Climbers do notice the dark coming on, of course. But it is difficult to believe how quickly and efficiently stress can short-circuit rational thought and allow your body to take over and simply keep you moving in the wrong direction. Like Couper and Lattey, they may know the right thing to do in an intellectual sense. But reason becomes a small, far-off voice, while their bodies tell them that if only they finish the climb, they'll be fine. Rest and hot chocolate lie ahead. Keep going.

Wilcox said Couper and Lattey "had this incredible failure to change their plans, this do-or-die attitude, even after spending four or five hours on the first pitch—and that's after the debacle of leaving the rope behind." But it's more subtle than that. The word "attitude" implies thinking. They were done thinking. They were effectively zombies.

Our fate is fashioned out of more than simple mistakes. However stupid our actions may seem to others after the fact, no one sets out to be stupid. In fact, everything we do makes sense to us at the time in terms of the sum total of what we have learned. And that learning takes place in the body, beyond the reach of consciousness. Couper and Lattey's biggest mistake was never having experienced the worst weather on Mount Washington. By the time they did, it was too late to learn.

· · ·

We know what happened to Couper and Lattey when they reached the top. Long years of experience have shown that people follow a pattern of behavior shaped by physiology, psychology, terrain, and natural forces. "People won't walk into the wind when they're lost in a whiteout," Wilcox says. "They arrived there after dark. Now they're faced with no visibility, wind over a hundred miles an hour right in their faces from the direction they should be going, and they decided to hunker down below the lip, where it's sheltered."

We can safely speculate that they thought of the tents and sleeping bags and clothing they could have brought with them. Rick Estes agreed. "Rule number one, especially on Huntington, is that you should always be prepared to spend the night out."

By dawn on Sunday morning, there were thirty-three high-angle rescue climbers, including Comeau and Wilcox, at the base of Huntington Ravine. As they began working their way up, the wind reached 127 miles an hour. Soon everyone was back down in the trees. They couldn't work safely in those conditions, which have been known to freeze eyeballs.

"The accident happened on Saturday," Comeau told me, "and it wasn't until Tuesday that we got to them. The wind stays for days here. People always think that if something happens, someone will come along. But we don't always come along."

Monday morning the wind reached 128 miles an hour with temperatures down to minus fifteen degrees. Comeau, Wilcox, and the other searchers had to crawl on their bellies to keep from being blown off the mountain, which would have meant falling two thousand feet. Wilcox surmised that Couper and Lattey had started to spend the night together as early as five o'clock. Lattey had decided to go for help but was turned back by weather and terrain. He was crawling back up when he died.

It was Comeau who found Monroe Couper. He was frozen, leaning up against a cairn with his hands reaching into his pack, as if trying to get his stove to make something hot to drink. With all the wind, it took Comeau some time to realize that Erik Lattey lay close by. His face was in the rocks, his arms reaching up toward Couper. "They were ten feet apart," Wilcox recalls. They were also only a quarter mile from an auto road and a way down. They had no map or compass.

· · ·

Most of our actions, most decisions about what to do next, take place without conscious thought. Joseph LeDoux, a neuroscientist famous for his research into how the emotional system works to generate behavior, has concluded that for the most part, we do things and then make up stories to explain what we've done so that it seems consistent with our view of who we are and what our lives are like. That sounds ridiculous if we think of ourselves as fundamentally rational creatures. But brain research dating back to the early 1970s is leading inexorably to that conclusion. So-called implicit learning or emotional learning is more powerful than conscious intellectual learning because it drives behavior. It is all the more powerful as a motivator of behavior because it is unconscious. We make decisions based on it all the time. Part of the proof for this is that people who have suffered damage in the areas of the brain that mediate emotional learning can't make decisions at all.

LeDoux writes, "In modern life, we sometimes suffer from the exquisite operations of this system, since it is difficult to get rid of this kind of conditioning once it is no longer applicable to our lives." That is why having a lovely experience in a place that can turn horrible may set a trap for us by shaping the way we unconsciously make decisions. It's like winning on your first visit to the casino. It will forever after seem like an attractive place, whereas in reality, you are certain to lose.

In other words, we have developed an adaptation to one environment, and we fail to take into account the fact that some environments—such as the seas and mountains and canyons and stock markets of the world—are subject to huge and sudden changes. At the same time, we give too much credit to our intellect and overestimate its power over the real learning we possess, which is buried within us: the emotional learning that resides in the body.

Many other scientists (such as Michael Gazzaniga, John Krakauer, and Antonio Damasio) are involved in related research. This new research has far-reaching implications, especially regarding hazardous environments. It suggests that conscious, rational, stepwise thought is not the giant we take it to be. It is instead a ghostly companion to our bodily behavior, only vaguely and imperfectly guiding it. Under stress or in high emotional states, it becomes a faint echo that is all too easy to ignore.

Certainly, the mind's ability to plan ahead is a useful and efficient tool. But in that very utility is a trap. We have to be able to continuously review plans in the light of new developments. We have to remain flexible.

Wilcox notes that he lives in the shadow of Mount Washington. Any day that the weather is nice, he can get up there in a short time, hike or ice climb, and "be home for beer call," as he put it. Thinking about Couper and Lattey and numerous others whose bodies he's retrieved, he adds, "They've been planning this for months. To them, it's the big trip, a once in a lifetime thing. Like Everest was for me."

Once the plan has become unshakable, it's easy to ignore new information or to unconsciously interpret it as favorable to that plan. For example, instead of interpreting "iffy weather" as meaning that it might be bad, you'll interpret it as "It'll probably be okay." Making matters worse, Couper and Lattey underestimated the severity of the cold they faced. Their lack of equipment (no down parkas, mittens, or tent) testifies to the fact that they had not experienced such extreme weather, had not had that crucial opportunity to let the body learn. Monroe Couper was a smart guy. A composer, he was also an associate professor of music at Kingsborough Community College in Brooklyn. But an inflexible plan—which had developed through stress, bodily innocence, and a few miscalculations—left him and Lattey vulnerable in an environment where everything they'd learned was wrong. They were operating in an imagined world that no longer existed.

. . .

Before I left Mount Washington, I sat in the lobby of the rundown Eastern Slope Inn in North Conway with Rick Estes, recently retired from the rescue service. Estes was a powerfully built man with the brush-cut moustache of a previous generation of outdoorsmen. He had the philosophical demeanor of someone who'd spent way too many years watching way too many people hurt themselves in the same predictable and avoidable ways.

Despite all the efforts, from public relations to legal remedies, the same accidents continue to happen year after year. "We had so many in 2000, I don't remember them all," Estes said. "We were running out of funds. Thanksgiving Day we ran out of volunteers. There were just horrendous cases."

The Falling Waters Trail leads up from Franconia Notch State Park to the summit of Little Haystack Mountain. The gradient is steep, and the drop-off from the trail is a long one. A favorite viewpoint is at a place called Shining Rock, a two-hundred-foot granite ledge kept wet and slippery by springs coming out of the forest. Estes recalled for me a guy and his girlfriend who were hiking up during that bad year. The girl got tired and decided to go back down, while the guy continued on up, taking his camcorder so he could show her what she'd missed. "He beat her down," Estes said. "We picked up his brain in a bread bag, which was all we had with us."

Estes watched the tape from the shattered video camera. It showed the man's feet on the green wet slime that covered the rock from which he'd slipped. Then: nothing.

The forest is littered with such stories, and most of them lead us back to simple principles. Estes and most others I talked to believe that as a nation, we have made ourselves less self-reliant by creating what he calls "magic wands," such as GPS and cell phones. But everything in our culture, from warning labels on McDonald's cups that coffee is hot to personal injury lawsuits, encourages us to hand over responsibility to someone else. In his novel *1984*, George Orwell called it "protective stupidity."

"You usually find people with brand-new packs and a stove that's never been started," Estes said. "They call and say something like 'I'm lost, but I can hear the cars.' What do you say to someone like that?" Estes had recently retired from the Fish and Game Department, which oversees search and rescue activities. He sighed, thinking over his career.

As long as there are moody places in this world, beaches and mountains and canyons and forests that can go from paradise to hell in minutes, there will be people lost and hurt and killed in them. In the larger system that puts millions out there each year—a complex system that arose from the availability of transportation, the inducements of advertising and hype, the money that allowed people to get there, and the proximity of people—there's no way to stop the accidents from happening. But we can stop them from happening to us.

· 2 ·

Change Redemption

THE LARGEST HUMAN penis in captivity hangs just off the lobby of Caesars Palace among the shops displaying Italian cowboy clothing and jewelry for the blind. It hangs from an immense reproduction of Michelangelo's *David*, and anyone passing through the vaulted hall of mirrors known as the Appian Way is suddenly confronted with David's mammoth toes on their pedestal. By reflex we look up: our view slides quite naturally skyward along the towering muscle-bound column of wax-white marble, and there, six feet up, illuminated in a spotlight diffused by smoke, hangs La Tremenda, the greatest *pinga* on earth, gently supported on the clement pillow of that stone-cold scrotum.

It's a shock. I know. But this is no place for shame. This is Las Vegas, home of Liberace, whose red-white-and-blue-sequined hot-pants tuxedo made Elvis Presley look positively Amish.

I checked in on a Friday. The room had Doric columns. The bathroom had a jacuzzi and glass walls, parts of which were transparent and translucent but none of which was quite opaque enough for a midwestern sensibility. When it comes to outhouses, we lean toward wood.

I do not try to hide the fact that I am an adrenaline junky. I like shape-shifting and rapid changes in altitude. But this whole thing—the giant penis, the glass bathroom, the guy on the house TV channel explaining how to play baccarat—made my hair stand up. Already I understood that sex and gambling were connected, that sex was the voltage that ran Las Vegas. The act of gambling tapped into something primal. Freud, who believed that it was a subliminal ritual of masturbation, spent a great deal of time analyzing Dostoevsky's obsession with gambling and how it seemed to propel his literary powers. When Fyodor would lose everything, he'd write real hard to pay his debts. There was nothing mystical or even symbolic about it.

For years I have traveled to exotic places to write these essays. For years I have asked my friends to join me on my trips, but few have accepted. There's always an excuse: family, work, obligations, inertia. When I said I was going to Las Vegas, my friends Jan and Don, who have a chain of bookstores, bought their tickets immediately and made our reservations at Caesars Palace. I happened to mention my travel plans to fellow writer Larry "Butch" DuBois, and he said without hesitation, "I'll drive over from Salt Lake City." When I asked him about the lure of Las Vegas, he said, "Gambling is the most powerful drug in the world. Second only to pussy."

When I told my Los Angeles movie agents, Rich Green and Howie Sanders, they said they'd meet me there and we could go over my screenwriting projects. Important agent-client bonding time, they called it. Tony Bill, another good friend, a producer and director from Los Angeles, flew his Cessna 310 out. ("The last time I was here," he said, "was at the Tailhook convention, and Helen got her butt pinched.") Fellow screenwriter David Klass (also a client of Rich and Howie) hitched a ride with Tony. A Rick and a second Don used some frequent-flier miles to join our growing group. Everyone I talked to about Las Vegas said, "Oh, I hate Vegas. It's too—tasteless. I hate it, I just *hate* it . . ." Before the weekend was out, there were ten of us gathered there, throwing dice and playing blackjack and giving away to slot machines dollars that we wouldn't have given to a beggar.

Caesars Palace was one of the few places left in the grand old tradition, booming at midnight the week before Christmas, jammed cheek by jowl with Cubano-smoking gamblers on a Sunday morning, while the cellar Christians were off to the catacombs to kneel and whimper. Caesars is a high-rolling casino for adult gamblers with a private casino upstairs for the highest of rollers who want quiet and privacy. The $7 million dollar suites are legendary. They are not for rent at any price. They are saved as comps for certain very special people who bet a great deal at the gaming tables, such as a Middle Eastern prince or a great sports star.

$$\bullet \quad \bullet \quad \bullet$$

As the elevator opened we were hit by blinding light and deafening noise. Jan and Don and I entered tremendous rooms of urgent concentration, vast sweatshops of citizens, rump to groin, bent to their tasks amid the stridor of singing machines, the clattering implements of their labors. They sat hunched over the radar screens of electronic poker like a thousand air traffic controllers guiding the airmail through Andean winter storms. There were no smoke-free environments in Las Vegas, except perhaps the intensive care unit, and a tawny pall drifted like a tapestry of seine nets through the measureless arena and was caught in the sheaf of beams descending from spotlights in the ceiling and twisted in them, breaking slowly into curlicues like tallow being squeezed out by these very animal labors at the hands of this seemingly impossible industry, in which the workers pay the proprietors for the privilege of their toil. And rising above it through the murk, a sign said, "Change Redemption." It struck me as an oddly spiritual concept in the midst of all this avaricious compulsion until I realized that it was referring to coins, not souls.

Don approached a pit boss surrounded by his fortifications of blackjack tables and waved him over. A moment later this clean young man in his good suit, like a maître d', brought Don a plastic clipboard with a carbon form to sign. They no longer call him a "pit boss." The word "gambling" is no longer in use. It's "pit manager" and "gaming." So this middle-management fellow signaled to the nearest dealer, who gave Don a single yellow chip.

"What's that?" I asked as we walked away from the transaction. Don handed it to me. My heart leapt when I saw the value. "One chip?" I asked. "A thousand dollars?"

"That's it," said Don, a lawyer from Chicago, who had been playing the stock market since the age of fifteen. As we crossed the casino, he flipped the chip like a quarter and mused, "You know, I trade hundreds of thousands of dollars in stocks. I move large sums of money around, and often the money is at just as much risk as it would be in this place. But my little five-dollar bet at the blackjack table gives me more adrenaline than forty-five hundred shares of Ford. Explain that."

Jan and Don selected a table and sat down. I stood behind them to watch. He flipped the yellow chip one last time and then pushed it across the green felt to the dealer, and I could feel my heart reach out to the chip: Good-bye, little yellow chip. Be safe. We could have had a pacemaker installed for that price.

The dealer, an attractive woman in her thirties, made change without looking up. There is no point in trying to impress a dealer in Las Vegas. They've seen it all. If you stood on your head and $1,000 bills flew out of your butt, they'd simply convert them to chips and deal another hand. Don pushed $500 over to his wife, Jan, and they ponied up a red chip each. The dealer dealt. I stayed to see her bust and pay Jan and Don and then deal again, setting the cards on the table with a soft and reassuring pop.

I crossed through whirling lights, insistent bells, and the clatter of coins as the slots paid off into metal buckets. I passed a cordoned-off area where a well-dressed woman fed $500 tokens into a machine and pulled the lever with wan disinterest and lost and pulled again and lost again. I crossed the immense sports book with a wall of televisions and comfortable theater seating. I pressed on to find a craps table that had my name on it.

I selected a five-dollar table where a number of people were playing with the concentration of cats watching a beetle. Nearly everyone was losing. Craps gurus say to watch before you play, to look for "a good table." My math wizard at Bell Labs, Lorraine, said that the tide of probability runs out, but it runs back in. Mathematicians call that "standard deviation." If you flip a coin, it might come up heads ten times in a row. That's standard deviation. But the longer you keep flipping, the closer your score will come to approximating a fifty-fifty split of heads and tails. It's those excursions of standard deviation that make it possible to win at games of chance, as long as you're willing to quit. And as long as you're betting at *correct odds*. In the case of flipping a fair coin, correct odds works something like this: If the coin comes up heads, you pay me one dollar. If it comes up tails, I pay you one dollar. You can reverse tails and heads and make the payout any amount. But the point is that we will wind up even if we play for long enough. In a casino, if the coin comes up tails, you pay the house a dollar. If it comes up heads, the house pays you ninety cents (or some other amount that is less than a dollar). That's why the casino always wins unless you quit while you're on one of the excursions in your favor. And that's why the casino wants you to keep playing.

I walked around the pit looking for someone to ask about my misgivings. I had played craps in casinos for money only three or four times in my life. But I had read about it. Now I sought out one last authority before putting my money down: the pit boss. She was an attractive woman of forty with a good suit and a sense of humor, and she told me to bet five dollars on the pass line (the minimum bet) and ten on the odds. That way the dealer could always pay me nearly the correct odds. It didn't matter what number came up. This is a critical concept: receiving correct odds on any bet was the only way to reduce the house advantage. Correct odds with a coin is simple, because there are only two sides to the coin and you're betting on an event in which either outcome is equally likely. A die in the game of craps has six sides. And the game uses two dice. So odds are more complicated, but the casino allows you to bet on those odds and is willing to pay out correctly on those odds, even while cheating you on the original bet of five dollars on the pass line. I know: I was confused, too, at first. But following the advice given to me by the pit boss is the best bargain in the house.

The pit boss wished me luck and said, "We want you to win." It's true. Since the casino does not pay correct odds, it makes money even when we win. Since experts call the house advantage "the most important concept in gambling," it's sad that most people aren't familiar with it. It's like playing tennis without knowing that the ball has to go over, not under, the net.

I remember standing with Jan one night, watching a man at the craps table. He had a long stack of pale purple chips in the wooden rack before him. The purple chips are worth $500 each. He was a studious-looking fellow with steel spectacles and a tweedy coat and scuffed tan sued lace-up shoes. He looked like a college professor in his forties. Thinning hair. Didn't say a word. After each decision, he'd play the pass line with one pale purple chip, and when a point was rolled, he'd back it with double odds—two purple chips, or $1,000, for a total wager of $1,500. We watched him carefully. He won and won, but when the tide of standard deviation turned and he began to lose, he picked up his chips and gave them to the dealer. "Color me," he said, and the dealer gave him chips in denominations of $5,000, which the man dumped into the big sagging pockets of his jacket as he walked away.

After my conversation with the pit boss, I returned to the table and dropped a $100 bill on the felt with a deep sense of the picayune nature of that denomination. This effect of relativity, I understood, was part of the strategy of the casino: Where else was a $1,000 going to seem ordinary, $100 seem trifling? And where else would their loss seem less than catastrophic? Everything in the casino was bigger than we were, and as we grew, we participated in that giddy bigness while escaping the sense of loss as we shrank back to our normal size once more. And we always shrink back unless we run screaming into the street to board the first taxi to the airport. The Alice-in-Wonderland effect.

Steve Wynn founded the Mirage. He's principally responsible for turning Las Vegas into a family vacation destination. Once he was going over the take for a single day at his Mirage, and the number in his hand was $3.6 million, higher than expected. You'd think that if games of chance are ruled by probability, Steve Wynn could predict the day's take rather accurately. Not so. Standard deviation rules (gamblers call it luck). The reason for the abnormally large take was a single baccarat player, who had won $1.5 million the night before during a standard deviation event in his favor. He had unwisely stayed at the table, losing a total of $7 million during the course of the evening. He got big. But then he got small again. Very small. Welcome to Wonderland.

The boxman shoved my trifling bill down a rabbit hole, and it was gone like a gum wrapper. The nearest dealer gave me twenty red chips. I love the way they handle the chips in that ritual transformation. There is a prestidigitation in the way a good dealer manipulates chips and in his coordination with the boxman in making money vanish and gaming chips appear. The fingers have such a sure grip on the smooth clay chips, which click and chatter like castanets as he stacks them up in exact accounts of change and wins and losses. I picked them up. The chips were cool and smooth and heavy. They smelled like new earth. They had a character so real, like phonograph records from the 1920s, it seemed they would break if I dropped them. A delightful attachment to them, a trembling wave of emotion, grew and swelled within me. Paradoxically, they were both money and not money. An experiment was done with apes in which they were asked to choose between two piles of candy, one large, one small. Whichever pile they chose was given to their mates. But the apes could not stop themselves from taking the larger pile of candy, even as they learned that selecting the large pile meant losing it. But when researchers gave the apes numerical symbols (i.e., chips) to represent the two amounts, the apes were able to overcome their survival instinct and make the correct decision, to take the smaller pile in order to receive the larger amount of candy in the end. Money is how we obtain food and clothing and shelter, our channel of survival on this earth. We are the apes in this experiment, and these chips are our symbolic candy. For most of us, it would be a stretch to play these games with real money. But the chips are also part of our ritual of magical thinking. They are played in a spiritual test of who we are.

I laid the chips in the wooden tray before me. Jan came up and slipped her arm in mine. "What's the word?" she said.

"You and Don winning?" I asked.

"A little. I want to learn craps," she said. "And I want to teach you roulette." Jan was a tall and fit and blond California goddess who played a lot of tennis and rode horses and drove a little red convertible that Don had bought her for her birthday. Jan had read just about everything that had ever been printed with ink, and I recall that in our youth the men fell before her as if they'd been hit by a stand of grapeshot. She was writing a big book on Los Alamos National Laboratory for Simon & Schuster. And in the late sixties and early seventies, we had been as close as two people can be.

A young woman in a red blazer was coming out, and the croupier was absently pushing six dice around with his stick, waiting for everyone to place bets. "Coming out" means throwing the dice for the first time in a round of play. The rules for the first throw of the dice are different from those for the subsequent throws. I dropped a red chip on the pass line, explaining to Jan as I went: "I'm going play the same way that that tweedy fellow with the pale purple chips played."

"God, I hope not," she said.

"I'm going to bet one one-hundredth of what he bet."

The croupier pushed the dice toward the woman in red and said, "Coming out." Fighter pilots and croupiers both have an economy of words that is almost codelike in its frugality. The woman picked up two of the six dice that were offered to her, the croupier returned the rest to the boxman, and the woman threw a seven.

"Seven a winner, winner seven," the croupier said and set a red chip beside mine in payment of my bet.

"That's easy," Jan said. "I can do that."

"Just do what I do," I said.

It happened fast, like the first time I rolled an airplane upside down. I didn't have time to worry. I felt the adrenaline, then it was over. Weird. It was only $5, so where did this sense of tremendous peril come from? You cannot buy $5 worth of any drug that will do that. Secondly, it was not even my $5. I was a journalist on assignment. I had a gambling budget of $500 of *their* money. I could lose $500 and still make a profit, because I get paid to write this stuff. So: Where was that hard rush coming from?

I picked up the $5 chip I'd won as the dealer paid off other bets. I left my original bet in place for the next roll. Jan placed her bet next to mine. I felt the pressure rising in my chest as the woman in red shot again. She raised her fist in the air and shook the dice in a decidedly Freudian gesture and then fired them off across the felt, which under the hot lights was as green as a hayfield at sunrise. Six.

"Now what?" Jan asked, sounding disappointed that she didn't get another red chip.

"She'll roll until the dice come up six again, in which case we win, or until she gets a seven, in which case we lose." I showed her how to put two more red chips behind the pass line for the all-important odds bet of ten dollars. This was the only bet in the house that would be paid at *correct odds*. It is interesting, therefore, that it is the only bet in craps that is not depicted on the layout.

New gamblers were drawn from the crowd by the woman in the red blazer, who rolled and rolled and did not lose. This is the meaning of craps: to have a beautiful woman in red roll and roll and never lose. The distant clamor of the casino fell away in a curtain of smoke, and the hard spotlight on the green felt seemed to define the only world we knew. I felt my heart race. My face grew cool with apprehension. Jan and I were winning. My heart soared like a hawk. With a sudden clarity, I saw how much sense this game made. I understood it. The dealer paid us twelve dollars against our ten-dollar odds bets, and we removed all except the single red chip for our next pass-line bet. I felt myself growing. I had thrown my test on the waters of fate, and the answer came back about who I was: I was a winner. My fingers worked the stack of chips in the beautifully constructed wooden tray before me.

The table was a lovely boat of handmade wood and Simonis number-two woolen felt, imprinted with the legends of the ancient game. I felt myself falling into the table. Yes. Jan and I would stay here forever. This would be our new home. I loved this table, this beautiful pea-green boat and plenty of money and the shiny red dice with their sharp and gleaming edges, honed to within one ten-thousandth of an inch, flying through the air and hitting the foam baffle at the far end. I loved the shooter, her blond hair flying, her well-cut blazer, and I imagined her in her other life, in her office back east (or west), commanding executive power. I loved the soothing murmur of the croupier as he commented on the play, cataloging the items being bought and sold in a constant stream of transactions like the barter on the floor of a commodities exchange, and I especially loved the clickety-clack as the dealer paid off bets and the boxman stacked the winnings.

The boxman sat hoarding his great piles of chips like a demon king, a knotted-up dwarf with horrible afflictions of the skin that had healed years before, leaving him with a waxlike countenance of ferocious unfriendliness and the grim certitude born of naked statistical destiny. His beady eyes peered out from the prison of his colorless flesh, and as he absently sucked on the stump of a cigar, a blue curl of smoke traced the outline of his bent head and filtered through his thinning hair.

I was struck by the pile of chips before him. There were the stacks of black hundreds, green twenty-fives, and red fives, dozens in each stack. There were tall pillars of purple $500 chips (called whites because they were once white). There were a couple of stacks of yellow $1,000 chips. And on top of all those stacks, scattered about in lonely profusion, were "chocolate" chips worth $5,000 each. I found the concept staggering and asked the dealer, "Do people really bet with those?"

He looked at me with contempt. "Yes, they do, sir," said a gravelly voice from a cave. "All the time."

The boxman's fat and nervous fingers, adorned with heavy rings, were guarding more than $500,000 at this low-end craps table. And everywhere hived within the thunderous drone of the casino were tables just like this one and, on each one, a pile as big or bigger. I felt myself growing faint at the concept of the amount of money that was gathered here—a million at least between us and the next table, and there were tables as far as the eye could see.

We were in a veritable mint, and not an armed guard in sight. The stuff had a gravity all its own, a power and pull, like some superelement so strong that it warped space and pulled light down into it.

Lost in my reverie, I heard the croupier say, "Seven out" as he raked our chips away.

"Can't win 'em all," Jan said, and the shooter's turn passed to her. She was suddenly alarmed. "I've never shot before," she said.

"Yeah," I said, "but you've trekked across a nuclear test site and hiked the Australian outback. You lived in Ecuador, and you can ride a horse backwards. Are you telling me you can't throw those two little dice across this table?"

"You're right," she said, shaking the dice, as an enormous gentleman stepped up to the opposite end of the table clicking a handful of hundred-dollar chips thoughtfully and scowled down at the green felt. Jan threw the dice as hard as she could, and they bounced off his chest, and one of them vanished into the big pockets of his workout suit. His regal countenance gathered in concentration as he digested the insult that had befallen him. Jan reared back a little. Then the man burst into a big grin, retrieved the lost die from his pocket, and tossed it back onto the table. The dice were given to Jan again.

"Hit the other end of the table," I said. And she did.

She rolled seven, and we took five each and left one down. She rolled nine. We added ten for our odds. She won again. We were in harmony with the rolling tide of probability, a mystical union such as surfers must feel entering the long blue luminescence of the tubular wave world.

Jan rolled and rolled. We won and won. She was blond and tall and graceful, and she smiled at me as she threw. "I like this game," she said. She was hot. She was red hot. This was the meaning of craps.

She asked the dealer, "How long have you seen a shooter go without losing?"

"More than an hour," he said with no expression.

Indeed, there are legendary stories about "the unfinished hand," supposedly the longest run in craps history, which took place between 2:00 and 3:30 a.m. in February 1947, at the 86 Club in Miami. A car dealer from Detroit held the dice for an hour and a half without crapping out, and the players at the table collectively won $300,000 before the casino managers declared the bank broke and shut the place down for the night. Not very standard but a standard deviation nevertheless.

When we pulled Don away from the table, he was up, too. With the self-satisfied smugness of winners, we went to an Italian restaurant called Spago.

We were gracious. The world fell before our footsteps. "Isn't this a great place to be the week before Christmas?" Jan said.

• • •

Some days I'd drive out in the desert and look back at Las Vegas and wonder what it was, this cracked crystal city swimming in a pool of its own yellow protoplasmic smoke, like the nucleus of some alien amoeba that had fallen from the stars and landed and lodged in the parabolic reach of the Mormon Mountains.

As I stood out in the vast and consuming beauty of the desert, among the upthrust rock formations, under a huge white setting moon that floated on a barge of clouds with its dipolar opposite, the rising sun, so bright I couldn't see in that direction, a cold wind issued off the last edges of the night. No cars came past out on this lonely highway, which grew faint as a thread and vanished in the shimmering distance. Like the shifting adumbral dreams of night being cast out, the mountains awakened from those shadows and the steeply rising land as the bowl of the land filled with luminescent mist. An inert snake lay cold on a rock, awaiting the first feeble rays. Moon dissolved in cloud. A mislaid flock of Canada geese crossed the desert sun.

Amid low yucca and sage brush, I headed into the Moapa Valley against a perfect blue sky. An hour later in Logandale I rolled past a cattle ranch that abuts the town's main street. Strange sights there to see: tumbledown grain silos very like the ones back home in the corn-growing Midwest. What history bestowed such monolithic reliquaries of rime-leeched masonry on this desert?

I stopped at the Lost City Museum, with its thirty miles of ruins from 1150 AD. The houses lay crumbling in the scorpion's northernmost habitat. From the asphalt parking lot, I crossed a small wooden footbridge over a narrow muddy stream and walked up the hill past the museum to look through an adobe ruin out back by the highway. It had been restored to its original conformation. I climbed into its rooms, none larger than a modern bathroom, some smaller. The Anasazi had vanished hundreds of years before, leaving only shards and pictograms. No one, so the sign said, knows why they went away.

It was eight in the morning when the old park ranger with a goatee arrived in a white pickup truck and got out in his army-green windbreaker and hard cotton slacks that were shiny from wear. He opened the museum house and stood outside smoking a Winston cigarette in the morning air. I said good morning and then asked him why there were grain silos out there in the desert. He snorted and laughed. "Ohhhh," he said, as if he'd been waiting for someone to ask that very question. "That's from the days when this whole valley was rich in corn and alfalfa and dairy farms."

"Corn?" I asked. "Out here?"

"Buddy," he said, "it was all irrigated off the Muddy River and the Virgin River."

"How?" I asked.

"It's these ditches you see everywhere," he said. "You walked over one right back there by the parking lot." His complexion was pale and wind blotched, and he wore black plastic spectacles. "In 1962 when I came here, this valley was green. I mean *green*. They grew cotton down there," he said, pointing east. "We grew all the tomato plants for the state of California right here. Had dairy farms with hundreds of cows and grew our own feed. And all of it irrigated from those ditches, just like the Pueblo Indians did a thousand years ago." (Las Vegas is Spanish for "The Meadows.")

He smoked and fell silent, and we both looked around. We were on a slight rise above the two-lane highway I'd taken here, standing in the middle of a vast desert surrounded by the shattered peaks of the Mormon Mountains and the Sheep Range. "What happened?" I asked.

"Doctors and city people bought the dairies and closed them down. They wanted the farms for a place to live, but they didn't want to work them. And their heirs don't want to work them, either. Buddy, kids won't work a ranch today. They're subdividing and selling off. When I came here, bottomland was five hundred dollars an acre. Now you'd pay forty thousand dollars for two and a half acres of sand up in them hills just to build a house on." He paused and took one last pull from his cigarette and then field-stripped it and crushed the burning ember with his toe as it dropped. "Buddy, you can grow anything in this valley."

Signs all over the museum said what a mystery it was that the Pueblo and Anasazi had vanished from this amazing miracle of fertility, which they had wrought from the sterile desert. But the park ranger knew the answer. For all the anthropology and geology and paleontology going on under fluorescent lights in glass vitrines in that building, the chips of flint, the stone tools, and the shards of pottery, there was no explanation of that culture quite as succinct as his. They should have put the park ranger on video and let him say, "Buddy, those Pueblo Indians vanished not because it was too poor but because it was too rich. They raised a generation of hip-hop kids who wouldn't lift a finger and who left for better things they imagined were right on the other side of these mountains. The Anasazi vanished in 1150 because they had other plans."

In human history, written and unwritten, that gold-rush mentality, the idea that you can get something without working, has made more than one culture vanish.

. . .

My friend, the award-winning Watergate reporter Larry "Butch" DuBois, came in from Mormon country the next day like the Road Runner on a column of dust. He's the one who got us to the MGM Grand, with its theme park that rivaled Disney World and paid homage to the success of the Universal Studios Studio Tour. He's the one who insisted on riding the bumper cars. Jan joined us, and we were probably the only three adults participating, certainly the only journalists intrepid enough for this adventure, racing and screaming across the rusty metal floor in a shower of sparks. The game seemed somehow ancient, both because of its character as a kind of motorized jousting and because of the unsophisticated and clearly hazardous machinery that propelled us. Butch and I finally crashed head on into each other seconds before the power was shut off amid our kamikaze scream.

"I was a fourteen-year-old kid again!" Butch shouted, as dozens of children departed in ranks, with their heads downcast in solemn contemplation. Butch, a tall half-bald man with a slash of white in his beard, leaped and gesticulated with excitement and cackled with glee. He wanted to go again. He begged us to go on the roller coaster water ride with him, but neither Jan nor Don, who had watched us from a bench among the swarms of families going to and fro in the great amusement park, wanted to get wet.

I had been in Las Vegas in the early eighties. I recall seeing a lot of old men with teenage girlfriends. Guys in shiny suits who'd never been to a health club. A few dismembered cadavers were still turning up in the desert with comforting regularity then. The only child I saw on that trip was Wayne Newton's daughter, who happened to be playing on the floor while Wayne's housekeeper made us hamburgers in his kitchen. Wayne. Good old Wayne. I was writing a profile of Wayne, and he let me fly his Bell Jet Ranger helicopter up the canyon to Lake Mead. Wayne was The Man back then. Wayne was a Las Vegas tradition. You went to Las Vegas, you went to see Wayne at his Aladdin hotel. But that year his show closed early because no one came. I remember hanging out in Wayne's dressing room before the show with Redd Foxx and the mafia bigwigs from the Teamsters Union eating Cuban pork and rice and telling tall tales. Red Foxx kept everyone in stitches with horribly off-color and racist jokes that wouldn't have been possible if he had not been black. These were the jokes he could not tell on TV or on stage. But that was another era.

Today Perego strollers made traffic jams on the strip. The Luxor was a *Raiders of the Lost Ark* virtual-reality world with a descent into the pyramid and families riding a river barge down an indoor Nile with real banana trees growing on the ersatz banks. For chutzpah, the Luxor the was the winner with its giant sphinx entryway and its 357-foot-tall glass pyramid. For pure size, the MGM Grand was king with its stupendous and dizzying *Land of the Lost* casino and its thirty-three-acre amusement park out back.

That night Butch and I prowled Circus Circus. We walked in the back entrance by the Sega R360 fighter plane simulator, and he grabbed my arm, halting our progress, transfixed by the sight of the silver machine with cries of pleasure and alarm issuing from inside the tumbling drum. Butch turned his grave countenance upon me and growled, "Who goes first, you or me?"

You have to picture him in his tweedy jacket with leather elbows like some Ivy League Graham Greene good-soldier type, lately retired from secret Cold War duty. He strapped into the fighter plane simulator with his sport coat on. I had to hold all the stuff from his pockets while he fought off the enemy planes. Spook turned fighter pilot. When he came out, grinning and sweating, his eyes rolling in their sockets even more than they usually do, he said, breathlessly, "I knew I had to hit more than six fighters, because that's what those kids were hitting. I had twelve kills in three minutes. *Twelve kills!*"

We wandered the vast and seamy reaches of Circus Circus that night. Circus Circus has a huge carnival arcade where no gambling is allowed, and at eleven at night, it was populated by abandoned children, feral *Lord of the Flies* savages who raped the electronic games with focused concentration and went wild at the old fashioned carnival setups—the china pitch, the teddy bear pitch, simulated horse races, and my favorite, a game in which the player used a sledgehammer to operate a catapult that launched a stuffed animal on a high trajectory toward a variety of aluminum cooking pots. The floor shook from the action. Ritalin-crazed kids on Sega motorcycles tilted into a virtual green landscape of road and forest, while hormone-powered girls in Indy motorcars raced to quadraphonic symphonies of Zulu drums, and desert tanks clashed in mimicry of the perpetual wars of the Middle East that had formed the backdrop of the children's entire lives.

Butch and I pushed through a distinctly blue-collar crowd down to the dark and sweaty circus level. A tawdry net hung beneath the grease-worn trapeze. Coke cups and gum wrappers littered the sticky floor. This then was the embodiment of who we are. Here was that empty-calorie, carny, white-trash world, the slack-jawed indolence of bad afternoon television, all come to suppurating life. It was the underlying spiritual and sociological arc of the middle American living room vomited onto a mammoth slab of roasted limestone concrete for mass consumption in the flesh.

After a while a man and woman in tights who spoke no English came out and performed quasi-sexual acts while dangling from a trapeze held high enough off the floor that it would hurt them pretty badly if they fell. Their lean and carnal strength was clear in spandex close and tight enough that they could have given anatomy lessons with their bodies, while the sexuality was subsurface enough that the kids, agape in horrified wonder, could see it, but their parents could not. The animal scent of the trapeze artists' twisting undulations hung in the humid, motionless air. Glistening with sweat, they coupled in the air like high-colored insects, hanging from each other's ankles and wrists and prehensile toes and finally teeth, squirming and dropping and catching each other with a trust few of us ever achieve with our partners for life. A quartet of secondhand musicians played from the orchestra pit. The drummer, a bald and bearded man in black glasses and a black turtleneck, thrashed at the snare as if trying to kill a rat, while the organist, in a sweat-stained golf shirt, rocked his head back blindly and groped the shattered keyboard of a scarred old Hammond B-3. Their shuffle beat echoed, hollow and forlorn, in the cavernous coliseum over the far-off din of screaming children.

We wandered down the strip toward the Mirage volcano, where 150,000 gallons of water cascaded every minute in foaming white spray, while gas jets spewed fire, and steam drifted across a crowd of families. "This is the fastest-growing city in America," Butch said. "And it's in the middle of the desert. Look at this. Water is everywhere. How can they sustain it? What are we doing to the ecology of the desert?" I say the answer is simple. We can't keep this up indefinitely. Because Las Vegas gets its water from the Colorado River and aquifers beneath the ground. Both are drying up. And when the water runs out, which it will, the desert will reassert its sovereignty in about four heartbeats.

Walking the strip at night, we found ourselves at the center of a cold and holy fire. The neon vagina of the Flamingo throbbed and pulsed with soft and lambent tentacles of pubic lightning. I turned back one last time to watch the volcano explode with luminous belchings of propane, great bubbles rising from submerged pipes and billowing into gaseous clouds of fire, while speakers blasted volcano noise, and crowds of people surged against the steel railing, and a cortege of cars crept past.

Steve Wynn thought up the thirty-two-million-dollar volcano and Treasure Island next door, which displayed pirate ships in combat. Cannons fired, pirates dived from the rigging, and in the end, a British frigate actually sank. If anyone doubts the power of the house advantage, that little 1.414 percent in craps, let them consider the fact that all this entertainment was *free*. This most amazing show on earth is what they give you just for parking your car. When the archeological record of our civilization is finally read, perhaps it will show a sudden mad nomadic evisceration as mysterious as the disappearance of the Anasazi.

• • •

I went back to the craps table the second night, while Jan was playing roulette and Don was playing blackjack. I like craps, the fast atrial fibrillation of the game. The wicked whiplash ups and downs of fate. I had about $160 in chips in my pocket. I played as I had that first night, placing a red $5 chip on the pass line and betting double odds on any point. I lost approximately $5 a minute until I found myself hitting the leather for another $100 bill, which vanished down the rabbit hole. The twenty red chips the dealer gave me began vanishing, too, at the same brisk pace, despite my assiduously sensible strategy for betting.

I could feel a cold stone growing in my stomach as my heart grew sick with fear and desperation. I recall one time being deep in the woods, high on a mountain in Glacier National Park, and stumbling upon a cascade of grizzly bear scat, a great, huge steaming pile of it, laden with berries, square in the middle of the path. I was about seventeen miles on foot from the nearest help, and I remembered feeling this sick sensation of my own feeble stupidity at being there at all as my guts turned to liquid. Well, there I was again, staring at a big tumbling pile of grizzly bear scat square in the middle of my path and even farther from help. Don told me, "Your best friend will lay down his life for you, but don't ask him for five thousand dollars." He's right. No matter how bad it gets, when it comes to money, you're on your own.

And suddenly, standing at that craps table, I jerked awake in a sweat: standard deviation was the bear that was eating me alive. The tide I'd ridden in on the day before was going back out, and I'd neglected to get off the bongo board.

I quickly gathered my remaining red chips, too ashamed even to count them, and jammed them in my pockets, and with black absorption, I slid off into the surging crowds of people jerking the slots.

I believe there are two schools of gambling. One is the school of fate, in which wild bets are placed on unlikely outcomes. The lottery is such a bet. The other is the school of control, which attempts to understand the rules and odds and to overcome them by skill and clever strategy and a Talmudic adherence to the rules. Losing the second kind of bet always hits harder. Don's method of playing blackjack was of the control school. He studied blackjack the way an accountant would study the tax code: for loopholes. He practiced at home with a special computer program designed for counting cards. He did not like to talk at the table, the better to keep score. While all around the constant stars wheeled in their random trajectories.

The other school was exemplified by one of my agents, Howie Sanders, who had come from Los Angeles with his partner, Rich Green. One afternoon Rich and I chased Howie all over the casino as he went wild playing craps and roulette. For him, it seemed, gambling was like the casting of a shamanic spell. The craps table was too mean and serious for him. It simply took his money faster than he could comprehend. He said it was like getting rolled. The roulette wheel really fixed his zoom lens, though. With a hundred dollars in one-dollar chips and thirty-eight places to put them, he could cast his spell. "Five and nine," he'd call. "Five and nine, and you're on the nine with me," he'd say, placing bets by way of a tip for the dealer. "And split the eight there on the corner, gimme two on the twenty-five." On and on he went in heedless exultation, like Toad of Toad Hall in his brand-new motorcar in *The Wind in the Willows*.

Amazingly, against the rotten 5.26 percent house advantage, Howie won for a while, hitting the magic five-and-nine combo that seemed to be his mantra that December afternoon. It was a great stunt, like that guy who tied helium balloons to a lawn chair and was seen some time later by an airline captain as he drifted by at ten thousand feet. But how long could he keep it up? I lay back on the sidelines and kept my powder dry. This was their day in Las Vegas. My original $500 stake was getting light. The craps table had given me third-degree burns, and I'd had a few sessions at the electronic poker machines that I'm ashamed to admit to. So I was feeling the need to conserve my gambling budget.

I was content to watch and to ponder my strategy, as Howie made wild excursions into the dizzying wonderland of randomness. Of all the people who came to play, Howie was the most fun. It was like watching rodeo. A small, compact, and gleefully humorous man, he would hang on for dear life until the bronco threw him, and then he'd get up and hang on again, whooping for joy. And when the money was gone, all he had to say was that it had been a hell of a great ride. A man of style and grace, Howie was not about to whimper. He paid for his entertainment even when his entertainment didn't pay him.

I was not as hale and hearty by any means. Trying to catch my breath, I grimly whispered to myself, "This is fun, this is fun, this is fun . . ." I pushed through colorful multitudes, the wall of sound and light, a clever effect achieved by the lavish and indiscriminate use of mirrors, synthetic reflecting materials, prismatic lights, and chromatic shifts of shadow and marble. I found Don at a five-dollar blackjack table. I crawled up behind him, gasping, "Help me . . ." and he turned and laughed. I remembered his own experience our first night out. It was late, and we were tired, so Jan and I went to bed, leaving Don deep in concentration at the tables. The next morning, we met in the mall at the New York Stage Deli for breakfast, and Don filed this report. "I broke my cardinal rule," he said. "I was down three hundred dollars, and I got stubborn. I decided I wasn't getting up until I had won it back. It's the worst kind of decision. I was tired, I was discouraged, and I was losing. But I stayed, and I played until I won it all back. Then I got up from the table and went to bed. About 2:00 a.m." He was tired but seemed satisfied that he had beaten the odds. "The only right thing I did was getting up from the table."

Indeed, he had beaten the odds in the only game where it's actually possible to invert the house advantage. First of all, you can make decisions about play during the game. In craps, roulette, and slots, the only decision is how to place a bet, after which an event occurs by chance. In addition, blackjack is the only game in which one event depends on another. The chances for a good hand change constantly as the composition of the deck changes. Some people can learn to keep track of what cards are dealt and then change the way they play accordingly.

One of my goals had been to conquer my fear of blackjack. I had lived in terror of that moment when the dealer would give me a supercilious glare and wait for my decision: Hit or stick? Split or double down? Do I scratch the table like a cat in heat? Do I pick my nose? Of course, I didn't want to lose. Losing was, well . . . for losers. But more than anything, I didn't want to be embarrassed. If I was doomed by the house advantage, at least I could look cool while getting skinned.

Don gave me a three-by-five card on which he'd written the crucial hands and how to play each. The dealer allowed me to put my little card right on the table and take my time reading it. She even let Don coach me on how to play.

Soon I didn't need a coach for most hands. And it became obvious that our friendly dealer was more than willing to help me play my hand, telling me at each deal of the cards when to stand, when to hit, when to split, and even when to double down. As the pit boss had said, they want you to win. Moreover, once a good dealer sees that you are playing standard basic strategy, she'll let you stand or make the hits for you automatically. You hardly have to signal. After a weekend of playing blackjack at Don's elbow, I was able to stand at a blackjack table and witness for myself exactly how many people were wagering significant money (hundreds, even thousands, of dollars) without a grasp of basic strategy. These players would wipe out in an evening. Jan and Don each started with $500 and were able to play a lot for the entire weekend.

But Don did something no dealer could do for me. Before we went to the table, he said, "When I start raising my bet, you raise yours the same amount." As the six-deck shoe gradually diminished, I'd notice Don going from a $5 bet to a $10 or even a $20 bet. I always bet what he bet, and when the bets got big, we'd start winning. The crucial effect of this practice was that when we lost, we lost in $5 increments. But when we won, we won in $10 or even $20 increments. By losing $300 the night before, Don had proved that when the cards are against you, there's little you can do. But winning it back, he had proved that this system can be made to work. Don is a card counter. Not big enough to be a threat to a casino. But a card counter nonetheless. And a good one.

. . .

By the end of the weekend, seven people had joined me there. Some of them had come and gone, but five of us were hunkered down dominating a blackjack table on a Sunday afternoon. The casino rose and rumbled and shrieked like the halls of hell. Music spit and crackled and crashed, while the din of bells and of coins clattering into metal buckets raked our nerves, and beneath it all: the low, strumming reverberation of human voices on the brink of combustion, a tremendous pulsing energy, which I could liken only to the sounds I'd heard in the biggest of the maximum-security prisons I had visited during my journalistic career. Brushy Mountain, where I had visited James Earl Ray. Marion, where I had met mass murderers.

David Klass, a friend from Hollywood, sat on my left. Beyond him were our agents, Rich and Howie. On the other side of Rich, Tony Bill (Oscar for *The Sting*) sat betting green twenty-five-dollar chips with dark concentration. The rest of us were betting red fives, and David grumbled about "not being man enough" to bet twenty-five dollars as Tony was doing. David had written many movie scripts, so he could afford the bet. TB was a skilled blackjack player, but he was losing. He was coaching me on my moves, and I was winning. Now *that's* gambling.

So it was that we settled in for our last quiet game of blackjack before they had to leave. When Tony's green twenty-five-dollar chips were gone at last, he pushed back from the table, dusting his hands off, and said, "I like that clear feeling. No money. No chips." And then we all pushed back and wandered out into the casino crowd. David was grumbling about not having the balls, not being man enough, to make the big bets when he should have, and as we passed the Wheel of Fortune, he stopped, transfixed by it. "What the hell?" he said with a shrug.

"Uh-oh," Howie said. "He's hitting the leather."

David put two dollars on a really bad forty-to-one bet, and the woman spun the wheel. We all watched as the rubbery dildo on the giant wheel flipped past the pins, the great rotating disc slowed and then miraculously came to rest on the bet David, in his despondency, had selected. David walked away with the eighty dollars he had lost at blackjack, but more than that, he had regained something else he'd left at the table. Perhaps it was his pride. Perhaps it was the world's largest human penis. Whatever it was, we all instantly understood it and cheered as he collected his bet.

I drove them out to the airfield, and over the wing of Tony's Cessna 310, I saw the moon rise, scorched and brown and yellow like a disc of crème brûlée. They climbed into the twin Cessna and took off into early starlight, Santa Monica bound.

· · ·

The Indian brave's rite of passage was three days fasting in the desert waiting for a vision. Mine was four days of eating at Spago in Caesars Palace waiting for a vision. I came out here in the desert on the fourth day. Chalk hills and accidental temples of stone where signs pop out on the path: "Climb to safety in case of flood." When the monsoon comes, there's nothing to soak it up, and it comes as a ripping, hell-bent cataract through the crack of this canyon. Other signs directing me to "bay" or "cove" or "beach" set up reverberating paradoxes in this desert.

When going to Las Vegas to gamble and play, it is important to whip out of town going south on Interstate 15 and look back at the creation of Vegas, how it fills the valley with wine-colored smoke and steel reflections and the white snail's tracery of cast concrete. It takes only minutes to shake off the rhinestone cloak of lights. Soon the dark prows of mountains draw athwart. To the west a single wall rises, faint and forbidding in the smog, a beckoning wilderness.

The Valley of Fire erupted as if it were still molten. The moment I saw it I understood the name. Dunes, bare and red as anthills in that raked Sahara, and the pale silver-green sage in endless undulations, and the impossible glassy lake of mercuric slag, with misty peaks gathered all around in hoards for hundreds of miles and tilting into the vanishing distance. Even with a road, escape seemed impossible from this ripped and creased and sandy earth, which slid away, littered with upturned plants and shadowed by immense caldera peaks. It was the density of the vision that made the elephant stand on my chest. And Lake Mead gleamed out of those wastes, an insistent, incongruous hallucination, deepening to royal colors as the sun drew high. There's no limit, it seems, to what the eye will accept. Unlike the stomach, it does not fill up. No matter how much of this landscape we put in, the eye takes it all, and we become euphoric on it, and yet we're just as hungry as before.

I came on a tremendous triceratops of red stone erupting out of the earth and stopped and climbed it and stood atop its fifty-foot peak above the desert floor and took it all in, wondering what kind of test it was of myself to guard this $500 I'd been given for gambling. What did I have to prove by *not losing* all the money? It was something to do with a story I told myself about who I was. And in the story, I was the good guy. I could have taken the $500 and pissed it away and laughed and said, "Hey, cool: they gave me five-hundred dollars to gamble with. Easy come, easy go." But no. I'd been guarding it. Hoarding it. And now the fact that I was still down almost $250 gnawed away at my miserly innards. "Loser, loser, loser," it taunted me. Even though all the books I'd read had told me to expect that kind of loss—more, really. The house advantage makes it inevitable: as long as you expose that money in a game, the odds will slowly eat it away as surely as this desert will suck the life out of you. Given the amount of action I'd laid down, I was doing pretty good to have gambled for four days and lost only $250. Howie and Tony had lost that much in an afternoon.

All around me on my windy perch the land was green and pale and silent. Gravity and light from the mountain ranges tried to pull me off the rock, but I held on tight. Monuments of stone. The red road silted out in ancient seas and froze like this, and millennia ago salts crystallized and formed the concavities, called tafoni, in the iron-red sandstone.

I climbed and scrambled down and went back with my jeans and jacket covered in red dust. I crossed through alkali heaps and green slag hills left over from the manufacture of the world. The team of ghastly gravel visages leaned in to inspect me from the sun-freaked shadows of this arid domain. This nearest rank of faces seemed scarcely credible, yet beyond was another and beyond that another misty enfilade of stone creations.

I caught a tour bus to the cafeteria on top of Hoover Dam. I dismounted and crossed the road that ran along the rim of the mammoth structure. This was where Superman almost lost Jimmy Olson. When the dam was being built, workers began pouring concrete one day in the 1930s, and they poured around the clock continuously for the next two years. I was surprised at how little stood between me and the parabolic slide to the gorge more than seven hundred feet below. One quick hop, and I'd be on a broad rim. Scoot less than a meter, and my feet would be dangling over the edge. Then just let go. What a ride that would be. The gorge was magnificent, rent and blown apart in wild striations like the birth canal of the world and now cleated with a cruel chastity belt of high-tension towers. So this was where the power came from to light the strip. To power the false volcano.

I crossed through traffic and crowds of sightseers to the Lake Mead side: tremendous fish like docile silver calves held steady in the stream among pilings big around as houses. Beyond: the lake like a bowl of mercury creased by the wake of a single boat.

The tour bus let me off at the parking lot. I drove back, watching Las Vegas swim in its own urine. Las Vegas: a sea of foam, a basket of snakes, a newborn volcano that erupts every half hour.

● ● ●

All of my friends had gone home, and I was alone in Caesars Palace. As alone as you can be when a thousand people are playing slot machines. A few more careless bets, and my $500 had dwindled to $200. I wandered the booming casino trying to decide what to do. There was Steve Schiff, straight-shooting New Mexican congressman, a fiscally conservative Republican from a largely Democratic state. A man who spends a lot of time talking all that right-wing belt-tightening stuff. Week before Christmas, and he's all alone, looking out of place in an ill-fitting sport coat and slacks and no tie, like a Catholic prep school kid who'd put on the coat because he had to. He sat at a blackjack table, placing $25 and $50 bets and looking bored and forlorn.

I decided to win back my $500. It was a strange decision, I realized, given what I knew about the odds, but I thought: If Don can do it, I can do it. If David was man enough, then so am I. I took my last $200 and went to the craps table and dropped it on the felt. A moment later I had a wooden rack filled with glorious soft red and green chips, and I was playing the odds once more. I didn't bet continuously. I bet with certain shooters and not with others. I felt my way along, my hands out before me in this dark hallway of randomness. As I was waiting out a round of losing deviations, a tall and handsome African American man came up beside me, wearing about $2,000 worth of colorful sporty nylon stuff. He dropped a long stack of $500 chips into the rack and calmly began placing them all over the layout. The dealer looked up at him and his stash and said, "You want to be rated?" The man said nothing but shook his head slightly: no. I'm guessing, but he probably lost $10,000 in less than ten minutes. I was transfixed. I didn't even place a bet. I just watched him. He was beautiful. He appeared to be in a trance, some misplaced football star wandered in here and this God's way of telling him he'd made too much money.

When he left, I started betting again and won $100 in about as much time as he'd taken to lose $10,000. I was finding it hard to breathe. I pushed my chips over to the dealer and said, "Color me," and he gave me three black hundreds and change. I didn't want to wear out my craps luck and get on the wrong wave. I walked around the casino, thinking, watching, wondering how I was going to make up the rest of my $500 stash. Everywhere I turned, they were giving it away. How to get them to give me some . . . ? Of course, anyone who knows gambling will tell you that this is absolutely the wrong approach. Accept the gift: you lost $200, not $300.

On an impulse, I put one of my silver $1 coins into a slot machine and won $25. Amazing. Already things were looking up. I crossed the casino again and stood watching a roulette game for a while, a perfect picture of random play. It had come up red about six times in a row. I put $15 on the black, and the dealer spun the ball. It clattered into the black, and I picked up another $15 and walked away. I hit a blackjack table for $30. I returned to craps for about $50. Another round of roulette paid $25. Thus I circulated around the casino in a kind of psychic trance, retrieving the money I'd scattered there during the long weekend. You see strange and subtle things in a casino like Caesars. A young thin Mediterranean-looking man with tragic good looks and black hair hanging half in his eyes. Walking with a cane, he came up during one of my roulette sessions and began placing $1,000 yellow chips all over the layout, perhaps a dozen of them cast randomly on the numbers. He wore a serious expression and an expensive light gray suit with a dark shirt and no tie. He leaned heavily on a stool as if his leg hurt him. When a spin of the wheel took all of his chips, he pushed himself up on his cane and, with no expression whatsoever, struggled through the turbulent domain to one of the many cash machines and withdrew more money and came right back.

It was nearly midnight when I retired to my room. I had recovered all of my lost money. I was going home the next day. I felt as if I had achieved my goal. I took off my shoes and started running the water in the huge jacuzzi in the fishbowl bathroom. I'd take a bath and watch TV and go to sleep. And yet something gnawed at me. Something was dreadfully wrong. Why had I guarded that money so jealously from the start? Why had I felt such a tremendous sense of ghastly failure at losing half it in four days? I had been treating the money not as a free gambling stake, a bonus, but as if I had a fiduciary responsibility toward it. I had been behaving like an investment counselor. Indeed, the thought of leaving Las Vegas a loser had filled me with a sickening discomfort.

I turned off the water in the jacuzzi. I put on my shoes. This is bullshit, I thought. I don't care about the money. I took five hundred-dollar bills. I locked my wallet in the small safe in the closet. I rode the elevator down. The casino seemed to explode with a shrill and stinking slo-mo violence, the gaudy flickering, the cigar smoke like burning insulation. People were swimming everywhere, cackling madly or sitting frozen in grim concentration. Was it a fire drill? Was it Thorazine? It could do anything but stop.

I crossed through, shouldering people out of my way, and approached a bored-looking dealer, who stood flicking the ball around and around the idle roulette wheel. I dropped the five bills on the felt. "Can I have a purple chip?" I asked.

"You gonna place a bet?" he asked.

My heart was going like crazy. I couldn't do this, I told myself. I just couldn't. Something in my upbringing. You don't want to throw money away. Even if it's not your money. "No," I said.

He called the pit boss over with a wave of his hand. "He wants a chip," he said.

"Give it to him," the pit boss said and turned away.

The dealer took my five bills and gave me a single pale purple chip, and I walked off into the crowd with my heart in my throat. What was this inhibition? I was a winner. But if I did this reckless thing, I would leave Las Vegas a loser. Was that it? What's the first thing anyone asks when you return from Las Vegas? Did you win?

These are important definitions. This is who I am. My stomach had been in knots for days over this very question. Why else would I have stayed up all night trying to win back what I'd lost? My old friend Marc, a shrink, would say it was a weird Freudian thing, but I was too rattled at that moment to recall much about my potty training. It didn't help any that all around me people were slinging $500 and $1,000 chips like they were Girl Scout Cookies. Why could I not simply bet the money given to me and go to bed and go home? Why did I always have to take everything to heart? God, was I really this serious? How boring.

I wandered the casino in complete confusion, clutching my precious little purple chip, feeling as if I stood in the door of an airplane with something strapped to my back that might have been a parachute or might have been some hippie's backpack that I'd picked up by mistake. And a little voice in my head was shouting, Jump! Jump! Yet I could not. Was I not more of a loser for my inability to take the risk? David had said it at the blackjack tables: "I wasn't man enough." Of course, it had nothing to do with being a man. That was nothing more than an expression. It had to do with evolution. It had to do with the ape experiment. It had to do with choosing the smaller pile of candy in order to get the bigger reward.

I had arrived at another roulette wheel far across the casino, where a lone and tired-looking young man was putting green $25 chips on the black and losing with every spin of the wheel. The weight of it was on him, I could see. I watched his play, fingering my chip. It was smooth and looked as if it had been hand-painted. The chip showed a man lashing the horses that pulled a chariot. It had pink and white hash marks on its edges and columns etched in its rim. It was a grand and pretty chip, and I was going to say good-bye to it and go away and not ever have this chance again. I cradled my chip. Good-bye, beautiful little chip. How I have loved caring for you. I have tended you so well on our weekend together. I had my notebook out, taking notes, and I outlined the chip on the page before me: a memento of our weekend in Las Vegas together.

The young man at the table kept putting his $25 chips on black one at a time and losing. He sat on a stool, and I stood behind him. I could sense his building frustration: Goddamn it, this has to change, he was thinking. The bleeping thing can't come up red for bleeping ever. Yet his pile of green chips had dwindled with every turn of the wheel, and I saw his hand move to pick up the last green chip. He hesitated. He held it poised in his fingers over the black, then thought a moment more and set it down on the red. He had given up. I could sense his defeat. I reached over his shoulder and placed my pale purple $500 chip on the black, and his head jerked around to look at me like *Who the hell are you?* Already I felt I had gotten my $500 worth just for that look. That's right, I thought. It's me. Roll over, Rover, the big dog's here to bury his bone. He didn't know that I was about to faint from trepidation. He didn't know that I felt as if I were having a heart attack. But that's what you pay for, isn't it?

The dealer noted the bet and called over to the pit boss, "White outside." The whole casino went out of focus, and the only sound that was left was the pounding of my heart. I saw the white ball go whirling around as the dealer spun the wheel. I think my eyes must have rolled back in my head for a moment. There was that sudden drop in blood pressure, the pulmonary rush, cardiac crash, as the ball slowed and painted a helical path down to the silver fins of the wheel and bounced twice and leaped into the air before coming to rest inside a black cocoon.

"Son of a bitch!" the young man said, standing and walking away from the table as the dealer took the man's last green chip.

"One white out," said the dealer, as he gave me another purple chip. I walked away with the two chips clicking together in the palm of my hand. I was shaking so hard I could barely walk. As soon as I was out of sight of the dealer, I sat on a stool by a slot machine and just waited for my heart to stop pounding. Son of a bitch, indeed. You can't get that rush at the ice cream parlor.

. . .

By chance, I ran into the same young man in the elevator. As we rode up, I felt him looking at me. "How'd you do?" I asked. He already knew how I did.

"Aw, man," he said. "I got crushed."

"At what?"

"Blackjack and roulette."

"Yeah," I said. "I was about even, you know. I'd gone upstairs already. I even had my shoes off, and then I just—"

"You had a feeling," he said.

"Yeah, I had a feeling."

"Yeah, I know. You had a feeling. I know. You got all my money."

"No guts, no glory," I said.

"You had a feeling then?"

"Yeah. I had a feeling."

I went back upstairs and lay in the jacuzzi for the longest time. The whole world was benevolent. Even the honking cars down on the strip seemed to call to me like nightingales. I felt like someone who'd just missed the plane that went down.

. . .

Leaving Caesars the next day, I passed through the Appian Way in order to bid good-bye to the world's largest human penis, Big Dave, who I felt had given me the fortitude to bet correctly. The Moby Ricardo, enshrined among the whore jewelry and pimp art. And as I drove down the strip toward the airport in my white rental car, I thought: I love Las Vegas.

A few days after I returned home, Butch called to say that Caesars World stock had been trading at forty-seven dollars on Friday when we arrived. "Over the weekend, while we were polishing the porpoise, ITT bought it at a tender offer of sixty-seven dollars. We were pulling the wrong handle," he said. "We missed the real game entirely."

· 3 ·

Stealing *Titanic*

WHEREVER WE GO, his stride consumes the landscape. I have to run to keep up with him. Bob Ballard is an imposing man, six foot two, with a flushed complexion and a rugged, windburned face. He has an urgent air about him, as if fleeing an imminent explosion. As we dash out of the chaotic construction site where his new Institute for Exploration is being built up around the Mystic Aquarium near the coast of Connecticut, he leaps into his black Mercedes and grabs for a Coke in the cupholder. It's only eight in the morning, but he's on his second or third of the day. He wears the same outfit he wore yesterday: white turtleneck under a navy-blue sweater, khaki slacks, tan socks, and comfortable penny loafers. His shaggy brown hair sticks out from under his blue Institute for Exploration baseball cap. A Mickey Mouse watch adorns his wrist.

Ballard rockets away and vaults across the bridge over the Thames River at well over eighty miles an hour. He slows to point out the New London Naval Submarine Base, the Coast Guard Academy, and the General Dynamics Electric Boat company, which builds nuclear submarines. Poking out of heavily guarded wharves are colossal black subs, dark symbols of a secret world. "This is a hub of US maritime strength," he says with the glee of a boy at Disneyland. And for good reason: the navy has been his Disneyland for roughly thirty years. For while Dr. Robert D. Ballard became famous for finding the RMS *Titanic* on September 1, 1985, his parallel career was that of a Naval Intelligence officer, developing undersea technology and performing top secret Cold War missions on the ocean floor.

He leans across the leather console, fixes me with his gaze, and shouts, "Cortés! I believe in the method of Cortés, who burned his ships and said to his men, 'We're going to Mexico City.'" He jabs me with a broad index finger. "It gets people's attention. I got my own attention at Woods Hole by announcing that I was leaving five years before the fact. I lame ducked myself. I blew up my life. I needed a new career, and that was how I got it." (Incidentally, Cortés didn't burn his boats. He had them dismantled.)

His cell phone rings. We pull into a parking lot. It's his wife. The volume is turned up, and I can hear both sides of the conversation. She has planned a special vacation weekend for him, a gift, involving theater, dinner, and a small celebration, and Ballard's secretary has scheduled his annual trip to Mexico to go dove hunting at the same time. His wife is weeping on the phone. "It's not my job to monitor your schedule," she said.

Ballard is abject, gentle, apologetic. "It's tragic," he tells her. "It's broken, and I've got to fix it."

I can hear him getting a royal ass chewing. "I don't want to spend any more time on this," his second wife, Barbara Earl, born on the Fourth of July to an old Connecticut Yankee family, says through her tears. This man is not one of her people. He is a cowboy, a wanderer from a family of wanderers, whose ancestors were shot down in gunfights out west.

"Rats," Ballard says.

"It's more than rats!" she screams.

When he hangs up, he sits for a moment looking deflated. The bluster is gone. His manic motion has taken him into a brick wall. "I haven't adjusted to the public demands on me," he says.

I ask what's going to happen. "Aside from eating a lot of humble pie . . ." he says. "Her schedule will lose."

· · ·

Until now, the seemingly flawless arc of Ballard's life has taken him from ROTC in college to the navy and on to Woods Hole Oceanographic Institution, where he discovered the world of manned submersible vehicles. He went on to distinguish himself as a marine geologist, a brilliant visionary, a daring scientist, and one of the foremost deep-sea researchers in the world. He has made 110 expeditions, many of them for the National Geographic Society, including the discovery of the German warship *Bismarck* in the Atlantic and the USS *Yorktown*, which was sunk at the Battle of Midway.

Now fifty-six and galloping through middle age, he has remarried and started a new family. He has stopped traveling to the bottom of the ocean. Instead, he is intent on bringing what he discovered undersea to his mammoth maritime institute. His fame has allowed him to help raise money—$52 million ($37 million of it from the state of Connecticut)—to build a monument to his discoveries. This, he hopes, will be the money machine that will take him further toward his lifelong goal of becoming the preeminent master of deepwater archaeology.

"Deep submergence has been my life from day one," he says. After careening through bare suburban landscape, he parks his Mercedes in front of his office in an anonymous strip mall but makes no move to go in. "I can't even tell you," he says, "when I first wanted to be an undersea explorer."

As a boy, he dreamed of Jules Verne. The son of the chief engineer of the Minuteman missile program, he craved adventure and a place in history. He spent summers on the beach, studying tide pools by day and poring over *Twenty Thousand Leagues Under the Sea* and watching old movies about *Titanic* at night.

"What's it like," I ask, "being down there?"

Ballard closes one eye and puts his hand to the other to make a tunnel through which to view the world. "Well, it's like this," he says, squinting to peer through. "It's the most frustrating thing in the world. You can't see squat." But those eyes have seen things few of us could imagine.

When Ballard came of age during the Cold War, America's nuclear submarines were among the most secretive operations the United States had. Indeed, because submarines—both the Soviet Union's and ours—were so mobile and difficult to detect and because their nuclear capabilities were frightening, the underwater games subs played became the real cutting edge of cold warfare. During those years, for instance, Soviet satellites could see when the navy sent support ships to work with undersea equipment. Soviet subs could then scramble to the spot to see what was going on. Consequently, any time the navy wanted to do something secret on the surface or below, it was of paramount importance to have other credible reasons for being there. The navy told some whoppers during those years. When the media once questioned why Howard Hughes's *Glomar Explorer* was cruising the Pacific, they were told the ship was mining manganese nodules from the seafloor. In fact, it was attempting to raise a Russian nuclear submarine that had sunk.

Inevitably, then, Ballard's scientific work took him unavoidably close to the navy netherworld of spying, spooks, and espionage. Beyond that, though, what made him so valuable to the navy was that his geologist's eye saw new strategic possibilities down under the sea. Ballard taught the navy to view the ocean floor as the battlefield of the future—an inky, liquid camouflage through which entire nuclear fleets could roam. To understand Ballard and how the push and pull between scientific research and military intelligence has shaped his career, you need look no further than his roles in searching for the vessels sunk in three of the most famous marine disasters: *Thresher, Scorpion,* and *Titanic.* Though Ballard couldn't admit it until the information was declassified, he was on the tail end of a secret navy mission when he discovered *Titanic.*

"*Titanic* wasn't really a cover story," he says. "It was a traditional relationship between the military and academia." But people who work with cover stories all their lives say that after a while it becomes difficult to find bedrock truth. Truth and fiction begin to blend.

USS *Thresher,* the first of a new generation of sub in Admiral Hyman Rickover's nuclear fleet, was one of America's deepest-diving vessels when it sank on April 10, 1963, off the coast of Massachusetts. *Thresher* was conducting dive trials to its test depth of thirteen hundred feet when, scientists speculate, a pipe burst in the engine room. Seawater, spraying out at more than five hundred pounds per square inch, shorted the electrical system. Orders came staccato as the crewmen, most of them in their twenties, fought for their lives. They dogged hatches and shut valves but faced uncontrolled flooding. When the electrical system shorted, the ship's nuclear reactor automatically shut itself off as a safety measure. With the nuclear fires out, the steam turbines stopped. With no steam, the propeller stopped, too.

For a submarine to move through the water, its propeller must turn. The nuclear reactor would take seven minutes to build up enough heat to restart the steam turbines—too much time, it turned out. The initial flurry of activity turned to a deadly hush. Even the air conditioning ceased.

Commander Wes Harvey ordered, "Full rise on the planes, maximum up angle" in the hope that it might carry the sub to shallower water. He radioed his escort ship, USS *Skylark,* which was steaming in a circle on the surface. "Experiencing minor difficulties," he called. "Have positive up angle. Am attempting to blow."

But efforts to blow the ballast failed.

Thresher spent the last of her momentum and began to sink backward. Harvey next reported to *Skylark,* "Exceeding test depth." His transmission could barely be heard.

A submarine can dive only so deep before its hull collapses from the weight of the water above it. Each crewman must have known that *Thresher*'s crush depth was fifteen hundred feet. As engineers watched the temperature gauges, hoping they'd get steam before the hull imploded, the rest of the crew was left with nothing to do but watch the walls and listen to the ship groan and creak.

The officers on board *Skylark* heard a dark, liquid explosion that must have cut them to the heart. Then they heard a second detonation that made an entirely different sound, crisp and dry and violent, like dynamite, detectable several thousand miles away by undersea hydrophones.

Death came quickly for the 129 seamen. At 750 pounds per square inch, a stream of water can cut steel. The submarine imploded and then quickly exploded, shredding the hull to scrap and flinging it into bits to the dark sea currents.

· · ·

In 1963, John P. Craven was chief scientist for the Polaris ballistic missile program. Eccentric and mysterious, Craven was regarded as kind of a Dr. Strangelove, operating on behalf of the military establishment from within the shadows of black security. But in the realm of diving technology, Craven's work set the bar—and the stage—for what Ballard would later achieve.

After *Thresher* sank, there was a public outcry. The families demanded that something be done. Craven was put in charge of developing a technology to locate and save sunken subs. He soon found money pouring into his budget to develop a deep-submergence rescue vehicle (DSRV). It was what Hollywood would have done with the story. The problem was, as Craven put it: "The probability that we might actually rescue someone was vanishingly small. DSRV was good cover because there's a mystique about rescue. But DSRV could never be used. We built it because it would give us tremendous capabilities to do other things. It was always tacit in these highly classified areas. Nobody said, 'We want you to give it capabilities other than rescue.' Yet we decided to give the DSRV the capability to lock divers in and out at great depths and decompress them slowly."

Eight years later, a submarine called the USS *Halibut* would leave for the Sea of Okhotsk off of Siberia with what the navy told the media was a DSRV attached to her decks. In fact, the device, shaped like a fifty-foot-long cigar, was a saturation diving chamber. Developed in secret, it allowed divers to work at previously unreachable depths. Upon reaching the target, divers emerged from the decompression chamber to tap into a Soviet communications cable. It was one of the navy's major coups of the Cold War. On its way home, *Halibut* stopped at a Soviet missile test range, where its divers retrieved enough fragments to allow engineers back home to assemble a nearly complete Soviet missile. Yet not even the best submersible could reach *Thresher* where she lay at a depth of eighty-four hundred feet. She remained there for the next twenty-one years.

On May 22, 1968, a second nuclear submarine, USS *Scorpion*, vanished on its way home to Virginia with ninety-nine souls on board. Soviet subs had been in the area, and navy brass immediately wondered if the Russians had sunk *Scorpion*—if, in short, we were going to war. To make matters worse, *Scorpion* was carrying two live Mark 45 ASTOR torpedoes fitted with nuclear warheads. (The best guess to this day is that a defective battery set off one of the conventional torpedoes, blowing the hatches and causing the sub to sink.)

Craven was put in charge of finding *Scorpion*, and on October 29, 1968, he did so, south of the Azores. Finding her was one thing, but *Scorpion* lay in 11,500 feet of water, beyond the reach of any of his submersibles.

. . .

Ballard was assigned to Woods Hole Oceanographic Institution (WHOI) in Massachusetts when *Scorpion* sank. Rushing about in his white uniform, Ballard seemed to be moving in a dozen directions at once—military man, geologist, would-be explorer, dreamer, and consummate salesman. They called him the White Tornado.

But Ballard's true motivation, his dream, was to dive where no one else had gone before. The perfect vehicle for that, *Alvin*, a twenty-three-foot, three-man submersible, was docked at Woods Hole. Craven had once used *Alvin* to locate a hydrogen bomb that the air force had accidentally dropped into the Mediterranean. Ballard spotted the white sphere of the submersible on his first day at Woods Hole and desperately wanted to take her for a spin. But even the senior scientists at Woods Hole would have had about as much chance of diving in *Alvin* as they had of going into orbit. Ballard knew that if he was to be taken seriously, he needed a PhD. By chance, a subject called plate tectonics was set to explode within the field of geophysics. Here was a dream come true: undersea exploration, adventure, and a doctoral thesis he could research in person on the ocean floor in a brand-new field of study.

Ballard also had an ace in his pocket. Woods Hole was supported largely by the navy. The young ensign happened to be the new liaison between the two: Woods Hole's funding went through Ballard.

Within four years, Ballard had found his way aboard *Alvin*.

At about the time *Scorpion* sank, though, *Alvin* was being lowered into the water when its lines broke. The crew barely escaped drowning. As they scrambled to safety, the world's most capable submersible sank in fifty-two hundred feet of water.

Alvin was ultimately retrieved in the summer of 1969, but she would need a complete refitting, and with the war in Vietnam raging, money was tight. Ballard's boss mused wistfully that what they needed was another lost hydrogen bomb to justify filling the coffers. Ballard shot back, "What we really need is for *Alvin* to go out and find *Titanic*." Ballard the salesman had an instinctive grasp of the romance and myth of the sea, and the story of *Titanic* was the ultimate seafarer's yarn. He knew even then that finding her could open doors in ways that not even the navy had considered.

Scientists at Woods Hole had wanted to refit *Alvin* with an expensive titanium pressure sphere. When the navy provided it, Ballard calculated that *Alvin* could dive to twelve thousand feet, where *Scorpion*—and *Titanic*—lay.

Ballard dove *Alvin* in the Gulf of Maine. Taking samples and measurements there, he completed his PhD (funded by the Pentagon's Advanced Research Projects Agency) and contributed to the theory of plate tectonics. He also extended to the ocean depths the range of geologists, who had previously been confined to taking samples on land.

On the strength of this work, he was invited to join the largest oceanographic expedition ever undertaken, the French-American Mid-Ocean Undersea Study (FAMOUS) in 1973 and 1974. In later dives, Ballard helped discover previously unknown chimneys that led from the earth's molten core into the icy ocean waters—the smokestacks on the roof of the factory that creates our world. In the process, he helped prove the value of manned submersibles in real science. And the team he was on made the first real advance in discovering the origins of life on earth.

By 1976 Ballard would dive on board *Alvin* to its full test depth of twelve thousand feet in the Cayman Trough, which he calls "one of the most spectacular submerged terrains on the planet." No sunlight filtered down to that depth. The seawater was as black as outer space. The pressure was fifty-five hundred pounds per square inch, 7.3 times that which had collapsed *Thresher* like a paper cup. Ballard said that looking at the shiny titanium hex nuts on the inside of *Alvin*'s hull was "like gazing into the maw of a loaded cannon." Every time the hull came in contact with rock, his mouth went dry. He was riding in a toy balloon, blown up to its absolute limit, that was being dragged and bounced along a jagged reef. If anything had gone wrong, no one would ever have known what had happened. They'd have hauled up nothing but a broken cable.

That was Ballard's life for ten years. The child who'd read Jules Verne had become him. But just as astronauts who'd been to the moon must have seen that they weren't going back, Ballard could see the era of manned undersea exploration coming to an end. And that's when he began to demolish his life.

On one of his early dives, Ballard had invited a marine biologist along to classify some of the life-forms he had found in the mineral-rich environment of hydrothermal vents—marine life that no human eye had ever seen.

"Imagine this," Ballard says. "You're the first biologist ever to see these new life-forms. You'd die to go down there, right?" But when they reached the bottom, the biologist turned his back to the window and watched the television screen. "What the hell were we doing down there?"

Ballard realized that his dream to journey endlessly on the ocean floor was essentially a doomed effort. When the quality of the TV picture became good enough, people would no longer bother going. It was too expensive, too dangerous, and machines would do it better. So Ballard decided he might as well be the one to make that happen.

In 1979, while on sabbatical from the navy at Stanford, Ballard had heard about fiber optics. He saw how this could be used on a tethered vehicle that would give realistic images of the ocean floor in real time. He began sketching designs for a new system. *Argo* would be a larger vehicle tethered to a surface ship. Inside the unmanned *Argo* would be a smaller robot, *Jason*, that could snake out and gather images in tight spaces—*Titanic*'s staterooms, for example, or *Scorpion*'s torpedo room.

Such an idea could not have come at a more propitious time. Yuri Andropov, the former chairman of the KGB, had just become the new leader of the Soviet Union. President Reagan had hired a hard-liner named John Lehman as secretary of the navy. Reagan was publicly calling the Soviet Union the "evil empire," while nuclear submarines played dangerous games of chicken beneath the sea. Nuclear war seemed closer than ever.

"Most people look at a Mercator projection and say, 'Wow, it's a long way from the Soviet Union to the US,'" Ballard says. "But if you look at a globe, you can see that from the Arctic Ocean, it's just a little lob." Ballard makes a popping sound with his mouth and an arc with his hand.

As submarine technology in America grew superior to that of the Soviets, the Russian fleet retreated. Instead of chasing around the American coastline, their subs chose to remain submerged in the Arctic Ocean for months at a time. They had the capability to burst through the ice and fire nuclear missiles "right over Canada," as Ballard explained. The complexion of the Cold War had changed.

By the summer of 1982, that atmosphere of uncertainty allowed Ballard to come up with the idea he'd been looking for, the seafarer's dream that would pave the road to *Titanic*. Ballard went before the navy's International Seapower Symposium at the Naval War College and talked of a new concept that he called terrain warfare. Submariners had traditionally viewed terrain as something to be avoided: you run into it, you're dead. But Ballard wanted to use terrain the way tanks do on land. You could hide the entire US Navy in one of those undersea mountain ranges, he said. The audience was riveted. When an impressed Secretary Lehman approached him afterward, Ballard pounced with his idea for deepwater imaging.

It took less than a month for the Office of Naval Research to sponsor *Argo/Jason*. The money streamed in, allowing Ballard to establish the Woods Hole Deep Submergence Laboratory.

. . .

Deep in the Connecticut woods one day, slaloming along two-lane blacktop in the black Mercedes, Ballard suddenly slams on the brakes and points to a narrow stream cutting through a yellow canebrake. "Look at that," he says. "Isn't that beautiful?" He watches the middle distance, seemingly at peace, as if he has escaped for a moment into the landscape. Then he stomps the accelerator, and we flee past the stream and dive once more into the forest at a speed that makes the landscape seem to revolve around us.

"Look, I'm a terrain person. I'm a geologist," Ballard explains. "I came into the navy having no idea that it was three separate worlds: surface, air, and submarines. I wanted to talk to these guys, but if you didn't have dolphins on"—he reaches over, grabs my lapel, and peeks under it, checking to see if I wear the insignia of the navy submarine forces—"the hell with you!"

And yet Ballard had a real advantage. He knew more about the deep ocean than the navy did. Submariners believe that they rule beneath the waves, but compared to Ballard, they'd only been skimming the surface. He was invited into the Pentagon's E Ring, where the navy's most senior officers worked, and was shocked to see the simple crudity of the charts on the walls. How little they knew of the submerged mountain ranges that were his workplace. In fact, the navy owned proper bathymetric charts, but no one seemed to grasp their strategic significance. They were locked away in a vault in Bay St. Louis, Mississippi.

Ballard flew to Bay St. Louis and had a three-dimensional model built from them. Then he took the model to Vice Admiral Ronald Thunman.

"Thunman was Op-Two," Ballard says with a sort of roaring, whispered, wide-eyed reverence. It's spook talk. "Do you understand? Oh two. He lived in a cell. This man was God!" Ballard was realizing how the game was played. Most of the world is underwater at an average depth of twelve thousand feet. If you're the world's top superpower, that's an important fact. The Cold War was being fought underwater, and these were the guys running it. And yet Ballard understood what not even Thunman understood: that the low ground is the high ground. And they didn't even have the right maps on their walls.

The vice admiral took one look at Ballard's model of the undersea terrain, and the lightbulb went on in his head. He gave Ballard *NR-1*, a miniature, ten-man navy nuclear submersible, designed by Admiral Hyman Rickover— and Craven. "The *NR-1* isn't a very good spy sub—Rickover just wanted the smallest nuclear reactor in the world," Ballard says. "So I took *NR-1* up to the Reykjanes Ridge and showed [Thunman] that we could live in that terrain, too. Reykjanes Ridge includes Iceland."

When I first met Ballard, he invited me into his tiny office, and we sat knee to knee because there was nowhere else to go. He said, "Why should I talk to you? You can't make me more famous." I went home a bit disappointed. When I told my editor at *National Geographic* what had happened, he called headquarters in Washington. *National Geographic* was founded by navy spooks. Soon I received a call from Ballard's office inviting me to come back. Now he seems at pains to impress me with his résumé.

"I was evolving a whole new strategy!" Ballard proclaims. "I'm a commander in the navy! You just ask Thunman or Lehman what they think of Bob Ballard's role in the navy. Call them and ask them. They'll tell you."

Yet Ballard laughs at my suggestion that he might be involved in the kind of spying that Craven did. "I got MIT started on designing terrain-involved warfare, not picking up junk off the ocean floor and certainly not tapping phones," he says.

By the time he started working with Thunman, Ballard was indeed a known quantity in the world of undersea science. His support ships from Woods Hole were a common sight out on the Atlantic. Stories about his scientific expeditions were published in *National Geographic*, which provided additional funding. That work was a perfect cover story—though a true one—for his other assignment: in the winter of 1984, the navy gave Ballard the go-ahead to test his new equipment by performing the first survey of the sunken nuclear submarine *Thresher*.

From its first passes over the remains of *Thresher* in July 1984, *Argo* delivered images just as vivid as Ballard had hoped they would be: a crew member's black rubber boot, a rubber glove knotted in the shape of a fist. Safe within their control van, a sort of mobile home full of electronic equipment mounted on the deck of a research vessel called *Knorr*, Ballard's crew looked on with reverential astonishment. They understood that they were visiting the naked graveyard of 129 men. A human hand had made that fist, a young submariner drifting through crush depth listening to the creaking hull. A last moment of resolve had closed his hand before a scalpel of ice water took his life.

Ballard shivers, remembering. "Those are my brothers who died here," he says in a quiet voice. "I knew I could be looking at myself."

The team watched the array of images as the *Argo* moved back and forth in a pattern known as "mowing the lawn." When *Thresher* imploded, dozens of steel gas bottles were released. Being heavy, they had streamlined directly to the bottom like bombs.

"They were about six feet tall," says Ralph Hollis, Ballard's pilot. "As we drove over them, it was like rows of tombstones."

A shipwreck in shallow water will form a field of debris a few hundred yards around at most. Yet as the lines on the chart table filled with paper, Ballard saw that *Argo* was revealing something entirely unexpected: a mile-long trail of debris.

As he watched the light debris pass across the video screen, he understood: the ocean is a fluid in motion. *Thresher* had exploded at around fifteen hundred feet, and the fragments had fallen to eighty-four hundred feet. The currents had worked with the debris for a long time before it hit bottom. The lighter the debris, the farther it traveled.

Ballard turned the vessel directly up the debris trail. Within minutes, a crew member called out, "Wreckage!" The submarine's rudder appeared at the edge of the impact crater. Suddenly it all became clear.

• • •

Craven believed that finding *Titanic* was a cover story for secret operations, just as Craven's deep-submergence rescue vehicle had been. He said that was just the way it worked. "Special intelligence projects have cover projects that are top secret," he explained. "Then you have secret projects covering the top-secret projects while confidential projects cover the secret projects. Each project covers the one below, all the way up to the public story, such as DSRV or *Titanic*, which is the story you tell the press and the public. But the trick is that they all must be true. They're not lies, they're real projects."

"My goal was to find the *Titanic*," Ballard insists. "No doubt about it."

I asked Craven if it would be fair to say that he had, taking the long view, led Ballard to *Titanic*. "Oh, we're much more Machiavellian than that," he said with a laugh, adding mysteriously, "The *Thresher-Scorpion* survey mission wasn't the seventh veil. It wasn't even the sixth veil."

Once Ballard had actually located *Titanic* and completed surveying the ship, he took off his explorer's hat and put on his Naval Intelligence hat. He declared all data from the site classified top secret before reaching port. Photographs were placed in safes, which had been put on the support ship, *Knorr*, by Naval Intelligence. The Naval Intelligence officer on board changed the combinations. When *Knorr* arrived at Cape Cod, she was greeted by a lawyer representing the secretary of the navy. Everything was rushed into a white sedan, which drove to Otis Air Force Base, where the materials were placed on a flight to the Pentagon. Ballard said that it was merely a way to control the release of priceless photos of *Titanic* to a hungry international press. This is undoubtedly true. This is undoubtedly one of many truths.

. . .

One morning I watch him tour his construction site with local members of the Mohegan Indian Tribe. The Mohegans, like the Pequots who run a nearby casino, are the beneficiaries of a booming tourist business. A dozen Native Americans in suits and ties and white plastic hard hats shuffle after Ballard, trying to keep pace as he leaps around the cast concrete molds, gesticulating and trying to shout above the roar of diesel engines.

The Mohegan elders nod in gaping solemnity as Ballard, in his rapid-fire military way, makes declarations of what his Institute for Exploration will bring to the area. It is meant to be the hub from which all of Ballard's future expeditions will be mounted. Ballard hopes the new aquarium will generate enough money that he will no longer have to engage in raising funds all of the time. He aims to create a self-sufficient museum for recording whatever history of mankind can be brought up from the ocean floor. The fruits of those expeditions would then be carried back to the institute for interpretation and display.

He's had other big ideas. Among them was the JASON Project, which has allowed two million junior high school students to travel on Ballard's expeditions remotely via the internet. While Ballard (or one of his robots) is down there inspecting a sunken wreck, the students can see in real time exactly what he sees. They learn how to manipulate cameras and in some cases are allowed to control the movements of the unmanned submersibles. In addition, Ballard has a long list of exploration projects—to the Mediterranean, the Black Sea, the mouth of the Hudson River, and other locations—stacked up into the future like planes over LaGuardia.

After Ballard finishes with the Mohegans, we once more sketch our jerky course into a wintry landscape under a cold Thanksgiving sky. As the black Mercedes gobbles up the picturesque landscape, I gently suggest that the US Navy isn't interested in Roman galleons that sank two thousand years ago in the Black Sea. Ballard plans to go there the next year, and the navy is helping to sponsor the trip.

Ballard says, "I think the navy has helped me because they genuinely have wanted to help me."

I respond with something like "Oh, come on. They don't want Roman galleons."

"No. No, they don't." At once his voice becomes uncharacteristically quiet.

"Okay," I say. "So what do they get out of it? Why the Black Sea? The Mediterranean?"

When I first met Ballard, he told me, "The navy has stopped doing secret missions. The war is over. There are no submarines left." Yet even his wife has been given secret clearances—just so she can be his wife. Some months have passed since Ballard and I began our sojourn together, and the story has evolved. Somewhat stiffly, he informs me that he is a senior scientist emeritus at Woods Hole Oceanographic Institution. "We have navy money for my Deep Submergence Lab to develop technology," he tells me.

"They want the technology that your expeditions develop?"

"They want technology. And they also ask me what to do with it. They send navy personnel on board with us. Look. Let me explain something. Take Saddam Hussein, for example. He put out a very crude minefield in the ocean, and it prevented the marines from landing. They were furious. Well, we could help. We live in their battlefield and know it better than they do. We know that environment. So we are developing mine countermeasures, robotics that could deal with undersea minefields. We're working on launching remotely piloted vehicles from torpedo tubes. We discovered internal waves that could flip a submarine. That's what I sold them, and that's why they want to pay to have me down there."

He describes an undersea gunnery range "on the tongue of the ocean," as he puts it. "It's wired up for war games, and they fire weapons there." The navy has donated a submersible called *Turtle* to Ballard's new aquarium. *Turtle* was conceived as a service vessel for that undersea war games field. It would scavenge lost weapons and bring them back. It was built down the road at Electric Boat on the Thames River. The navy is constantly looking for new toys like this, and Ballard is one of the chief players in that business.

The war is not over. They still do secret missions. And there are plenty of submarines left.

"Besides," Ballard sums things up, "I'm good news. I'm not Tailhook or Watergate. They can point at me and say, 'Look. Look what he's doing.'"

"So do you think John Craven's crazy?" I ask. Craven is convinced that Ballard is the navy's new Dr. Strangelove. Based on what Ballard has just told me, that sounds about right.

"Not crazy. Eccentric," Ballard says. "He wants credit for his career. Everything he ever did was secret. Who wants their life shredded when it's over?"

I appreciate the fact that Ballard can't tell me what would prompt the navy to be interested in his visit to the Black Sea. So I ask Craven his opinion. "No, I can't tell you, either," he says. "And yes, you can figure it out for yourself. Is this an area of strategic and military concern? Do you think that military hardware of significance has been lost in the Mediterranean or the Black Sea? Do planes that land on carriers sometimes not land and sink instead? You want to know what's in the Mediterranean and Black Sea? This is Davy Jones's locker. You just have to ask yourself, What's in Davy Jones's locker?"

· · ·

Ballard has fallen silent as we drive out toward the spot on the Connecticut River where he is building a new house for his new life. The Mercedes enters Old Lyme, gliding through forests and horse farms. "The family comes first," he says. "I'm allowed five weeks a year at sea. I don't have any family, so it's all my wife Barbara's family." He drives more slowly as we approach the house. Periodically he stops to admire the beauty. Their new house is surrounded by a nature conservancy. "These fields can't change," he says, as if casting for one fundamental truth that will remain constant instead of becoming an ever-shifting dream.

As Ballard turns onto a mud two-track and cuts through woods, we catch glimpses of a huge edifice through the tangle of black branches. As we get out, Ballard says, "I'm going to grab a tree" and vanishes into the woods muttering, "Too many Cokes."

Construction debris is everywhere, and workers dance on the roof. Ballard returns from his errand, and I attempt to follow as he runs from place to place, vaulting up stairs, naming the rooms. The inside of the house is barely framed up. Everything smells of pine sap and fresh concrete.

A separate, smaller house is attached to the big house through the garage. He seems like the kid at school who is so unsure of himself that he has to work overtime to impress you. "Wait'll you see my office," he says, as we climb a plank on which rubber treads are nailed. "Then you'll see that I know what I'm doing." It commands a view of a marsh, where a silvery channel of water dips through a swale of reeds below the house. "Barbara's lap pool will be down there," he says. "This is her project. She's on budget and on time."

We crawl through a hole in a wall and wind up in the main house, where he shows me what he calls "the kids' play area—as far away from my part of the house as possible." Ballard has a five-year-old son, Ben, and a daughter, Emily, who's one and a half.

Down another level, the bare concrete basement breathes a cold humidity. He shows me the locations for the building of the gym , the family theater, and what he calls his Yankee workshop. "I'm a homebody," he says. "I love to stay home and fix up the house."

We climb back to the main level and stand in the family room, looking down to the head of the estuary. The sun etches a mandala of yellow light on the dusty plywood floor. "I have completely retooled my life," he says, thoughtfully. "But I think I got it right this time. I have a new wife, a new family, a new job—everything."

We drive back toward Mystic through dappled sunlight and shade. He is quiet, introspective. He speaks of collecting wine, and of the upcoming Thanksgiving dinner with Barbara's old-line Connecticut Yankee family, and of a life he envisions in which he is connected to the world electronically and never has to leave his house. "When fiber comes down Route 156, I'm building a teleconferencing center in the basement. This is the future. I think the internet is reinventing the family, the old days when Mom and Dad were home. I spend more time with my wife and kids than ever before, and my productivity is up. What's wrong with this picture? It's a great adventure. Ben woke up melancholy this morning, so I got him all snuggled up in my arms, and we lay on the couch and watched the sun come up." He smiles. "Pretty good stuff," he says. "Pretty good stuff."

Ballard slouches in the leather driver's seat, flicking through the turns with one finger. "This new career will take up the rest of my professional life. So there's no question of 'I wonder what I'm going to do when I grow up.' I'm happier than I've ever been, and I'm nicer than I've ever been. Barbara calls me the 'kinder, gentler Bob.' I don't have anything to prove. I'm done with impressing the world." He sighs. "I feel I've dropped anchor for the first time in my life."

He drives on in silence, and after a while he seems to forget what he's just said. I can see his eyes go far away, and he comes back sharp and focused. He paraphrases Joseph Campbell to preface the thought I can see developing. "Life is the act of becoming," he says. "One never arrives."

He straightens up in his seat and looks at me. "I want to be the father of deepwater archaeology," he announces. "I'm going to have to earn that. Let's roll up our sleeves and get at it!"

• • •

There had been other expeditions to find *Titanic*. In each case, they had laid down search lines less than nine hundred feet apart to avoid missing her hull. *Titanic* was 882 feet, 9 inches long. That constraint meant staying on station a month. A month at sea costs a fortune, and those searchers were inevitably driven off before they could finish.

On August 12, 1985, a year after surveying *Thresher*, Ballard was poised to set sail for *Titanic*. But he raced to the site of *Scorpion* instead. The nature of the mission was secret from everyone on board except a few key people who had to know. Steve Gegg, the navigator, said, "Whole areas of the vessel were closed off. The control vans were secured. Big red signs were put up that said, 'Restricted.' Any displays of our position were shut off."

In sending Ballard to scenes of disaster, the navy was interested not only in getting good pictures. It was worried about radiation leaks from the subs, particularly from the *Scorpion*'s plutonium warheads. In addition, the cause of *Scorpion*'s demise was still a mystery.

Argo mapped the site in four days. Then *Knorr* raced toward *Titanic*'s resting place, arriving on the twenty-fourth in good weather.

Thresher had shown Ballard the secret. Since 1912, everyone had held the same mental image: a nearly nine-hundred-foot-long hull, lying in two thousand fathoms like a model in a vitrine. Ballard had imagined it that way, too. But *Thresher* had opened his eyes and put *Titanic* within his grasp. To find a deepwater wreck, you don't look for a hull a few hundred feet long. You look for a trail of debris a mile or more long. And when you find it, it will take you directly to the heaviest debris, the ship itself. You didn't need to "mow the lawn" over small areas of the bottom to find a single locus of wreckage. You could scale a search to cover much larger areas, needing only to spot part of a long debris trail.

Ballard calls this discovery his Rosetta stone for finding *Titanic*. And because it was classified top secret, he kept his new technique to himself. *Thresher* had taught Ballard that his search lines could be almost a mile apart. *Argo* could cover the whole "box" in ten passes.

Ballard bet everything on this theory. The good news was that it would take him only six days to search the hundred-square-mile box. The bad news was that there wouldn't be time to try again if he failed. And if something broke, the show was over.

The control van was at its emotional and physical capacity: jammed with people, filled with cigarette smoke and the aroma of fresh popcorn, pulsing with rock music. The salty sea air drifted in through the door as crew members came and went. Each team member had a specialized task. The captain piloted *Knorr*, towing the vehicle on its lateral grid, while navigators kept track of *Argo*'s position with acoustic transponders. Technicians controlled her altitude with a joystick. Sonar operators hovered at their consoles, collecting images of the bottom, while a video monitor displayed images from the camera. Photographers documented the expedition, while Stu Harris, chief designer of *Argo*, stayed on the computer, solving problems as they arose.

They worked around the clock. Tension rose as the crew waited, knowing that it was just a matter of time before some component of this Rube Goldberg machine failed. To make matters worse, a storm was approaching. Three interminable days passed as the crew watched nothing but images of the empty seafloor. Malfunctions multiplied. People began seeing things. There was near mutiny when one crew member insisted they backtrack to look at a shadow.

Ballard began to doubt himself. The comparison with the captain of the *Titanic* wasn't lost on him. It was Captain Edward J. Smith's hubris that had let him steam ahead through the night while other ships were heaved to in the North Atlantic ice fields. Ballard now saw his secret navy life, his brilliant insights, even his clever inventions, gang around to mock him in the night. His more traditional scientific colleagues disapproved of his "publicity stunt." If Ballard failed, it could do permanent damage to his career. In fact, finding *Titanic* would do permanent damage to his career, too, but that was what he wanted: to blow up his life on his own terms.

Yet as gloom descended, Ballard noticed something on the chart table. A French ship that had previously conducted sonar searches of the box had been blown off course as it laid down its first line. It had missed the northeastern edge of the box—that was the only portion that had never before been searched. It was a triangle five miles long, barely a mile wide—but large enough to contain *Titanic.*

It was Saturday, August 31, Labor Day weekend. Ballard checked the weather as the sun was going down. The approaching storm had increased to a force-eight gale, which meant they'd soon have to haul *Argo* out of the sea and begin fighting for survival. He studied the charts. After this line, number nine, *Argo* would encroach on the uncharted terrain. It was their last hope. Ballard couldn't stand to watch. He had a beer and a sandwich and went to bed.

At midnight plus forty-eight minutes, September 1, Ballard was asleep when a young tech named Billy "The Kid" Lange watched a dark shape crawl across the video monitor and cried out, "Wreckage!"

Stu Harris hit a switch, lighting up the seafloor.

The navy sonar officer called, "Hard contact!"

A tangled pipe slipped beneath *Argo*'s cameras and crept away across the screen. Once more they stared at emptiness. It was as if it hadn't happened. Ten agonizing minutes passed. Then a huge section of steel plate heaved into view. The rivets made it impossible to deny: it was part of a ship's hull. But in a major shipping lane, it could have been any ship.

Jean-Louis Michel, who was running the French wing of the expedition, looked up and saw that *Argo*'s ninth line had hit pay dirt in the exact spot where his ship had been blown off course. All at once, tons of debris filled the screen.

The ship's cook ran to wake Ballard. Michel calmly opened a book of *Titanic*'s construction details and turned to a page showing a boiler. Ballard sprinted from a dead sleep to the control van in time to see Michel holding in his hands the same image that appeared on the monitor. Theirs were the first human eyes to view *Titanic* since she sank.

Tortured sections of deck railing passed, a bronze porthole, deck equipment, a fragile unbroken lightbulb, dinner plates, wine bottles with their corks pushed inside by the pressure of the sea.

Unable to contain his elation, Ballard poured a toast. As they drank, though, he realized that they were approaching the exact time of night when more than fifteen hundred people had died horribly in those icy North Atlantic waters.

The crew followed him up on deck. At 2:20 a.m. the navy sonar officer raised a flag, while the crew observed a moment of silence. *Titanic* had sunk on a starry night in calm seas, a night just like this one. All Captain Smith would have had to do to avoid the disaster was to stop. But some people just can't stop.

As first light fell on the gray and heaving ocean that morning, *Knorr* found herself in the middle of bombers and P-3-Orion sub-hunting aircraft thundering overhead. Ships cut across the seas, which rolled with the approaching storm.

It is a stretch to believe that after the ship had been lying on the bottom for seventy-three years, *Titanic*'s position was discovered coincidentally by a NATO antisubmarine exercise on the same morning that Ballard discovered it using the navy's own secret underwater search equipment. Craven believes that Ballard was using *Titanic* as a cover for something else and that the navy was overhead to make sure no Russian subs got close enough to spy on the operation, whatever that might have been.

"The navy was oblivious," Ballard insists. "It was complete coincidence the navy was there."

Craven said this about what occurs underneath cover stories such as the investigation of *Thresher* and *Scorpion*: "We'd also need another cover that's unclassified. Okay, well, we have the *Titanic* down there right in that region, and we can do our missions while using *Titanic* as cover. As we do that, we discover to our shock and surprise that our old buddies from the Soviet Union are out to do the same mission. They've shown up with their *Mir* submersible. Ballard goes out of Woods Hole; Sagalevich, one of Russia's chief ocean scientists, goes out of the Shirshov Institute, which was the KGB's oceanographic institution; and nobody is fooled that it's anything other than top-level spying. The Soviets don't spend money to hunt for *Titanic*."

Ballard became famous overnight. He had achieved one of his lifelong dreams. But even as he gained prominence from his books, magazine articles, and documentaries, his personal life was suffering. In the summer of 1989, his son Todd was killed in a road wreck. Ballard's life began to come unglued. He filed for divorce and looked for ways out. Like Cortés, he began to dismantle his ships.

. . .

On our last day together, we drive out to the University of Connecticut at Avery Point in Groton, where Ballard keeps one of *Argo*'s descendants, a remotely operated vehicle for undersea exploration. Ballard lunges through the glass doors into the old Marine Science and Technology Center and charges down the dimly lit, yellow-painted cinder-block corridor. He points to an office. "Dick Cooper is in there. He's a pioneer in saturation diving." Saturation diving. That's how Craven tapped the Soviet communication cable. We stop at another lab, where Ballard discusses new projects with his colleagues. Then we go back out into the wind and cross through gleaming sunlight toward an old lighthouse and a stone castle, which are situated on the rocky verge of the ocean. Flags snap in the fresh breeze, and Ballard looks at the waves and says, "It's not a good day to be out to sea. They always say, 'The storm went harmlessly out to sea,'" he laughs. "You don't work in a wind like this, you survive."

We climb down to the shore. Lobster pots float in the dark water, bobbing in the breakers. Seabirds wheel and cry. We sit in the sun on the stone rim of the sea. There is no sand, the beach is one huge slab of stone as far as the eye can see.

"It's beautiful here," he says.

We walk the granite shore, and he kneels at a hollow place in the rock. "A tide pool," he says. "My roots. Where I began as a child. It's a microcosm, and it changes every twelve hours. The tide comes in and changes out the pool. You might come back and find a fish stranded there. It's taken out to sea, and then it's handed back to you. It's such a neat thing. I love rocks that have been in the ocean." He looks around, and his face takes on a wry expression. "Some sadist dumped us here. There's a part of each of us that wants to know about our world."

He lowers his hand to the rock shelf and feels its surface. "This is New England granite," he says. "This rock is probably Ordovician, about four hundred fifty million years old." He studies the striations, then launches into an impassioned speech. "You see," he says with quiet excitement, "most people start with the Atlantic Ocean opening, but they're missing a few billion years, because before it opened, it closed." He explains that the rock beneath us was continental shelf when North America collided with Africa. One tectonic plate shoved under another, and the rock we are touching was actually thrust into the molten earth's magma. Suddenly I feel as if we're handling a meteorite, something that has visited another world and returned transformed by its journey.

He runs his hand over it, feeling for more information. "Subduction melted the continental shelf and made granite. And then other forces heated it again later on but not enough to melt it. See here? Just enough to bend it." He shows me the curved lines in the rock face. "Then it cracked, and hot fluids, geysers like the ones you find in Yellowstone, pushed through the crack, and this light line is the result. See how it goes all down the beach?" He points.

Chemicals have precipitated out of the fluid and formed a line two inches wide, which flees down the seashore along the angled gray plates of granite.

Perhaps for the first time, I think, I'm seeing the real Bob Ballard. Removed from his circus, he's just a kid again, trying to understand the story told on these tablets that the ocean has thrust before us.

We stop in front of a boulder that comes to Ballard's eye level. He leaps up onto it with effortless agility. He looks out to sea, and after a while he turns completely, standing to his full height on the rock. The waves curl, metallic blue and white. Suddenly he stretches out his arms in a gesture made famous by Leonardo DiCaprio in the movie *Titanic*. And he shouts, "I'm the king of the world!"

· 4 ·

The Zendo, the Dojo,
and the Superbike

UNLIKE THE MOTORCYCLE shops I remembered from my youth, Pro
Italia in Glendale, California, looked like a clothing boutique. In fact, half of the
shop was devoted to leather suits that could cost up to $3,000, stylish canvas
jackets with logos on the back, costly Italian boots, and hand-painted helmets
that ran from $1,000 up. Pro Italia was decorated in a spare modern style using
subdued colors. The few motorcycles on the carpeted floor seemed more like
sculptures than vehicles, capricious by design, with a plastic fluidity that suggested at once motion and an Einsteinian conception of space. Some of them
bore price tags above $30,000.

The display case at the counter was laid out with shining objects. The character played by Lee Marvin in *The Wild One* could not afford (and would not
want) a $395 titanium gas cap. So who was buying all of this?

Bobby Carradine, one of the notorious Carradine brothers (Keith,
David), came in with his producer, Michael Goldstein. Goldstein was trying
to decide whether to take up riding again after two years of physical therapy
following his horrendous crash on the Crest. The Crest is local parlance for
Highway 2, known as the Angeles Crest Highway, which runs from the border
of Santa Monica and Los Angeles up into the Angeles National Forest and over
a geological formation that takes the form of a crest. The object of going up the
Crest is to proceed as fast as possible through a series of sweeping curves to a
restaurant called Newcomb's Ranch. The curves on Highway 2 are not tight.
Their slow unfolding beauty invites dangerous speeds. If you can ride the Crest
going 120 miles an hour, you are considered competent. But it's not a racetrack.

It's a street. So there are factors we can't control. A patch of oil or tar. A minivan crossing the double yellow line.

Goldstein's crash: Like fighter pilots, motorcycle riders have their own language. No one speaks of a crash. They say, "I stepped off." They call it "an unanticipated dismount." Or they say, "I took a soil sample." So Goldstein stepped off at about a hundred miles an hour and broke every bone in his body, give or take a few. He got a helicopter ride, as they say. Meaning: to the hospital.

Goldstein didn't ride for two years. Now he stood in Pro Italia hungrily eyeing the Ducatis, which seemed to melt and move in the liquid light. It was hard to tell that Goldstein had been injured so badly. He walked a bit stiffly. He couldn't quite decide if he was ready to buy a new bike. He still belonged to the Clubhouse with Bobby and Lyle Lovett and the others. He went to the meetings. He even drove up the Crest (in a car) to have breakfast with them.

The Clubhouse is a loose affiliation of riders who meet just down the street from Pro Italia at eight o'clock on Sunday mornings at a steel shed where they keep their motorcycles. From the outside the shed is nondescript. Inside it looks like a church. There is a sort of chancel-and-narthex feeling to the room, and at the front, where the altar would be, Lyle's Ducati holds a place of honor. Ranked in two rows on either side of the long room are the other motorcycles, mostly Ducatis, along with some Moto Guzzis. The lighting is subdued. Chairs are set in neat rows. The floor is carpeted, and a lectern stands at the head, though I've never seen anyone speak at it. The leather suits hang on a rack at the entrance like brightly colored vestments. A lot of lime-green lightning bolts on expensive cowhide adorn the legs and arms.

The first time I rode with the Clubhouse, I hadn't been on a motorcycle in twenty-five years. The last motorcycle I'd owned had had a kick starter. When Earl Campbell, who owns Pro Italia, offered me a new Triumph, I stared at it with the dumb realization that I had no idea how to use buttons that were placed on the handlebars and around the instrument cluster. As the others were warming up their engines, I wondered if I'd even get out of the parking lot. Rick Nelson, Pro Italia's sales manager, came over to me and said, "Ride your own ride. Don't get sucked in." And walked away. It was like hearing a Zen koan.

Suddenly, everyone roared out of the parking lot, and reflexes I hadn't known since I was a teenager returned to my hands and feet. We passed through a desolate region of poisonous restaurants and stucco malls and began the climb out of Glendale on Highway 2. The leaders pulled away into the national forest. The last I saw of them, they were leaning hard into the curves at angles that defied what I knew of physics. Small in the distance, they looked like cartoon motorcycles hinged to a toy track by invisible springs that would make them lie comically flat, then pop them up again, then make them lie flat again, as fake mountain scenery revolved on a drum past the stationary bikes.

I thought to follow them, then immediately recalled what Rick had said: "Ride your own ride. Don't get sucked in." My bike had no hinge, no spring. If it leaned over that far, it would stay down. I saw them recede through several more curves, and then I was alone. When I say "alone," I mean that I was the only person on a motorcycle. I was, in fact, surrounded by great zeppelin-like sport-utility vehicles full of children.

With no more effort than it takes to pull the trigger of a pistol, I could have passed all the cars, but I was afraid. I loafed along behind a titanic white land yacht, riding beneath the weeping gloom of rock walls, which vaulted hundreds of feet straight up. At length, I reached Newcomb's Ranch and found the group finishing breakfast. The restaurant was one huge dining room of makeshift tables with plastic tablecloths. The floorboards were bare, the walls unfinished, and a woodburning stove, which appeared to be made out of the cast-off boiler of a ship, dominated the center of the room. A bar faced the road and parking lot. Helmets lined a high shelf. The guys sat with their leather suits peeled down to the waist, exposing T-shirts. One T-shirt said, "Ride Fast. Take Chances." Another was printed on the back with the legend "If You Can Read This, The Bitch Fell Off."

No one said, "Where have you been?" No one made fun of me. They were gracious and self-deprecating and said things like "Riding good isn't riding fast" and "I'm not fast at all." They said it because they had seen people killed and it had really gotten to them. There was a coffee can on the bar for donations and a crudely lettered sign that said, "WHEN YOU CRASH, the first people to reach you will be volunteer paramedics . . ." It went on to ask for donations for emergency medical equipment. The Crest was a notoriously dangerous stretch. Several motorcyclists died there every year. Nobody wanted to tempt someone to go faster and then have to watch him die on the side of the road. Even so, this didn't slow them down. When we left, they all zoomed away before I could remember how to get my motorcycle started.

When you fall down, they are even more solicitous. On another day I was following a professional rider. We had been on a freeway on our way to the pretty roads. I followed the rider off the exit ramp, which curved onto an access road. As I leaned into the turn, I found myself under the motorcycle in deep gray mud. My left leg and foot were pinned, and it wasn't at all comfortable.

Within seconds I was surrounded by riders. Though they were part of my group, I couldn't recognize anyone behind the tinted face shields of their helmets. I couldn't help thinking: Alien abduction.

Someone was saying, "Don't try to do anything. Your adrenaline is going to be really high. We'll take care of it." But my adrenaline wasn't high. I wasn't even hurt (thanks to an Aerostich suit reinforced with lots of padding and Kevlar). I just felt stupid. I'd scratched up a really nice motorcycle.

They lifted the bike off of me. They all came over and touched me, asking, "Are you all right?" It seemed like a ritual, this touching. The pro I'd been following gave me his motorcycle to ride and fixed the one I'd dropped. We rode on to a café, where we stopped for coffee. There were perhaps two dozen of us, and as we stood around in the parking lot, they came to me one by one and touched me and said, "Are you all right?" Some told stories. "If it'll make you feel any better, I stepped off last year . . ." They all seemed to be saying: There but for the grace of God go I.

Riding a motorcycle is about the most dangerous thing most people can figure out how to do. Emergency-room physicians invented the term "donorcycle." A man I know who runs a heart-transplant program for a major hospital told me that victims of motorcycle accidents were the best source for fresh hearts, because "where else can you find a perfectly healthy young person whose only difficulty is that he's brain dead?"

There is a sliding scale of danger in riding a motorcycle. As the speed increases, the danger increases. And as the path of the motorcycle turns, the danger increases exponentially. The reason is simple physics. An object in motion tends to stay in motion *in a straight line*. The faster a motorcycle goes around a curve, the less there is holding it to the road. The safest way to ride is slowly in a straight line. But the whole point is to get as close to the limit of traction as possible.

Many of the riders I rode with, in fact, had attended Freddie Spencer's school in Las Vegas (sponsored by Honda) to learn how to drive to that limit and recognize it. "There comes a point in leaning over," said one student, "where if you touch the throttle, you're going to go down. That's the point where you want to be riding. That's what Freddie's school is about." The reason to ride there is that it makes the world disappear, leaving only the beating of your pulse, the beating of the engine, and a heavy g load crushing your body into the suspension of the machine. Not everyone likes that feeling. But when it's over, the world returns in saturated colors. You feel more fully alive. Everyone around you is smiling about that shared secret. I had known the feeling in other sports—diving, gymnastics, snowboarding, and flying stunt planes. It took me months to achieve that state on a motorcycle. And I was able to do it in part because I met Dirk Vandenberg, who was the chief motorcycle test pilot for Honda of America.

. . .

Tim Carrithers, a writer for *Motorcyclist* magazine and a former racer, attended a motorcycle safety course with me. "Is it dangerous?" he said. "Hell, yes. You see this fifty-pound suit I'm wearing? Well, I don't wear it to garden in." He was referring to the Aerostich ballistic nylon suit most of us wore, which has viscoelastic padding in strategic places, Kevlar in others. Tim said he wouldn't ride around the block without it. "If you can't accept the risks, don't ride. Japan has never understood that nobody *needed* a motorcycle. Motorcycles are not for everyone, no matter what Honda would like to think. So you have to make people want them, and you can't make them want them with purely logical reasons." He used the Triumph Motorcycle company's new engine technology as an example. It had three cylinders. Why wasn't it a tried-and-true four or else a sporty V-Twin? "Because," Tim said, "*Speed Triple* sounds bitchin."

I met Dirk Vandenberg at the Motorcycle Safety Foundation course. At the time, I had no idea how funny it was that Dirk was taking the course. Later I understood that it was a bit like Max Planck taking remedial math. Dirk wasn't the sort of guy who drew attention. He stood less than six feet tall, smiled innocently, and never bragged or even mentioned what he did for a living. He wore black plastic glasses with cracked frames and a throwback moustache. His black hair had been cropped short (at a discount, it seemed). He wore square clothes, and when he drank, he drank Black Russians made with Maker's Mark instead of vodka. He smoked cigars, which he carried in a leather case in his shirt pocket, along with pens and pencils. He looked like a cross between Clark Gable and Ernie Kovacs, only cleaned up so that he might be mistaken for a high school algebra teacher. I knew vaguely that he did something under the sprawling umbrella of Honda's marketing department. The truth was, as Ray Blank finally admitted to me, Dirk was Honda's secret weapon.

Ray Blank was head of marketing for Honda of America, which supplies the world with cars, trucks, vans, motorcycles, all-terrain vehicles, electrical generators, and other types of machines that are powered by internal-combustion engines, even lawn mowers and Weed eaters. "Honda," Tim Carrithers said, "is the eight-hundred-pound gorilla."

To understand what Blank meant about Dirk, it's necessary to understand a bit about the design of motorcycles. Motorcycles are designed for different purposes. The Clubhouse riders, whose wish is to go very fast through canyons, ride sport bikes. Sport bikes are several steps away from Superbikes, which are the fastest racing motorcycles on earth. Sport bikes are designed to lean way over so that riders' knees touch the pavement and to have a head-shocking range of power such that opening the throttle makes riders feel as if they are going to be ripped off the seat and left on the road while the bike shoots ahead on its own. This has been known to happen.

Cruiser is a term applied to bikes that look like a Harley-Davidson, the company that has dominated that part of the market. When the Japanese manufacturers got into the cruiser market a few years ago, Harley-Davidson sued, but the courts decided that, as Carrithers put it, "you can't patent soul." Cruisers are heavy, loud. They do not lean well (the bike I fell off of was a cruiser), and they vibrate dramatically. Cruisers are often covered with chrome and tassels. "They're more a fashion statement than a motorcycle," Carrithers said. But they are more comfortable than sport bikes, especially on long road trips.

Then there are touring bikes, enormous jukeboxes meant for driving long distances across country, such as Honda's Gold Wing. They are just a roof short of being automobiles, and most of them have large windshields and fairings to stop the wind. (Motorcycle purists say that having the wind in your face is the *whole point*.) Touring bikes have stereos and luggage racks. Some have heaters. One of Honda's models even has a reverse gear.

Dirk's job was to design, develop, and test sport bikes for Honda. Only Honda tests sport bikes on American roads, and so there was no one like Dirk in the entire industry, no equivalent at Yamaha or Kawasaki or Suzuki. Dirk kept Honda ahead of those competitors for many years.

Dirk's name was never mentioned in the press. Ray Blank—indeed, all of Honda, right up to Soichiro Honda before his death—lived in fear that personal injury lawyers would discover the existence of Dirk-*san* (as he was called in Japan, where he had traveled more than a hundred times in the course of his twenty-one years at Honda) and find out how much one man had to do with the development of each sport bike that Honda put on the street. Because there were grisly accidents in which people were jammed under the steel Armco barriers on the sides of roads. Plaintiffs' lawyers would have a field day. They'd have someone to blame. Honda executives awoke in cold sweats sometimes, thinking how it would sound to hear Dirk's nickname reverberating through a courtroom. His colleagues called him Dangerous Dirk.

Honda sport bikes represented Dirk's art form, an expression of his very elegant answers to very knotty problems of physics, fluid mechanics, and engineering. Dirk worked like an artist making lithographs, who creates an image and then takes it to the printer to work out the final product. Honda engineers in Japan would build a prototype from their own concept or from Dirk's. Dirk would go to Japan to test and help to perfect it. For most motorcycle companies, that's where the process would end. But Honda went a step further. Japan would send the prototype to America, where Dirk would ride it not only on a test track but also on the street. "They can make them work perfectly on a test track in Japan," Dirk once told me, "but they won't be ridden on a test track. They'll be ridden on roads under a wide range of conditions."

When a prototype arrived at Honda in Torrance, California, Dirk would take the bike apart and put old body parts on it, a scuffed and dirty gas tank, ugly tires. "We'd never wash it," he said. The point of that exercise was to make the motorcycle look like some sort of anonymous beater—like Dirk himself—so that no one would know that he was testing Honda's latest technology. Then he'd ride the streets of America, a secret man on a secret mission. He looked like a dork on a ratty mongrel motorcycle that might at any moment leave him walking. In reality, he was the lead astronaut of Honda, riding a state-of-the-art instrument from one of the most sophisticated teams of engineers in the world.

Dirk loved his anonymity. He told me of the thrill—well, the laughs—he'd get pulling up to a stoplight next to a bunch of kids on Kawasaki Ninjas, one of the fastest production sport bikes. Dirk would grin that innocent grin of his and gun his engine provocatively. They could see his black plastic glasses behind his face shield. He'd give them a chance to mock him and his dirty no-name bike. And then he'd leave them in his dust while he wheelied away. Dirk could do a wheelie half a mile long. Longer.

A wheelie, of course, is that maneuver that results when the back wheel gets so much power that the front wheel comes off the ground. I remember, when I first started riding with Dirk, asking if he had any particular advice. "Cut your toenails," he said. I was puzzled until he told me about learning to do wheelies. When the bike would rear its head up so far that he'd go over the back of the seat, Dirk would hit the ground standing. Since he was usually going about fifty miles an hour by the time the bike went over, his feet would be jammed into the toes of his boots. "My toenails would all turn black and fall off," he said. "I learned to wear tight boots and cut my toenails real short."

Like motorcycle racers, Dirk enjoyed a relationship to pain quite different from my own. I regard pain as something to be avoided. I think Dirk regarded pain the way I regard the skin on an orange. He didn't really think about it. It was a flimsy barrier, which he went through easily to get to the good part.

Dirk, of course, didn't work alone. The final product represented the work of teams spread across the globe. But in a tangible sense, Dirk led Honda, and Honda led and defined not only the sport-bike industry but also the very culture of motorcycling. Since the early sixties, all the other manufacturers have been in a constant struggle to keep up with Honda, which year after year has taken the awards, won the races, and enjoyed the praise of the industry press. During his two decades at Honda, Dirk not only helped to define that company's success but did more to define the entire Japanese sport-bike industry than any other individual.

The odd thing was that Honda had no one to replace him. Many contributed, but Dirk alone actually climbed onto the bikes to ride and said: Here is what it has. Here is what it needs. He had no assistant, no protégé, until late 1997, when he brought a young racer on board and began to teach him the trade. Dirk's position was unique in all the industry, and Honda let him work in his own way with no real plan in mind other than to capitalize on his gifts and to keep him secret for as long as possible. That was the Honda Way. It was part of the spirit of Soichiro Honda, which had made the company not just successful but dominant in everything it attempted.

The company has always followed one man, Soichiro Honda, who said, "Before technology, there must be a way of thinking." Mr. Honda's Super Cub, a small motorbike that was introduced in the late fifties, still holds the distinction of being the best-selling motorized vehicle in history. Honda has sold more than a hundred million of them. The change in the culture of motorcycling, which enjoyed a defining moment when the Guggenheim Museum displayed *The Art of the Motorcycle*, can be traced to the work of Soichiro Honda. Through Dirk, it can be traced to the enduring present.

• • •

"We are an outpost of the magic kingdom," said Ray Blank. The magic kingdom to which he refers is not the one in Disney World but Honda in Japan. An intense, compact, bearded man who smoked filtered cigarettes as he walked between buildings on the Torrance campus (because there was no smoking inside), Blank spoke of his work in spiritual, even mystical, terms. "We have a lot of magicians in the race shop," he said, referring to the tidy garages where the motorcycles were prepared for racing. "Sorcerers in training, fabricators who are alchemists."

He's talking about people such as Tom Jobe. He had a drag racing team in the sixties called the Surfers. They had no sponsorship and so had to do everything themselves. Tom built an engine that could run almost pure nitromethane when all other drag racing engines could run only about 70 percent without blowing up. He wound up in the Drag Racing Hall of Fame, which to most people might be an honor equivalent to having a pool ball named after you but is impressive to the members of another racing team. Tom is the fabricator for Honda Racing. Ray Blank calls him a magician. Ray Plumb, the crew chief for Superbikes, raves about Tom Jobe. Tom, a big man with a broad Germanic face, has a special deal with Honda Racing. His contract says that he comes in when he feels like it or when they need him and they pay him a lot of money. The rest of the time he can do whatever he wants. He has a dozen computers in his house and spends a lot of time with them, like someone obsessed with gerbils. When the computer department at the Torrance campus can't solve a problem in the system, they call Tom, and he solves it. The word is that Tom can build anything out of anything. I saw a swing arm he had built that was considered a revolutionary design. I asked him if he used a computer to do the calculations. "No," he said. "I just looked at it for a couple of weeks, and it came to me. It's kind of like baking a cake."

Among his many other assignments, Blank was in charge of motorcycle racing at Honda of America at the time when I got to know him. He oversaw the expenditure of $10 million every year, which is what it cost each of the Big Four (Honda, Yamaha, Kawasaki, and Suzuki) to try to solve the technical and spiritual puzzles of moving a two-wheeled vehicle around a curved track faster than anyone else. (It sounds like a lot of money, but Honda spent ten times that to race a car at the Indianapolis 500.)

It would be easy to dismiss Blank's spiritual interpretation of his work, but it can be traced to Soichiro Honda at the time of World War II. The philosophy of which he spoke permeates and defines the company from top to bottom. Anyone who spends time at Honda will hear the workers refer to the Honda Way. It may be someone busing tables in the corporate cafeteria, or it may be the head of the company.

"The Japanese place a great value on the founder's words and philosophy," Blank said. He referred to Honda as a dojo, which is a training camp for martial arts. "The dō is the way," Blank said. "The system. The founder's way. In a sense he is viewed as a holy man." And in the same sense, that philosophy permitted Ray Blank to regard Dirk as the holy man's disciple. It permitted Dirk to work with no net. Honda had no plan B, no one to replace Dirk like a spare part if he broke. In that way, a whole corporation was, like those who ride its motorcycles, living on the edge of traction. The fragile life of one man was defining the experience of riding Honda motorcycles in the real world. And he might, at any moment, fly off into space.

Dirk, like Soichiro, seemed bent on consuming the vast landscape in huge gulps. Honda sponsored a ride for journalists in the area around Temecula, halfway between Long Beach and San Diego. The company had rented the Rancho Valencia villa in Rancho Santa Fe for our comfort. A *Miami Herald* photographer, Candace Barbot, sat backward on Dirk's bike, her feet propped precariously on the foot pegs, holding on to nothing, gorgeous blond hair flying from under her helmet, so that she could take photographs of us all coming toward her in a gang, up the hills and around the curves. Candace was demonstrating the way. She and Dirk almost immediately fell in love, in a purely spiritual sense, of course. They had found in each other kindred spirits. As Dirk fled past us at riot speed, he and Candace would laugh and shout, "Responsible riding!" mimicking the war cry of the new motorcyclist that Honda was trying to create.

Ours were no random meanderings through Julian and Rainbow Canyon. No one at Honda went off half-cocked. Dirk had gone out the week before and made a detailed "trip book," which showed each turn (with mileage and road diagrams), including notations that might help us to avoid a crash ("sand in road") or appreciate a point of interest ("Jim's Nut Farm").

I followed Dirk through an avocado plantation that covered land that had once been Mexico. Here and there a stream broke across the road, and we splashed through it in sun-glinting rooster tails. At one ford, a white German shepherd lay in the shade of a spreading tree on the edge of a ranch. He feinted at Dirk and then chased me lazily. I had the impression that if I had stopped, he would have licked my hand.

A quarter mile later we climbed a cockeyed, off-camber road that angled up at a dizzying twenty-seven degrees—Dirk had measured it. Leaning into the turns was a trick since the road banked the wrong way. At the top we all stopped, perhaps ten of us, to take in the view, while Dirk went back down. Dark palisades of mountains fled in ranks that made a monster mandible beneath the sky. The valleys in between the teeth had filled with a buttermilk mist all the way to the Pacific Ocean.

We heard his motor first and looked down the wicked incline. Then came Dirk, roaring uphill, ascending the whole way in a continuous wheelie, Dirk's trademark.

Tim shook his head, saying, "Man. Dirk-*san* is the king."

Dirk liked to wear a North Face vest. North Face has nothing to do with motorcycles. It's more the kind of gear a backpacker would wear. When we asked him about it, Dirk explained, "When I crash, I tell the emergency room doctors that I was hiking or bird-watching." Why? we all wanted to know. "In order to skew the statistics about the danger of various sports," he said. The month before he died, I was walking through the Torrance campus with Dirk and Ray Blank. We were crossing a parking lot, heading toward the race shops, when we passed a white Honda van parked among the other vehicles —motorcycles, trucks, cars, huge red semis. The van caught my attention because it was completely smashed from the front end back to about the second seat. It had also been defaced with graffiti written in Magic Marker. The inscriptions read like the ones people put on a cast when someone breaks a leg. Most of them were addressed to Dangerous Dirk. One said, "Don't tell my wife." A month earlier, I had been riding dirt bikes in Baja California, staying at Mike's Sky Rancho up in the mountains south of Ensenada, and everyone had been talking about some guy who had driven a Kawasaki into the swimming pool a few days earlier. It turned out that it had been Dirk.

When I asked Dirk about the wrecked van in the parking lot, he said, "Oh, *that* . . ." and went on to say, "No, honest, it wasn't my fault," as if I had assumed it would be. He had been streaking down the 405 in the van at about seventy-five when the car in front of him did a 360. Dirk plowed into it broadside. "The airbag wrapped my glasses around my face," he said. Other than a long bruise from the seat belt, though, he hadn't been hurt. But the inscriptions clearly suggested that everyone had assumed that the crash was Dirk's fault. Dirk, who had once sawed the cast off his broken arm so that he could surf. Dirk, who had learned to juggle and to ride a unicycle.

When someone crashed (they always do on these rides), Dirk would be the first on the scene. He took charge with a calm, gentle wisdom. He'd been there. He knew he'd be lying there again. Most people get hurt pretty badly in those falls. The country we ride in is beautiful, so it's all cliffs and ravines. The beauty and danger are the two sides of the same coin. Dirk would get the injured party to lie still, to stay calm, while someone else called an ambulance and others put out flags to warn away the oncoming cars. No matter how many crashes he witnessed, including his own, Dirk never slowed down. He certainly never entertained the idea of stopping. When we saw him ride, it appeared almost a foregone conclusion that he would die horribly, though exactly how horribly we could not have predicted.

• • •

The Honda Way combines equal parts of audacity and humility. Dirk's character and work formed its perfect expression in the same way Soichiro Honda's had. I never met Mr. Honda. So I can't know nearly as much about his character. But his deeds are revealing. Honda was the son of a blacksmith. The biographies have it that the first time Honda saw a motorcar, he ran down the street after it. He found a puddle of oil it had left, plunged his hands into it, and wiped it all over his arms in sheer joy. He dropped out of school to become an auto mechanic's apprentice. In time, he opened his own shop, and from it he raced cars until he crashed and had to spend a year recovering from his injuries. (That is a fairly typical story. Ray Blank, just to give one example, had to give up motorcycle racing because of a crash.)

At the age of thirty-one, Honda returned to school to study metallurgy so that he could manufacture better piston rings. He manufactured piston rings until the end of World War II and then began selling bicycles that were fitted with small war-surplus engines. He began development of an original motorcycle right after the war and in 1948 founded the Honda Motor Company. The next year he introduced the first Honda motorcycle, the Model D, known as the Dream. The name was not a marketing ploy. It was Soichiro Honda's dream. But it was also a dream to ride, because it had an electric starter and was quiet.

Soichiro Honda personally held 470 patents by the end of his life, none of them trivial. Each contributed substantially not only to Honda's seemingly boundless profits but also to the technical development of motorcycles and the cultural development of those who rode them—even to the way they viewed their world. If Mr. Honda (and Dirk for the last two decades of the twentieth century) formed one leg of the tripod, and his engineers formed the second, then the third leg has always been racing. Honda's emergence into racing began the long, sweeping shift in the culture of motorcycling away from the image of the Hells Angels and toward what it is today.

In 1954 Mr. Honda announced to the world that his company intended to win the world's most prestigious motorcycle race, the Isle of Man Tourist Trophy. The established forces in motorcycle racing, British and American manufacturers, greeted that declaration with grave skepticism and a certain sense of hilarity. At that time, when a Chevrolet could still be expected to last twenty years, "cheap" and "Japanese" were considered synonymous. Japan was known for transistor radios and bad copies of American engineering. Suggesting that a Japanese motorcycle could win at the Isle of Man was like suggesting that Mexico was going to put a man on the moon.

But Soichiro Honda gave no sign that he was discouraged by being the object of ridicule. A modest and self-deprecating man, he traveled to the Isle of Man that same year to see what he was up against. He found competitors whose racing machines developed three times the horsepower of anything Honda had.

Mr. Honda went back to Japan and began systematically developing a new motorcycle for the race. Never one to go off half-cocked, he spent almost five more years in the process of development and testing. To this day, Honda engineers frustrate the people in marketing and sales and even in racing because of their obsessive attention to detail, their adamant refusal to let go of anything until it is perfect. It can make the wait for a new motorcycle seem interminable to someone who wants to win a race with it or sell it on the showroom floor.

When Mr. Honda left the Isle of Man and vanished for five years into what was then the *terra obscura* of Japan, people on the American and British racing teams reasonably assumed that he'd seen the folly of his bold declaration and had retired to making silly (if profitable) little scooters. Five years is a long time. Certainly no winning team was trembling in fear of Soichiro's "rice burners," as they called them.

Then in 1959, Honda finished sixth in the ultra-lightweight 125cc class and won the manufacturer's trophy in that class. But 1961 was the year that changed everything. Honda showed up with new bikes in both the 250cc and 125cc categories and won first, second, third, fourth, and fifth places. The world of motorcycle racing was devastated. In the course of a single event, Mr. Honda had brought to an end the decades of unchallenged dominance the British and Germans and Americans had enjoyed both on the street and on the track. It was a defeat from which they never recovered. It was the beginning of the end for British motorcycle manufacturers, and the Americans (i.e., Harley-Davidson) never again held a dominant position on the track. In the years immediately after that, the mid to late sixties, my friends and I rode British bikes, Triumphs and BSAs. In 1969 when Honda introduced its in-line four, the CB750, it was a revolutionary act. Engineers around the world were trembling in their labs, knowing what it meant, but we on our Triumphs laughed at the guys on Hondas. We said they sounded like sewing machines. They sounded alien to us because we'd never heard the sound of a motorcycle running properly. While we were stuck at the side of the road, kicking and kicking our starters, trying to get a dead BSA going, the Honda guys zoomed silently past us, waving and smiling. Mr. Honda had not yet concerned himself with what we called "soul," the sound of a poorly designed engine, on which Harley-Davidson believed it held a patent. That would come later. At that time, Honda had one thing in mind: the irrefutable act of going faster than anyone else—forever.

Our motorcycles, when they ran, sounded like thunder. Even in our youth, we were the old guard. We were the Four Horsemen of the Apocalypse. We were blind to the future and to the significance of Honda's engineering perfection. Decades later, Honda would have to engineer great, lobed crankshafts that would mimic in a well-designed engine the vibrations—the thunder—that took place naturally in a poorly designed one. They literally stole Harley's thunder. The bike was called the Shadow, perhaps as a nod to the old Vincent Black Shadow.

During the seventies, Honda spread its influence throughout all categories of motorcycle racing. It wasn't just because of good work, perfectionism, hiring the best riders. It was official company policy to win. It was a spiritual mandate. It was the Honda Way. And Honda didn't merely win. He destroyed his opponents. When he announced that he would win at the Indianapolis 500, it sent a shock wave of fear through the automobile industry. By then people understood what such a declaration from Soichiro meant, and as in a B-grade horror movie, they could see the dark shadow lengthening as Honda returned to Japan to spend another six years developing a racing engine and a chassis that would blow away the British Cosworths and the American engines, which had held a lock on car racing until then. When Honda took an interest in your sport, it was a death sentence. You knew he'd catch you. You even knew approximately how long you had to live.

But racing was never an end in itself, not any more than meditation in a Zendo is an end. Sitting in silence is a means to the goal of enlightenment. Koichi Amemiya, who held several top positions at Honda over the years, says that the "racing spirit" is the driving force within the company.

"Racing is the crucible of development," Ray Blank told me. "Racing is the only way to develop anything. Engineering excellence comes from a basis of competitive elements that are found only in racing. There is no thought at Honda of ever getting out of racing."

Honda not only competes with the world. It competes with itself. Blank showed me Tom Jobe's work in the race shop one day. We marveled at the ingenuity of the device, a finely machined ellipse within another ellipse, used for tightening the drive chain. "Japan has already thought of this, I'm sure," Blank said matter-of-factly. "But they won't tell us. That's part of the discipline. We are their children." The Honda Racing Corporation in Japan does not give Blank motorcycles to race. American Honda must purchase them, develop them, and support itself on its own. "We are a *gempo*," Blank said, "a distributor responsible for our own development and marketing." Each year American Honda purchases two Superbike race packages, each for around $600,000, from Japan. The package is essentially a motorcycle (some assembly required) and spare parts, including a spare engine. It's like receiving a model in a box. More than that, it's like receiving a puzzle. The mechanics and motorcycle "tuners," as they are called, then must take the parts "and bring this bike to life," as Blank put it. "What they do in the shop dramatically changes it. Development of the bike never stops." The Superbike that Honda raced at the time I was visiting carried the designation RC45. "It's eight years old and still evolving," Blank told me. Perhaps most frightening to its competitors at Suzuki, Yamaha, and Kawasaki (Harley-Davidson was no longer a serious competitor, and the British didn't even enter the big races by then) was the fact that the RC45 was an antique by Superbike standards. Yet it continued to win against motorcycles that had been introduced that same year. At one event at the Laguna Seca Raceway in Monterey, California, race officials wanted to inspect the RC45 for possible violations of the rules, because they couldn't explain how it could keep going faster and faster every year.

Despite what people say, winning is everything, and Honda's sweeping victory at the Isle of Man in 1961 was the defining moment in the history of motorcycling. The romanticized American tradition of grease and gumption were shown to be no longer sufficient to the task. A strong scientific method, along with the Japanese way of addressing a job with fierce dedication and Zen patience of oceanic depth, had proved to be the only formula for winning both on the track and in the marketplace. And the world of motorcycling began its gradual turn away from the image of the Ugly American Biker. When the cultural compass had finished its swing, it pointed due east. American motorcycle culture turned to the perfectionism of the Zendo. (Harley-Davidson remains nothing more than a fashion statement.) There are even those who argue that our very consciousness of the term "Zen" can be traced to Japan's motorized vehicle industry. It appears now even in the way the racers talk about themselves and their work.

. . .

At the time I met him, Rich Oliver, thirty-six, was the oldest rider in the Superbike class, having moved up in 1997 from his position as "the all-time winningest rider in AMA 250 Grand Prix history with 32 career victories." In that type of competition, however, the bike he rode had been more like a street bike that anyone could ride, though admittedly not the way Oliver rode it. "And when I won, I won by a mile," he said. He was actually modest, soft-spoken, and articulate. As we sat at dinner one night, he described to me what it was like to ride when he was winning. "I was in the zone. It was as if I wasn't there." He said that he would take the energy of the crowd, the team, of everyone who was watching as well as racing, and in some ineffable way, he would let that energy pour through him. He described it as a transcendent state in which he was not thinking at all. "I was hardly there," he said more than once, groping for an expression that would capture what he had experienced.

Crossing the finish line was ecstatic. "I couldn't figure out how I did it," he said. Like jockeys, most motorcycle racers are lean and lightly built. Rich wore a goatee, his black curly hair was neatly trimmed. Although his education had ended with high school, he had a large vocabulary and picked through it carefully to create thoughtful sentences. "I suppose in any athletic event people have that experience," he told me.

He was distressed because, as he put it, "I spent ten years learning how to ride supersport and 250cc bikes. And when I moved to Superbikes, everything I learned suddenly became irrelevant. It was worse than knowing nothing. Jamie is just starting out," he said of another racer, Jamie Hacking, who was ten years younger, "so he doesn't have anything to unlearn. But now I do what I know how to do instinctively. And I crash. It's very discouraging."

Worse than that, worse even than losing, was the spiritual loss of not being able to ride "in the zone." He could no longer transcend. Contrary to what a rider might say (and even believe), he did not ride to win. Winning, which is an absolute requirement for the industry, is secondary to the best riders. Oliver said that he raced in order to reach that transcendent and timeless interval in which he could lose himself to the machine, to the energy of momentum, and to the myriad forces that he at once battled and recruited to his purpose. Oliver hoped (and perhaps did not yet believe) that in time he would recapture that essence on the Superbike.

Part of the reason that the racers find their work so deeply spiritual may have to do with the fact that they begin riding at a very early age. Mat Mladin, a former Australian Superbike Champion, started when he was four. Doug Chandler, who eventually wound up in the American Motorcyclist Association Motorcycle Hall of Fame, started when he was five. When Miguel Duhamel was a baby and couldn't sleep, his mother would strap him to her body and ride around in the night air on a motorcycle. In the American Motorcyclist Association (AMA) Superbike series, he won thirty-two times, second only to Mat Mladin. Incidentally, they all began on Hondas.

In order to succeed, the racer's mind must tell him that everything is all right when his engine is at its breaking point and his body is traveling at 185 miles an hour. At 14,500 revolutions a minute, the engine sounds like a human cry.

I asked Oliver to explain why the transition from supersport to Superbike was so cruel. One would think that a motorcycle is a motorcycle, and racing is racing. "The Superbike is so much heavier," he said, "that its momentum works against you. And it has so much power, so readily available, that it requires a completely different touch." The Superbike can accelerate its 355 pounds of mass to more than a hundred miles an hour in the equivalent of a city block. It takes about three seconds.

Given the power and sensitivity of the instrument, the precision required of the rider is difficult to imagine. A typical rider's lap times may vary within no more than two-tenths of a second. A lap may take a minute and a half to complete. At some tracks it's two minutes. It is a variation of less than 0.2 percent.

During a turn, the back wheel spins from so much power, while centrifugal force causes the front wheel to slide. The bike is going sideways as it completes the turn. If the slide remains steady and the weight is distributed evenly between front and back, the rider drifts through, straightens up at the end, and continues in a new direction. But applying as little as 5 percent too much power can cause the rear tire to slide more than the front tire. "In a 250 you can actually flick it back in line with the throttle and with your body. You can kick it back. The Superbike is so heavy that once it gets away from you, momentum carries it around. You can't save it." Instead of one body composed of man and machine in perfect coordination, it becomes like two men in a donkey costume, and the back steps out ahead of the front. In supersport racing, as racers say, the throttle is your friend. After the transition to Superbike, you're no longer friends. And the same is true for the street rider who decides to go 120 on the Crest.

· · ·

The gulf between American culture and Japanese culture would not be bridged quickly and not by victory alone. There was still the problem that a motorcycle was, in America—if not in Europe or Asia—a completely nonessential product. Honda's concept—that motorcycling was a family pastime for everyone—was wrong when it came to America. In Europe and Asia, people rode motorcycles because gasoline cost too much there, because cars were too big and expensive, and because there was simply not enough room on the streets.

But Americans couldn't imagine going without a car. Owning a motorcycle in the United States was like owning a pair of skis. There was no practical reason for it. But that was a difficult concept for the people at Honda to understand.

Honda's success in America would depend on its ability to satisfy an ineffable American hunger. It required a deep comprehension of a purely American lust. It had to do with attitude, with soul, with styling. It had to do with the fact that the American market was a mile wide and an inch deep and was dominated by products that were often pure style. Honda seemed unable to comprehend that concept and therefore needed a surrogate in America, essentially someone who could think for the company.

The American surrogate was Dirk Vandenberg, whom Ray Blank called "the mind of the American motorcyclist." It was his job for all those years to take the achievements of the Japanese engineers, developed through racing, and to wage a campaign (and sometimes bitter battles) to transform sophisticated race hardware into a rough, tactile, sensual experience that seduced the broadest possible range of American thrill seekers. Even after Honda had begun to win races worldwide, there was still a wide range of technical problems that needed to be solved, and Dirk was often at odds with Japan not merely about how to solve them but even about which problems were worth solving. When you dominate the world of racing, it's difficult to admit that you have problems. It was Dirk's freakish gift that in a sort of T. E. Lawrence fashion, he could cross those cultural boundaries. He could communicate with the Japanese (though he knew little Japanese). I saw him do it with gesture, grin, and pidgin. He could bring the two worlds together in the manifest and undeniable reality of a red motorcycle, which, when placed on the showroom floor, sold like there was no tomorrow, which was exactly how Dirk rode.

Dirk's role in creating the VTR 1000 Superhawk was emblematic of his struggle. When I first returned to motorcycling with Lyle Lovett and the Clubhouse, the Italian Ducatis at Pro Italia were the sine qua non of sport bikes, bikes on which a rider could lean hard and fast around the mountain byways, contesting Newton's right to define the rules that govern how we move about our planet and how our planet moves around the sun. The problem with a Ducati is the demands it places on even a highly skilled rider. A Pro Italia mechanic named Ed irks his boss, Earl Campbell, by riding a Honda to work. Earl ranted and raved and ordered Ed never to mention the name Honda again. I asked Ed what he thought about the Ducatis on which he spent his days working, and he said, "They're not for most people. They'll just spit you off if you don't know what you're doing."

I spent several days riding up and down the Crest on a variety of bikes to see which bikes I could ride the fastest. The top Ducati, the 916, proved to be my slowest ride. The reason was that it was uncomfortable and it frightened me. Confidence equals speed. Rick Nelson, who had warned me to "ride your own ride," said, "Oh, you just need to get going over eighty, and the wind kind of lifts you up off the handlebars and takes the stress off your wrists." Tim Carrithers told me that the 916's steering didn't really function well below that speed. Dirk understood the mind of the common motorcyclist. He understood that riders of my skill level weren't going anywhere near eighty on the Crest. He understood that we might like to ride a bitchin' bike that through its inherent engineering qualities would give us a natural and confident feeling. He understood if we felt that good on the bike, it wouldn't matter how fast we were going.

It took him twelve years to convince Honda to manufacture the Superhawk. Honda didn't want it. The reason was strictly a cultural one. Honda had spent decades developing the best motorcycle engines in the world, most especially a V-four, used in the RC45 Superbike. It had a perfectly good street bike built around that engine called the Interceptor or VFR 750 (later increased to 800), which could, in the hands of a competent rider, whack a Ducati on the Crest.

During the seventies, Soichiro Honda, through his studies of metallurgy and his patented designs, solved the problem of how to make a small engine produce tremendous horsepower. But European bikes still handled better. (Honda won races, but most people don't race.) The main problem was the frame, which would flex in a turn. Steering was unpredictable. As a result, the bike did not impart great confidence in the rider. The nose wandered. Tim said, "The Japanese didn't figure out how to make a motorcycle go around a corner until 1980," which was about the time that Dirk began testing.

Dirk explained that the object of his work was to develop a motorcycle that would adhere to the road and behave predictably, that would give the rider that all-important feeling of confidence, which allows him to push himself to the limits of his skill. But at another time, one night after a few Maker's Mark Black Russians (called Revolvers in the world of bartenders), Dirk explained it like this: "Men want three things: money, horsepower, and pussy. Women control all the pussy and eighty percent of the money. All we can give men is horsepower."

Of course, he meant more than horsepower. He meant a sense of inner control. Suspension was the key to the feeling of control. "The reason you feel instantly comfortable on the Superhawk," Dirk told me after I'd ridden it up the Crest a few times, "is the suspension." When he says suspension, he means not just springs that absorb bumps but also the frame itself and other components that connect the wheels and motor to the rider and to the road. Over the years, to solve the problem of flex, manufacturers had made the frames more and more rigid. "But that means that every bump the back tire hits is transmitted to the front wheel," Dirk said. "On a perfect test track, that's fine. But in the real world, it makes the bike hard to steer." With Honda engineers, Dirk began to reinvent flex, to give up some rigidity in favor of more control at ordinary speeds on imperfect roads. I rode a dozen motorcycles, but only the Superhawk gave that sense of lovely and effortless control. "The engine is a stressed member of the frame. The swing arm is bolted to the engine," Dirk explained. "The engine is bolted to the frame with six bolts, but only one pair are solid." The rest are hollow, allowing for flex. Because the rear wheel is disengaged slightly from the front wheel, the front remains planted firmly on the pavement, with the result that the steering feels rock solid. Dirk also changed the weight distribution, which traditionally puts half the weight on each wheel. Dirk put only 47 percent of the Superhawk's weight on the front. Since the front was firmly planted, extra weight could be used to allow the rear wheel to grab the pavement more efficiently during acceleration. The result was a subtle but undeniable feeling of settling into the machine, of becoming one with it, and most importantly, of trusting it to go where you point it. "This is the most connected bike we've ever made," he said. On the Crest, going fifty on the Ducati 916, I felt as if I was going to crash. Going seventy on the Superhawk, that feeling never entered my gut. And of course, the gut is what makes you buy the bike in the first place.

Once the horsepower game was over (and long before the Superhawk), the Big Four understood that handling was destined to be the dominant factor in motorcycle design. In fact, when the motorcycle reaches a speed of around 195 miles an hour, the air is compressed so much that the rear wheel begins to spin on the pavement. The bike hits a brick wall and parks. Although more horsepower is available, the air won't let the bike accelerate, and then here comes another curve anyway, so the rider has to slow down. The race of the future was going to be won by the frame, the suspension, and the tires, because everybody was already going as fast as they could go on the straightaways.

Turning, as it happens, embodies the greatest mystery of motorcycling and the greatest challenge faced not only by the engineers and by Dirk but by the race teams as well. Because turning incurs such severe penalties at the hands of physics. It is in the turn that races are won or lost. It is in the turn that the rider going 120 miles an hour up the Crest experiences his death. A motorcycle doesn't crash going in a straight line unless a car makes a left turn in front of it.

David Thom, a researcher at University of Southern California's Head Protection Research Lab, had joined us at the Motorcycle Safety Foundation course we attended before our ride through the countryside around Temecula. Thom helped to write the Hurt Report, published in 1981 by the Traffic Safety Center at the University of Southern California, which set out to analyze the causes of motorcycle accidents and identify what could be done to help prevent them. The researchers conducted an exhaustive investigation of nine hundred accidents. The Hurt Report has not been brought up to date, and critics believe that the industry doesn't really want to answer the question of how safe motorcycling is. The answer, intuitively, is: you don't have to do a lot of research to know that a motorcycle turns you into a human cannonball.

But one of the findings of the Hurt Report is not intuitive. Hurt's research confirmed a mystifying phenomenon that until then had been anecdotal: one-third of all riders "*did NOTHING* in the way of evasive action in the pre-crash time," said the report (Thom's emphasis). "The ability to intentionally counter-steer and generate the sudden swerve was generally unknown by these riders." In other words, most riders never learned how to turn a motorcycle. They didn't know how to ride.

During the safety course, I discovered that I didn't know how to turn, either. I had never thought about how a motorcycle turns. I knew that I couldn't get it to do exactly what I wanted in a predictable way. Sometimes I'd think *left*, but it would just keep on going straight. Or it would go left but not exactly when and how I wanted. I'd never heard the term "counter-steering." The truth was, I'd been lucky until then.

That inability to turn results in one of the gravest dangers, as both Thom and Dirk agreed, which is doing nothing. No one believes he'll simply freeze like a deer in the headlights. But late one night, sitting in front of a fire at Rancho Valencia, Dirk's wife, Donna, who along with Candace was one of the few truly hard-riding women I got to know, told me about a trip that she and Dirk had taken. The lead rider had missed a corner entirely, failed to turn, and driven off the road. "Four other motorcycles followed him right off the cliff," Donna said. "Dirk and I were on the fifth bike, and we managed to stop." That is the definition of the phrase "getting sucked in." Which is why Rick Nelson had said to me on that first mad dash I took with Lyle and the Clubhouse, "Ride your own ride. Don't get sucked in." Those guys drove off a cliff because they got sucked in.

There is good reason that so many people are confused about turning. To go left, the front wheel has to be turned to the right. Imagine doing that on ice. Newton's law would make the bike continue in a straight line, against the direction that the front wheel has been turned. But since the bike is stuck to the road by the friction of tires on pavement, it won't slide, it will begin to fall over, to lean (toward the left in this case).

Sensing that the bike is falling, the rider will turn the wheel back toward the left, as if to stop the fall. All this happens in a fraction of a second. Once the bike is leaning and the front wheel has been realigned toward the left, a left turn is established. All that maneuvering sacrifices a lot of energy to friction and heat, so the addition of a little power continues the turn. To come up out of the turn, the front wheel actually has to be turned deeper into the left turn, which has the opposite effect and rights the bike. It happens unconsciously for the most part. I've talked to Superbike racers who couldn't explain how they turned, but they are different from us. Without a thorough understanding of counter-steering, ordinary riders will crash. It's only a matter of time.

Since engineering for the racetrack always trickles down to the street, a new generation of more sophisticated riders evolved during the eighties and nineties. Once they became aware of what it felt like to ride a bike that (in Dirk's words) was connected, nothing else would do. That type of knowledge was very new, almost secret, when Dirk began to wage his campaign for the Superhawk in 1984 and cobbled together his first prototype. He tried to sell it to Japan and failed. "They thought the market was too small," Dirk said, "and they were right." But Dirk was ahead of his time, even ahead of the engineers in Japan. Honda was working on suspensions and had a perfectly good V-four engine. Why build a twin (which was what the Superhawk would be)? The answer was that the efficient four-cylinder engines sound like sewing machines. A twin vibrates. It has a throaty sound. It feels and sounds like a real motorcycle. The perfect motorcycle not only had to have horsepower and to handle beautifully. It had to have soul. As good as the Japanese are supposed to be at understanding mysterious things, they didn't understand American soul.

At that time, the only V-Twin sport bikes were the so-called exotics, the ones I had seen lately at Pro Italia in Glendale—Ducati, Moto Guzzi, Bimota—which could cost $30,000 or more. One Super Bowl Sunday at Pro Italia, Rick Nelson, the sales manager, had mused on the Ducati mystery. "The Suzuki has a stronger motor and it's cheaper," he said. "But the Ducati is the best. It's a Ferrari. For me sound is the soul of a bike. If I can't get off on the sound of it, then it doesn't matter what the cost is. And sometimes with those Japanese bikes, it gets so technical and refined that you lose what the thing is about. I can bypass technology for soul."

Dirk said, "We wanted to capture the riders who had passion. We needed something with soul."

Tim explained it this way: "You say, 'I want a Ducati 916 so bad my gums sweat.' Why? Because it's the kind. Then you get out on it, and you find out that it is, it *is* the kind. But you can't use it. It wants to be ridden hard, and nine-tenths of the time, you're going out to Dunkin' Donuts, and on that slow ride through traffic, a 916's going to beat you like a redheaded stepchild. You can ride the Superhawk anywhere, anytime, and in the hands of a good rider, it'll spank the 916." Honda wasn't the first to think of this. Suzuki had the same idea a little earlier with the TL1000S. "But it's ugly as a mud fence," Tim said. And it's not connected the way the Superhawk is.

Shortly before his death, Dirk finally succeeded in getting Honda to put the VTR 1000 Superhawk on the market. The miracle of Honda's answer to Ducati was that a rider of ordinary skills could go really fast up the Crest (or Decker Canyon or Latigo Canyon) and also could feel confident going to Dunkin' Donuts. Lyle, a confirmed Ducati guy, wasn't all that sure he liked it at first. "It's like a Ducati with power steering," told me. But then he bought one. It is, after all, an engineering marvel.

Dirk introduced me to the Superhawk on that first extravagant weekend, that incredibly expensive Honda hoedown at the Rancho Valencia villa in Rancho Santa Fe. This was where Dirk's wife, Donna, had told me about riders going off the road because of failing to "ride your own ride." This was the press event to promote motorcycling as a family activity, fun, safe, joyous, and clean. Honda had sent out a semitrailer truck full of motorcycles, all its models on board, including the Superhawk.

We ate lobster and lamb chops in the huge dining room under a beamed ceiling, attended by liveried servants before a leaping fire. Afterward, over Armagnac and a selection of Cubanos, Dirk's boss, Gary Christopher, told us of a dream he'd had. Gary was not just a corporate executive but also a man possessed by motorcycling. He was the honest goods, a true believer. In his dream, Gary was doing a wheelie. Only it wasn't just any wheelie. It was the wheelie to end all wheelies. It went on and on, fifty, sixty, seventy miles an hour, down the road. And he was happy in that dream. Everyone leaned in and listened as he told the story, and I kept waiting for the punch line, but there was none. When Gary was done, we all put our fingers to our chins. Tim nodded solemnly. I nodded, too. Dirk and Candace nodded, and even Donna nodded.

Everyone understood. He told us how happy he'd been, and we all got it. It was deep. It was a tale from the Zendo.

The next day we went riding through avocado and tangerine plantations. We stopped on a quiet road to rest, to trade bikes among ourselves, to get our bearings, and to zero our odometers before entering the mouth of the dragon, fifteen miles of curving, intestinal switchbacks and long, decreasing-radius turns that would suck you in and then spit you out if you weren't concentrating. We were somewhere in the vicinity of Mount Palomar on roads known to be the best motorcycle routes in the country because of their serene beauty and the jagged technical demands they placed on both rider and bike. Dirk had been riding with Candace on the back of the brand-new Superhawk, which had not even been released for sale, and now he offered the bike to me.

We stood around looking like fighter pilots in our Aerostich Roadcrafter ballistic nylon suits, and for a few minutes, we compared notes and studied our route, taking cookies and bottled water and apples and juice from the open back of the big white support van in which Beverly and her assistant, Kim, were following us. A few years earlier, Beverly St. Clair had been hired by the Big Four to set up a group called Discover Today's Motorcycling, which would attempt to correct the problem of sagging sales. Beverly undertook a media blitz that sought to instill in the public mind an image of motorcycling as stylish and responsible. During the first half decade of DTM's existence, motorcycle sales doubled and doubled again, as did DTM's budget. Beverly had given us all cell phones so that we could stay in touch. Each time we stopped she mentioned "responsible riding."

I mounted the Superhawk and roared into the narrow bituminous channel that had been cut through a shaggy old eucalyptus forest. I found myself behind Dirk and Tim, thinking of Tim's rules of life. For example: "Never be the first kid to jump off the garage roof." Tim was tall and looked like a serious athlete. His short hair, which tended to spike on its own, still retained a bit of the red color from the night a tall and beautiful woman named Sally had decided to dye it for him. Tim had been hoping for something more intimate, but it had turned out to be something of a Samson and Delilah night. I had ridden the Crest with Tim and had turned five hundred off-road miles in Baja while eating adult portions of his dust. I had come to trust him. I knew he wouldn't kill me—not on purpose. So I settled in behind him and Dirk and thought: Whither thou goest, I shall go.

We entered the shade of the eucalyptus trees, whose branches came together overhead to form a tunnel. The road was black and soft and narrow, barely wide enough for two cars to pass each other. On either side were neatly tended *ranchitos* with painted fences and flowering bushes and cropped lawns. Tim referred to these as "potpourri plantations." The smell was intoxicating.

Soon the road fell away and began plunging and leaping through a series of splits, spikes, and bullwhip curves, returning to itself like a river driven mad by gravity.

Once again, as always, I found myself alone. But presently I rounded a curve and saw Tim politely waiting for me. Dirk had gone ahead. Tim sat athwart his cycle, ass cocked to one side like a racer, arms and legs dangling with slack-limbed indolence, one finger languid on the throttle. Michelangelo could have sculpted him. But the motorcycle's tail looked venomous, wasp-like, and as Tim's head swiveled, the face shield glinted like a compound eye, and I remarked how this image of him combined the utterly human with the completely alien and how that was exactly what Dirk had worked so hard to achieve. Odd how the Japanese had failed to comprehend what he was after. Tim could have been an image in a Japanese comic book.

He raised a hand and urged me on. He was going to show me how to do it. I was to follow him into the Gretel darkness.

Tim slipped his six-foot-four frame back into riding position. His bike surged forward. I tucked down on the Superhawk and found that the gas tank accepted my abdomen in an almost sexual embrace. So this was the missing piece of the engineering puzzle: me. I grabbed a handful of throttle. The bike was drawn effortlessly in behind Tim's. We were welded together, brothers in Aerostich armor. Suddenly my life—all life—made sense. I thought: This is a test. It's about trusting myself, about trusting my friends, about trusting Dirk's machine. Dirk's machine could do anything that I had the hair to attempt.

Commitment is more than a word: once you fly into a turn carrying speed, you can't decide that it's a bad idea. Tim had told me, "If you want to wad up your beautiful new VTR 1000 faster than junior-jet stink, just grab a big handful of that floating front disc brake while you're in a corner." So to find the path out, he'd said, go deeper in. Look through the turn. Steer your way out. Which sounded like a pretty good set of rules for life.

Tucking in behind Tim, I asked myself: What's the worst thing that can happen? The bike isn't going to fall down by itself. There are two sixty-pound gyroscopes, otherwise known as the wheels, keeping it up. It will run wide only if I let it. The iron armature of this earth will keep me solid on these curves.

Tim was showing me how fast I could safely run the reaches of that river as we searched for Dirk, our Kurtz in that heart of darkness. I saw the formula for unknotting that road in the lines that Tim drew for me.

As our speed increased, the Superhawk settled into a rhythm, and I settled in with it. I concentrated on being smooth and relaxed. Into the next curve I went, counter-steering. All that was required to make a deep left bank was to shove the left handlebar away from me—a touch would do it. A gentle urging of the throttle would pull me straight through. I understood that motorcycles make noise, but the world was oddly silent, save for a musical tone as the suspension vibrated like a cello string.

We rounded an especially tight corner that took me by surprise. All at once I knew I was going too fast, and all I could think of was to grab the brakes, to slow down. The centrifugal force was like that sudden sensation when you know you've drunk too much and you're going to throw up. Suddenly I didn't know whether to push or pull. For a hair-ball moment, a black terror gripped my heart. I had the almost irresistible urge to grab the brakes. Keeping myself from doing so was like trying not to pull my hand away from a hot stove. Then I heard Dirk's voice in my head. "The throttle is your friend," he said. Counter to every instinct and on the strength of my faith in him and Tim, I cranked on more gas. The curve magically straightened out. The throttle pulled me through. The engineering Dirk had worked twelve years to perfect actually worked.

As we rolled into the straight, I saw Tim catch up to Dirk. He slipped into his sideways racer's slouch. His compound mantis eye seemed to smile back at me through the proton shield, and he jerked his fist into the air triumphantly and gave me a thumbs-up sign with a Kevlar-gloved hand.

• • •

Nights passed at the faux-Italian villa in Rancho Santa Fe, and days passed riding through orange groves and little towns that looked like Mexico, where any individual we passed might earn less each year than one of our bikes had cost. I had come to understand that I would never know what it was like to be Dirk unless I rode like Dirk, a patently absurd possibility. It was Candace who gave me the idea to ride on the back while Dirk took the Superhawk through a canyon. I trusted Dirk's skill implicitly, yet the paradox of my trust didn't escape me. For even then I understood in some vague way that he would certainly die while riding a motorcycle. Even at that early stage, I was sad about it, for we were fast becoming friends.

The sun was going down in the canyon when I mounted up, one arm around him, one hand reaching past his waist to brace myself on the gas tank so that I wouldn't slide into him when he got on the brakes.

Late sunlight peeked beneath the front wheel as we entered the shadowlands. In the first turn, I could feel that Dirk was testing our weight and balance against the Superhawk's authority. Even so, my gut sensation told me that we were in a long crash, certain but not yet ended. G-forces pulled us toward the cliff of naked rock to our right. We dove deep into the apex of the curve. I could feel Dirk roll on the throttle.

The next corner was a complete 180, and it was marked with a yellow sign that said, "15 MPH." Dirk hit it at well above fifty, and when he flicked into the turn, I saw a wooden cross with fresh flowers. I could smell the flowers as we passed. I knew that we were too far over, too close to the edge of the road, that a bit of steel-belted radial the size of a dime could not possibly meet the demands of our speed and our eight hundred pounds. Once on an oil rig I'd been dangled fifteen stories over the Atlantic Ocean on a cable as thin as my old Parker 51 fountain pen. It had taken a supreme act of will then not to weep from fear in front of a group of grown men. But I trusted Dangerous Dirk. We vaulted out of that turn and into the next and the next, and my heart, while it didn't settle, began to merge into the physics of the situation. Dirk's feats appeared dangerous to everyone else, because if we tried them, we'd be wearing that Superhawk like a hat. But he was Dirk and we were not.

We stopped to turn around in the final moments of daylight. Dirk had explained that with a clean, well-engineered road, a rider of ordinary skill could double the speed on the yellow warning signs without undue concern. Candace, who had ridden behind him for much of our trip, reported that he was tripling those speeds routinely. The sign coming up said, "45 MPH." At the apex of the turn, the right-hand mirror traced its invisible line to within three inches of the steel Armco guardrail. It gave me a chance to watch his precision and smoothness. It was a long sweeping curve, and the distance between mirror and guardrail remained the same, as if we were traveling along the length of a gray galvanized razor blade. There was no wobble, no searching for the line. We were dialed in. We were connected. We seemed to stay in that turn for a very long time. I could see the dimpled pores of the metal as if I were looking through a microscope. Here then was the clarity we seek. If we could not manage it in our lives, then at least we could glimpse it on this razor's edge.

As we spun back through the final series of curves, the night advancing through the canyons, I was left with a feeling of joy and trust in Dirk and the bike he'd built and his good-natured accommodations to the impersonal laws that governed its movements.

. . .

One quiet weekday morning, we ascended to six thousand feet on Mount Palomar. Before we started up, Tim told me, "Anything I do, you can do now." Tim followed Dirk, and I followed Tim, losing them only once or twice. Pinning it in one long and ever-tightening curve, I thought: At last, this is the knot I can't untie. I felt like Houdini handcuffed at the bottom of the bay. It was an unnatural act, and it took all my faith. I simply flicked the left handle-bar away from me—I think I actually punched it—and one part of me fully expected that action to upset the bike. But the Superhawk lay submissively on its side and then greedily ate up the turn as I opened the throttle. It was magic. I know it was magic, because I believed it to be impossible.

At the top we found ourselves in a cedar forest near Mother's Restaurant, one of those legendary breakfast spots where bikers gather. Giant oaks had scattered acorns underfoot. Snow, which lay melting by the side of the road, where it had been pushed by plows, persisted in patches in the woods. The only sounds were from birds, the trickle of snowmelt, and our own soft voices as we looked over Dirk's trip book. The view of the Pauma Valley drew us in. I'd had little time to look while riding, when all my concentration had been taken up with task saturation, the Zen of the beginner's mind.

I parked the Superhawk and told Tim, "I think they're going to erect a statue here. Our Lady of Centrifugal Force or something. Because it was a miracle that I got through those curves alive."

"Nah," he told me succinctly, "you're all right. You're in the hunt now."

I made my way down from the road and stood in the cool shade of the forest. Bright sunlight filtered through in towering shafts, seeming as solid as columns of yellow stone. I came on a single giant cedar tree with a fairy cavern worn into its trunk by weather and rot and animals—it looked big enough to sleep in. I could hear Dirk talking with Candace and Tim up on the road. They were talking about a series of wheelies he'd done, and I heard him say, "Don't tell Beverly."

. . .

Dirk was at home taking care of his children. Beverly and I had hoped to meet him for drinks at the Ritz-Carlton in Dana Point, but his wife, Donna, also an executive at Honda, was working late. Beverly and I had been in the bar for half an hour when Dirk tiptoed in, carrying the younger boy, who was three, and followed by the older one, who was six. Dirk looked like a little boy sneaking out of school himself. "Don't tell Donna," he pleaded. "She'd kill me if she knew I'd brought the boys to a bar." Then he added, "Well, hell, they've got to start sometime."

Dirk ordered his Maker's Mark cocktail and leaped up from time to time to chase the younger boy around the vast carpeted bar. Several stories below the windows white breakers creamed and curled against the dark ocean. Dirk's older son was gentle and protective toward the baby, just as Dirk was gentle and protective with them both. I sat admiring Dirk for what he was, true man, journeyman, a rare hybrid of wild and tame, out drinking with the gang with his moveable nursery. I could see Dirk in the older boy, who was already riding a small Honda dirt bike at home. Dirk had only one drink. Then he said he had to get the boys home. He had them in bed before Donna got home.

Dirk and I exchanged frequent emails. Going over them now, I see that they always involved schemes to go riding. "Beverly said she's really close to the Campbells," Dirk wrote, referring to Earl and Linda, who own Pro Italia, "and she will make some inquiries to get Harrison on board." Earl had built a motorcycle for Harrison Ford, and we were hoping that Harrison might come to Freddie Spencer's school in Las Vegas with our group to find the limit of his traction. Harrison liked motorcycling because he could be with the guys, and as long as he didn't take his helmet off, no one knew who he was.

"Nov. 17 and 18 are reserved with Freddie Spencer for his racing school," Dirk wrote me a few days later. "Please confirm with Lyle that he can attend and yourself, too. Ray Blank, Gary Christopher, myself, and possibly Pete ter Horst (our new press manger) are all planning to attend, too. Let me know if you and Lyle can make it." He gave the dates and then added, "Most of this is subject to change without logic!! Sideways is best! —dirk"

And a few days later: "Will Lyle be able to get to Las Vegas the evening of the 16th? (Sun)?? After school on the 17th I'll arrange for all of us to drive Legends cars on the small paved oval course next door to the track. Could be too much fun!! Did you get with Harrison Ford's people?? Should I try on this end??" Dirk had been trying to interest me in race cars, especially small go-karts, which he called shifter cars. From what Gary Christopher told me, they were some sort of suicidal steel cages with huge engines, no seat belts, and a tendency to get inverted without warning. "I always end up covered with bruises when I finish racing," Dirk told me, adding with glee, "It's great fun! You have to try it!"

Just before we were to meet at a big Superbike race in Florida, Dirk wrote, "About winning: I think we have as good a chance as anyone, but Daytona is a very special race. Long and hard on tires and equipment. And Scott Russell is really good at Daytona. He's tough but Miguel Duhamel has beaten him there."

We met at Daytona in the middle of Race Week, which is actually two or three weeks of the worst kind of debauch imaginable. Half a million motorcycles arrive all at once in an effort to make Mardi Gras look like a Girl Scout Jamboree. Most of them are Harley-Davidsons, which we don't consider to be real motorcycles, because they're ugly, they don't turn well, and they don't make horsepower efficiently. But they are extremely popular, and everyone was tricked out in leather Third Reich gear. I saw a beautiful woman sitting on her Harley with a decal on the back of her black skullcap helmet that said, "My Other Toy Has A Dick."

There were strange kinds of motorcycle races taking place all over town. We watched oval flat track, which involves bikes that have no brakes. We went to a Supercross competition, which is a gazelle-like leaping contest for dirt bikes. We even saw vintage races with old motorcycles like the Triumphs and BSAs and Nortons I used to ride in the sixties. Dirk and I rode new Hondas everywhere, watching races into the night, sometimes two or three in a day. Dirk couldn't seem to get enough of it. We ate hot dogs and drank beer and weaved our way through traffic jams that took hours to get through in the limo. (Yes, Beverly had limos working the event for us, but we'd thrown our cell phones into the pool and were out AWOL on motorcycles that could not see traffic but went through it like neutrinos.)

On Sunday we went to the big race, the Superbike race, and watched Miguel take the lead away from Scott Russell in the tenth lap and then crash in the chicane turn. As he slid away on his back, a hundred yards through the grass (unhurt), Miguel's Superbike vaulted end over end "at about twenty-two thousand dollars a bounce," as one of the mechanics put it. When race mechanic Al Luddington put it on the laser transit to measure the frame, though, it was dead on, and within a couple of weeks, it was racing again.

The Daytona race took place on March 8. May 20, 1998, Dirk was back at Honda in Torrance when he forwarded me an email he had received from his old friend and colleague Joe Boyd, an engineer at Honda. It was a fake "new product intro," obviously intended to poke fun at Honda. The press release Boyd had written announced the Built-In Orderly Organized Knowledge device (BOOK) and went on to describe its technological advances: "Compact, portable . . . can be used anywhere—even sitting in an armchair by the fire. Yet it is powerful enough to hold as much information as a CD-ROM. . . . An optional BOOKmark accessory allows you to open the BOOK to the exact place you left it in a previous session—even if the BOOK has been closed."

A week later Dirk was testing a new sport bike on the track at Willow Springs near Rosamond, California. Boyd, a senior motorcycle engineer, was there to observe. At one point before the test, Boyd and Dirk were seen talking, though no one overheard what they said. Boyd had a small point-and-shoot camera, and a number of people who were there assumed that Dirk had asked Boyd to take his picture as he came around the turn. Dirk always wanted photos, and he was excited about the beautiful prints that Candace had made for us all. Boyd had accommodated Dirk before in this regard. Boyd walked out onto the grass and stood beside the track as Dirk ran his laps. Boyd looked through the viewfinder as Dirk approached the turn. Point-and-shoot cameras have short lenses, which make objects appear farther away than they are. Dirk was probably going seventy miles an hour. As he entered the turn, Boyd stepped onto the track with the camera to his eye. Dirk was leaned hard over, right on the edge of traction, where no maneuvering is possible. Such a high-speed race line, once begun, cannot be altered, as I had discovered on my rides behind Tim. Dirk and Joe were such old friends, we could all imagine it. Dirk thought: Well, Joe's not going to step in front of me. And Joe thought: Well, Dirk's not going to run me over.

Dirk's side mirror hit Boyd in the head and killed him instantly. The force of the impact slammed Dirk into the gas tank, crushing his sternum. The handlebars whipped around and crushed his chest from the side. The bike went down hard, and Dirk was thrown to the pavement. Paramedics worked on Dirk, whose heart had stopped. They were able to get his heart beating, but it stopped again, and the second time, they couldn't get it started again. Dirk was forty-eight years old. Joe Boyd was forty-nine.

· 5 ·

Hill Fever

I HAD NOTICED a badly healed scar across the border between South Dakota and Wyoming. I'd heard tales that it had bewitched Custer's regiment and rendered them simple with its pleasures in the summer of 74. Rolling through the Black Hills two years before their doomed meeting at the Little Bighorn, they had picked wild flowers from their saddles and had even dismounted to play the first game of baseball in the West. The Indians would not venture in there. The place was too powerful for all but a few shamans and vision seekers. The Black Hills had some of the world's largest caves, they said, and glorious rock-climbing on crystal towers. It had the highest mountain in the United States east of the Rockies, Harney Peak.

So it is that I find myself in a Ford Explorer piled with gear, heading west on Interstate 90 one blue-sky day, taking in the burning autumn colors and listening to Lucinda Williams sing, "Some laws should be broken from the start."

Yeah, I think. Gravity, for example.

At first light, the moon sets through the pines, looking like a faceted ivory lens. The air is full of wild red and gold leaves, fluttering around like broken butterflies. Far in the distance, I can see Cathedral Spires leaping into decks of pink clouds against a blue-gray sky.

We're going out to attack those spires with tight rubber shoes, a few lengths of rope, and a jangling rack of metal wedges. I can't help thinking, I'm going to fall. My instructor, Sue Schierbeck of Granite Sports in Hill City, South Dakota, tries to reassure me while regaling Bobby Model, our photographer and a top climber himself, and Julia, his tobacco-chewing assistant and half sister, with stories of horrible climbing accidents.

We hike around Sylvan Lake, passing through a narrow slot in the granite beneath boulders jammed in the crack above our heads. Even though it's

October, the temperature will gradually rise to eighty, but at the base of the seventy-foot stone face near the lake, it's still comfortably cool. Sue has placed bolts at the top, and now I watch Bobby climb the sheer face to place a rope. He goes up fast. Nothing holds him to the wall. It's like watching a spider.

Yesterday I worked some bouldering problems with Bobby and watched him execute a move called a barn door on a smooth overhanging rock perhaps twenty-five feet straight above me. Gravity just politely stepped aside and let him through. So seeing him walk up this rock face the way I'd walk up stairs did little to give me confidence.

At the base of the wall, Sue says, "I just want you to stay right here and work your way across laterally to get the feel for it. Just look at your feet and find places to put them. Take your time."

Everyone has to start somewhere. The route was only four feet off the ground and crosses the rock laterally for about twenty-five feet toward a big vertical crack. My goal is the crack. I move easily across until I get within about two arms' lengths of it, at which point the wall becomes glassy smooth.

"This is a five-ten move," Sue informs me, "but you can do it. Just study it for a while."

I catch sunlight winking off of a tiny blue crystal just above my head, and for the first time, I notice how beautiful the rock is. It is a great dark medium studded with a rainbow of colored crystals. Then somehow, I'm in the crack. An earthquake can't move me.

"Aw," she says, feigning disappointment. "Most people fall the first few times. Okay, let's rope up."

Be careful what you pray for, I think, as I tie the knot through my harness.

I begin climbing. This is easy, I think, grabbing big fists full of rock. Just like when I was a kid climbing trees.

I go ten or fifteen feet up, and Sue calls to me, "Lean back."

"What?"

"Lean back. I've got you." I want to do no such thing. I want to clutch the wall. My rushing adrenaline turns to a shrinking feeling. But how can I refuse to trust her here if I plan to trust her farther up? I prepare myself for the ridiculous move, then let go and fall. I'm in the air, feeling gravity grab me. Here I go . . .

Then the rope gives and springs up and down as my harness catches my hips, and I hang there with my toes gripping the wall.

I let my pulse return to normal as she holds me on belay, and a sudden joy pours through me. I'd forgotten that feeling from my childhood, when gravity gives you a big hug.

"Pretty cool, huh?" she calls. "You can't fall."

Yeah, I think. Unless the rope breaks.

"Climbing," I call.

"Climb on," she says.

I find myself concentrating on the puzzle made up of feet and fingers and rock. At no time do I look down at the ground, for fear that my fear will freeze me.

I come to a place where I make a move to a tiny dime-edge crystal and find myself fascinated that it can hold me. My left foot smears on a rounded place, and I'm hanging on to a slim edge with my right hand, looking for the next move across an expanse of granite that appears for all the world to be mirror smooth. There has to be something here, I think, or this wouldn't be called a 5.6.

Just then Bobby appears in my field of vision and shoves a camera lens in my face.

"Smile," he says, snapping the shutter. Then he scrambles down and around to my other side without effort.

I've reached the crux, the most difficult part of the climb. I'm about halfway up, where the crystals vanish, leaving a blank space about five feet high and rounded out just enough to get in my way. As Bobby scampers past me and onto the summit, I'm still searching for something, feeling like a blind man with my left hand as my calf muscles begin to tremble. I can see that in one more move, I'll have a place to stand, but there's nothing in between. I desperately want to go down but remember an old Danish saying: "Pissing in your pants will keep you warm for only so long."

Damn it, I think, I know fear. Come on, old buddy.

I slap my left hand against the rock—a motion like trying to open elevator doors—and move my right hand to another tiny crystal. I set my right foot up, smear my left, and just push hard, feeling the blood in my face. The bottom drops out of my stomach, and with a rocket rush of adrenaline, I make a long reach and grab a bucket, as a slight depression in the rock is known. I'd thought that it was out of range but I'm solid now. I shove my hip into the rock, reach, and move over the hump. I tag the summit just to say I did it. Then I call to Sue to lower me. I lean back and walk down the rock. I am filled with a familiar joy at coming into this scarred old land.

· · ·

Rod Horrick is in charge of mapping Wind Cave, the sixth-largest cave in the world. An intense man of medium build with brown hair and blue eyes, Horrick discovered caving while on a trip with his father at the age of seven. There is not a hole he won't scramble into or an element in it that he won't stop to explain.

As we enter Wind Cave, I can already feel my chest tightening as a suffocating sense of claustrophobia descends on me. I've never gone caving before and irrationally expect a neat hole like the Lincoln Tunnel with big rows of fluorescent lights. But as we leave the mouth of the cave, we find ourselves descending through the bronchioles and down into a chaotic world of tremendous breakdown, man-size holes that appear beneath our feet. Each hole seems to lead down to sharp rocks and more sharp rocks.

That's why we're equipped with helmets, head lamps, gloves, heavy knee and elbow pads, sturdy boots, and rough clothing as we plunge ahead. You have to see the cave to believe its chaos, a fractal world of riven rock so complex that it's impossible to take it all in. At first, I try to look everywhere at once, to get a hold on my environment. That sets off a flutter of panic in my chest. Then, gradually, I begin to focus on details. It takes me a full hour to get the sense of how to move through the cave, not so much physically but emotionally. For one thing, the beam of my own head lamp is all the light I have, and if I swing it around, it's a bad movie. Monster shapes charge at me, and creeping red rock fingers reach out to grab me. There is no floor, so we're always balancing on one rock or another. I pause and look down from one such perch. The nothingness descends to infinite blackness.

As we move on and on, I begin to get a sense of some hidden order. We climb huge boulders to a narrow passageway where I have to crawl on my belly. I have to push my pack ahead of me as I drag myself through on my elbows.

At last we emerge into a huge room whose size is made difficult to comprehend by its complexity. As I shine my light down the side of the boulder on which I sit, it falls away through the branching of countless convoluted passageways—leads, Horrick calls them, the very lungs of the moist earth.

"Where does it go?" I wonder out loud.

Horrick points out that this question is the first step in being seduced by the cave: wondering where something goes and then following it.

Horrick coaxes me off my boulder. "I want to show you something," he says, hopping nimbly from rock to rock over crevasses that descend to the iron armature of the earth.

I claw my way up beside him. I find him lying on his belly, pointing his head lamp into a small grotto. I lie down beside him. Look: beneath an over-hang, a sea anemone. White domed body with thousands of long and sparkling hair-like feelers.

"Don't breathe too hard," he says. "It's incredibly delicate."

"What is it?" I ask.

"Those are gypsum needles," he tells me. "Calcium sulfate. The same stuff that Sheetrock is made of."

The creature is a stone, and although the air never moves in here, I have the illusion that it's waving its tentacles in the sea of near-100-percent humidity in which we breathe. It's cold enough that I can see my breath. There's an entire ecosystem down here in this land of the lost. At the bottom of the chain is a tiny mite that eats minerals and lives through chemosynthesis, an exception to the rule that all life depends on sunlight. The food chain moves up through a sort of hopping insect all the way to wood rats, which mark their meandering trails with urine in this Bible-black world, and bats, which are blind and use sonar to find their way.

Horrick's voice shakes me from my thoughts. He's telling me about a room he found that was filled with bones, including bones of bison and other mammals. That seemed an impossibility, there being no source of food. Horrick studied the bones and noticed that they appeared rounded, as if worn in a stream. "I could see tree roots, so I knew we were fairly close to the surface, and I had a theory."

Horrick hauled an antenna back into the room, while others triangulated with radio signals from above, pinpointing the spot, which turned out to be in the bed of a stream. The roof was only eight feet from the surface, and Horrick figured out that at one time, there had been an entrance to the cave there. The bones of dead animals had been washed down the stream until they fell into the Chamber of Lost Souls, as he named the room. Gradually, the stream bed silted up, sealing the cave once more. Horrick believes, in fact, that over the years, the cave opens and closes its mouths, providing access to different areas at different times. It's like this huge breathing beast of living rock, lying half-asleep beneath thousands of acres of land.

After six or seven hours of exploring, Horrick says that he needs to go find Bobby, who has been taking photographs elsewhere in the cave. I tell Horrick that I'd like to be alone. He has quite a long scramble to get to where Bobby is and back before we start the arduous climb out of the cave. He hesitates as he considers my request. "Look," he says, "if I leave you, don't move, okay?"

"I won't."

"I mean, don't move at all. Don't go anywhere, do you understand me? Just sit where you are."

"Okay," I say.

He studies me for a long time and restates his warning in stronger terms: "Because if you go anywhere at all, I won't be able to find you." It's the first time since we entered the cave that I've seen him display any concern at all. But I understand. The beast will swallow me if I slip from my perch on this boulder. And Horrick is asking himself: Is this guy a flake, or can I trust him? Then he scrambles off. His light bounces around and vanishes at last.

A silence such as I have never heard descends on me. And if the cave swallows Horrick, I have no idea how to get out.

So I turn out my light.

The absolute sensory deprivation of the cave grips me then. There's nothing to tell me that I even exist except the hammering of my heart, my shallow breathing. Maybe this is what it's like to be dead. With twenty stories of rock and earth blanking out all of civilization, I'm as close to escaping as I'll ever get.

But gradually, sound intrudes. I hear a scraping. Something approaches. At last, a dim flickering of light plays on the rocks, growing until I see once more the bouncing beam of Horrick's head lamp and hear him climbing over the rocks toward me. I flick on my own lamp and see the look of relief on his face when he realizes that I haven't vanished. He exhales. "Let's go," he says.

• • •

I meet Noah Daniels, Horrick's assistant, while in Wind Cave. He's talking with Bobby and Julia and gets all excited when Julia asks about mountain biking in the Black Hills. Noah, like Julia, is a competitive mountain biker, and it turns out that the mountain biking, not the caving, is the real reason he came to the Black Hills. "It's unreal, man!" he tells her. "There is some of the best single track in the world in the Black Hills!" And then, sotto voce: "Most of it's unofficial, of course." We find something pretty unofficial near the Mystic Trailhead parking lot.

Bobby, Julia, and I scramble through brush and buckthorn until we find a faint pathway and set our bikes on it. It rises gradually for about fifty yards and then takes off uphill so sharply that it just seems to suck Julia and Bobby into the dark forest like one of those pneumatic tubes at the drive-in bank. My bike has fingertip hydraulic disc brakes, and I get a taste of them right from the start. As I struggle uphill, my front wheel comes off the ground like a snake-bit stallion, and I lean forward to bring it under control. On a short downhill section, I grab the brakes and nearly endo the bike, sliding around and running off into the woods a few yards with my rear end up in the air.

Then I get on the main track and grind to a halt, heading up at a forty-five-degree angle. The track is twelve inches wide and scattered with sharp chunks of shale. As I climb two hundred, then four hundred feet, a wall of trees and stone rises to my right, while the drop from my left foot approaches the vertical. It's heavily timbered and populated with big, sharp rocks. My bike's titanium and carbon frame is nice and light, which comes in handy, since I carry it most of the way up.

I don't mind going slowly in that dense and beautiful forest. The woods of the Black Hills are a spooky spirit world, with vestigial Ice Age flora and the ghosts of Cretaceous monsters still lurking in the limestone and luminous schist. Already in the early evening light, a yellow moon is rising full on the wind as the woods exhale a tangy spoor of mint and sage. In the leaf-fractured searchlight of late cathedral sunbeams, I can see golden aspen leaves whirling down to decorate the pines as if they're Christmas trees.

Half an hour later, I've slogged the thousand vertical feet to a logged-off area of crepuscular shadows where I find two hunchbacked figures astride their bikes in the mist, conferring with their helmets touching. It gets cold at night, and we have no lights for night-riding, so they've decided to race back down. Julia's going to descend as fast as she can while Bobby follows, snapping pictures. He has a camera mounted on his bicycle and will trip the shutter by clenching the remote shutter release in his teeth.

When I express my wariness of the tiny track, Bobby says, "Oh, no, going down is a piece of cake."

Julia adds, "Actually, um, going down this is gonna be pretty radical for a beginner." She shows me how to use my feet and brakes to minimize my chances of inverted flight.

Bobby clamps his Nikon at about chest level, and he takes off chasing Julia down the narrow track. I bring up the rear, judiciously using fingers and toes to keep from flying straight off into space. As I scatter rocks and hop fallen logs, it's all I can do to keep my wheels on the narrow cut in the mountainside.

Julia is expertly screaming along the hairline track with Bobby on her tail, his wild-man blond hair flying out from under his helmet, teeth bared in a wild snarl, as he clicks off shots with his incisors.

I'm now starting to get the hang of these high-speed turns, spitting chunks of shale into the forest as my tires slide off the edge and somehow jump back into place. Hey, this is fun, I think. Julia suddenly shoots ahead of Bobby, bent low to her handlebars, shouting, "Duck!"

Bobby rockets down the track, hard on her rear wheel, sitting fairly upright to keep his chest clear of the camera and the metal spike that holds it. His bike seems to hesitate for a moment in midflight. Then it lurches upward, his front wheel comes way off the ground, and I think: If it looks bad, it is bad. I hear a cracking noise as a tree falls across my path, and Bobby disappears off the edge.

Not exactly. By the time I skid to a stop at the point where Bobby went airborne, I can hear him cursing and groaning. Several pieces of equipment are still leaping and crashing down the long hill through the underbrush, and one of them is obviously a strobe, because it goes off, illuminating the dark forest with a blast of light.

Bobby has come to count on incredible luck. He was once swept across a glacier by an avalanche and avoided being dumped into a crevasse only by leaping at the last second, snagging the far edge with his fingertips. He spent sixty days getting up Trango Tower in Pakistan, nine of them in a hanging tent stapled to a wall three thousand feet above a glacier in blizzard conditions. His backpack had snagged a tree limb, bringing the whole tree down and sending Bobby over the edge. This time, he fell into a pile of branches and stopped about twenty yards down the eight-hundred-foot slope. But soon Bobby and Julia were chasing each other down the hill once more, and as I watch, I understand their secret: Bobby and Julia are running, too. They're just running faster than I am.

· · ·

Practically from the moment I arrived in the Black Hills, I started hearing tales of Jan and Herb Conn, who caught hill fever right after World War II and settled here in 1949. With the crudest equipment imaginable, they would eventually lay the foundations for all the climbing and most of the caving in the area.

So it is perhaps inevitable that one day I find myself sitting in a circle beside their woodpile at the base of a low and rocky hill, out on the warm grass in a boulder-strewn grove of aspen and pine on their land near Calamity Peak. Sunlight streams down, igniting the mica chips scattered across the ground. The mica gives an impression of pixie dust, as if a magic spell has been cast on this place.

Jan, seventy-seven, and Herb, eighty-one, are both less than five feet tall and have an air of quiet mischief about them. When we first pulled up their drive, Herb was standing there as if he'd been expecting us, this tiny man with an unruly shock of white hair and a quiet, knowing grin. I had heard people in the area describe them as reclusive, but that's not quite accurate. For Herb and Jan, people are absolute volcanoes of energy with all their noise and restless motion. Most of us can filter all that out, but the Conns find it intolerable.

"Herb and I always shied away from making contact with people if we didn't have to," Jan explains. "I've always hated cities," she adds, and when I ask why, she says, "Well, trying to figure out what all those people are thinking can plumb wear you out."

An almost mystical reverence surrounds their history. We heard tales of elfin shamans, their fingers reading the Braille of unroped routes where mortals fear to tread, literally flying up the rock faces on antigravity beams. We also heard that they live in a cave.

They don't. They built an enclosure of rock set against a seven-foot-high rock face and covered with a tin roof. They stayed there while constructing their spacious house (no plumbing, water, or electricity). But when the house was completed, they could never quite bring themselves to move in. They liked the smaller space. "Anyway," Herb tells me, "you can heat it with an armload of wood."

The door is four feet, two inches high, and there's just enough room inside for Herb and Jan to squeeze past each other. Once inside, I feel like a giant. Every bit of space is densely packed with their belongings, from Herb's typewriter, on which he writes short stories, to wooden cups hanging from the ceiling, tools of all sorts, and stacks of paper. A shelf is fixed to the rock face at shoulder level and thinly padded to make a bed beneath a small skylight cut in the tin roof, "so we can see the stars," Jan explains.

Standing there, attempting to make some sort of sense of it, I realize what they've done. From the start their love was born of and based on rock. As the 1959 climbing season came to an end, Jan and Herb met Dwight Deal while climbing in the Needles, just a few miles from here. He invited them to join him on a trip to map Jewel Cave. They accepted, not expecting much out of it. But there was something about the rugged, tortuous, yet intimate contact with rock. There was the labyrinthine confusion of the passageways littered with boulder fall, the slithering through flinty canals, fit only for an incubus, then being born into virgin cathedrals, great billowing duomos with stained-glass crystals and fretwork no human eye had ever seen. There were the startling discoveries of mysterious aragonite frostwork and gypsum cave cotton, a million years in the making. On top of that, the endeavor required all their technical skills as climbers as they stemmed up chimneys into black nether heavens. In one such place, Jan found a dripstone cascade, a frozen waterfall of rock, and found that its flutings played like a xylophone when she tapped them.

The cave had gotten inside them. They had gone in to help survey a bit of it and emerged instead with a map for the rest of their days: Jan and Herb spent the next twenty-two years in Jewel Cave, eventually surveying some sixty-five miles of it.

Given their love of rock, it stands to reason that they arranged to live on a rock face. Their bed is bolted to it like a portaledge on a big wall climb. They sleep on the rock face every night, curled up warm above a woodburning stove made from a milk can, the constellations framed in their skylight, the comfort of a rock womb always close around them.

Bobby is trying to get them to tell us about their great pioneering climbs, but they're simply too modest. In their view, they didn't pioneer anything. They were just having fun. While they are credited with creating the ground-up ethics of the Needles, Jan says, "I don't know why they get so excited. You climb for what you get out of it, not for what someone else thinks."

At one point in our talk, Jan leaps up and runs to a shed and returns laden with the gear they used to make their historic climbs: an alarming collection of rusted pitons, F. W. Woolworth $1.99 sneakers, and a US Army–issue brown hemp-nylon rope circa 1945.

"No harness?" I ask.

"We just tied the rope around our waist and went up," Jan says. "Of course, if you fall more than fifteen feet, you'll break your back, so you don't want to do that." While we all handle the gear, like people marveling over the first space capsule, Jan asks, "Herbie? Do you think we can get these people up Juniper?"

Soon we are racing through the woods along a secret path that Jan and Herb have cut, as they giggle about the Forest Service's disapproval of their unofficial trails. They make them hard to find and hard to follow on purpose. As we proceed through airy pines over rough terrain, I can see that all around, the green heads of rocks are trying to be born out of the ferny earth's placenta.

We reach Juniper Rock. At least that's what Herb and Jan call the ninety-foot spire wedged into a hillside at an angle. They scramble away like squirrels and vanish. We have, of course, no ropes. Julia, beside me on the rock, is realizing that her clogs are inadequate to the task at hand. Jan appears far above us, peering over a flake of rock, and assesses the situation. Then she calls behind her, "Herbie? Why don't you throw your shoes down? We'll worry about getting down later."

Herb makes the summit in a few more deft moves and then sits to take off his shoes, which he throws to Julia. They're all up there eating peaches and nuts out of their packs by the time I get close enough to hear what they're saying. Jan and Julia are engaged in a discussion of composers. Jan favors the impressionists, such as Debussy. She comes up here to play her flute.

Now I see why Jan wanted us up here: the entire world is spread before us, Calamity Peak ridge to the northwest, Cathedral Spires to the north, and not a road to be seen. A bird flies up to me at eye level, then veers off, as surprised by the encounter as I am. But Jan and Herb sit chatting, their feet dangling over the edge.

I notice Herb watching Bobby, who is bouldering on a twin peak that juts up about twenty yards away. Now Herb climbs down eagerly, finds a place to cross between the two, and scrambles up to where Bobby stands. Herb says, "I've got to see if I can reach that handhold." Clearly, he has seen a move Bobby made and wants to try it.

I watch as Herb makes the climb, gets to the same point where Bobby moved for the top, and reaches. Herb is balancing on his toes perhaps sixty feet up on the slim edge of a flake, reaching as high as he can. He makes a small jump, and his toes leave the rock. For a second, he's suspended in midair, touching nothing, then his hand gets purchase on the rock, and he hangs for another second or two, then drops back to his toes with the balance of a dancer. He nods, satisfied that he could do it. When he turns around to face me, he's smiling, his sky-blue eyes twinkling with contentment. In another moment, he has scrambled back to Jan's side. It's what a scientist I know calls "a hummingbird problem." You know it's impossible. He's bleeping eighty-one years old. But there it is: you can see it. When Herb and Jan descend the ninety-foot spire, it's like watching firefighters slide down a pole. I'm the last one down, of course.

• • •

I awake to the sound of Bobby screaming, "We're gonna die! We're all gonna die!"

It's been a bad night on Harney Peak. I've been awakened numerous times to find myself, by turns, in Sue's arms or in the arms of her dog, Jake. Well, paws, jaws, tail, tongue, teeth—it's been a little hard to tell with Julia kicking me in the face as she struggles to find comfort. Two beautiful women, two studly guys, and a golden retriever: if this sounds like the cast of a rollicking good porno movie, try it in a two-man tent being pounded with the Zydeco rhythm of a blizzard with forty-knot winds, blowing snow, and freezing rain on the edge of an icy cliff on the wrong side of the mountain in the middle of the night.

Now, at last, as daylight drips like cold chicken fat through the yellow nylon, I notice an ominous weight over my head. I reach up and shove, and an old-fashioned avalanche heaves and slides off our roof with a seismic sigh and tumbles a hundred feet down over the cliff at our feet.

"This is bad," I say, and Bobby starts up again, screaming that we're all going to die. "Hey, hypothermia is no joke," I insist lamely.

"Yeah," Julia says with a yawn. "How are we going to make espresso?"

Is there no way to impress these people with the gravity of our situation? Sue is still sleeping soundly.

Yesterday began mild and sunny, and we took our time getting up here from Sylvan Lake. We'd already had two weeks of near-tropical weather in the Black Hills, with warm, sunny days of mountain biking and rock-climbing, wild nights in Pringle at the Hitchrail, where a gutted elk lay on its back in a pickup truck in the parking lot, casting a rheumy eye on the wicked hieroglyphic constellations arcing slowly overhead. By the time we made our push to Harney Peak, the highest point east of the Rockies, we'd been lulled into complacency and were due for a rude awakening.

So here I sit, my frozen claw digging into Sue's shoulder, trying to wake her to this shameful reality: "We have to get off this mountain, Sue. Like now."

"Don't worry," she says, rolling over in her bag. "We'll take care of you."

"Frostbite is a serious thing," I say. "Pretty soon I'll be snipping off your black and shriveled toes." No reaction. "Snip, snip, snip." Nothing. She's asleep again.

I tell myself to be thankful: I nearly made the hike in shorts and flip-flops. But something in the air last night told me that it just might be chilly at seventy-two hundred feet, so I brought a few extra layers. Still, it's been snowing hard—sideways—all night long, and it shows no sign of letting up now. And we have no gloves.

We had solidified into a light assault team to tackle this daunting project: to recce and then get a headlock on this enchanted land. Seen from space, the Black Hills look like a giant scab straddling the South Dakota–Wyoming border, an old necrotic wound that healed badly. But ground truth shows that wound to conceal more exceptional climbing, mountain biking, hiking, camping, caving, and all-around woods-and-wilderness delirium than any place I've seen in a very long time. Unfortunately, our crew is not very well acquainted with the better part of valor, and I have been concerned for some days now that one of us might get killed, never mind embarrassed.

Bobby is by far the worst. He has Fitz Roy in Patagonia and even a near summit of Everest notched on his rack. So I can understand how he might not consider our little blizzard to be a very big deal.

Julia is a marauder on a mountain bike. She's only recently taken to climbing but has never learned the f-word. "Fear" is not in her lexicon. An MRI would show that in place of her amygdala, the fear center in the brain, are the McDonald's arches. She might be the first and only woman to pee off the top of the Brooklyn Bridge, which she did while filming Philippe Petit, who walked a tightrope between the two towers of the World Trade Center in 1974. And Sue was born and raised in these dark hills. She runs the climbing school and guide service here. But while Sue's ceaseless optimism is bracing, she's the one who decided that she and I didn't need to bring a tent for ourselves on this overnight.

Now she is reluctantly rising, as I realize that I left my new Montrail hiking shoes out in the snow all night.

Bobby shoves Jake out into the screaming wind, and the dog is swallowed by a snowdrift. Three of us are sitting up now, but no one's making a move to actually leave the tent.

We reached the lookout tower at Harney Peak late yesterday afternoon to find the hills spread before us in every direction, fading to infinity in a gathering mist, shot through with a soothing golden sunlight. We hiked around to the west side of the mountain across jagged rocks and arêtes to find a place to camp in an area of small but ancient pines. Eons of erosion had lined shallow crevasses with soft soil, moss, grasses, and low-growing evergreen shrubs. Bobby and Julia set up their tent on a flat and sandy cliff edge where the wind seemed to accelerate through a venturi of towering rock steeples.

While Julia and Bobby began unpacking dinner, I watched the eighty-by-sixty-mile crazy quilt of rock spires begin to drown in evening mist. It looked like a bowl filling with milk. From high above, I could see mobs and gangs of rock towers surrounding us, leaning in, dark, hoary, atavistic monoliths, urging us on. We could see white mountain goats grazing the ridges.

As we looked north, I commented, "Looks like a front." In fact, I said that the fast-moving cloud deck looked like a prelude to precip, but no one was listening.

I found a sheltered spot about two hundred meters west of camp on the edge of a cliff, where a depression of soft earth with overhanging pines made a perfect bed about the size of a bathtub. I laid out my pad and bag and returned to camp, where Bobby and Julia were fighting, appropriately, like brother and sister, over why the MSR stove wasn't working. We polished off a bottle of Coppola white and a half-pint of Dewar's before we even got the water boiling.

Then Julia was standing on a lone spire on one foot hundreds of feet from the ground, arms outstretched against the evening, singing at the top of her lungs, "High on a hill stood a lonely goatherd" and then yodeling into the distance. The rock walls answered, "Yodel-ay-hee, yodel-ay-hee, yodel-ay-hee-hoo!"

It might have been nine o'clock when we said good night. The weather was still good, though the overcast had moved in. We could see the lights of Custer far below.

I bundled myself down in my bag, and Sue followed me and laid her bag out next to mine, saying, "Mind if I join you?"

We talked for a while of imaginary climbs and adventures far from home, dozing now and then. At one point, I awoke thinking that my face was being attacked by insects. I sat up. There was enough moonlight filtering through the clouds that I could see my pack, covered in white. It wasn't insects, it was ice pellets. "IPs," I told her.

I woke Sue, and we decided that it wasn't really happening—denial, that primal killer. Moving farther up under the pines ought to solve the problem, we agreed. Jake, of course, was sleeping with us and moved accordingly so that he was almost on top of my head. That's okay, I thought. He'll protect me from the IP hornets.

Then we fell into a dead sleep. We woke hours later with a start. Everything was glowing white with several inches of ice and snow. Our sleeping bags were soaked through. Our packs and shoes were encased in ice, and the long way back over steep rock was gleaming with a new and slippery surface. The drop to the next level was nowhere less than a hundred feet.

"Oh boy," Sue said. Given her penchant for understatement, that alarmed me. Sue has a very matter-of-fact way about her, which conceals a wealth of knowledge and experience. She is qualified in high-angle rescue, emergency medicine, and wilderness medicine and is a first responder for search and rescue, including cave SAR. She has climbed all over the world. I suspect, too, that the world has climbed all over her.

"Welp," she said breezily, "let's get in the tent, I guess."

She had her new Black Diamond Moonlight with the four LEDs, and it was a good thing, too, for as we scrambled over the icy rock, I could see that it would be a very long way down if I missed a step. The wind was driving IPs parallel to the ground, and they dug into my face and hands as I followed her, both of us dragging our pads, our sleeping bags blowing freely in the wind behind us. Jake bounded happily ahead.

We made our way around the last spire and shouted to wake Bobby and Julia in their tent. Then began the agonizing process of wedging ourselves into the space meant for two. By the time we got settled, I couldn't feel my fingers, and Sue had to zip the fly of the tent for me.

Jake turned in circles and found a spot to settle down on top of my legs. During the half hour of agony while my hands thawed, we all turned and squirmed, kicking and grunting, trying to find a position in which to sleep, until at last, exhausted, we fell into a sort collective coma and listened to the wind-driven ice attack the tent.

In that fashion, the night passed, while I took mental inventory of what we hadn't brought, thinking about what it would be like trying to traverse the iced-up rocks to reach the trail off this godforsaken mountain.

Even Julia could tell that something was dreadfully wrong when, at first light, she unzipped the fly to look outside. "Oh my God," she said. We all looked out. There were many inches of new snow on the ground. The wind was blowing spindrift off the cliff edge just inches from the tent. Beyond that we saw nothing except white. *Praeter solitudinum, nihil video.* And all our gear lay scattered out there beneath the snow and ice.

That was first thing in the morning, when Bobby began screaming, "We're all gonna die!" and we all practically wept with laughter, because it was just so stupid. What are we doing up here in October without winter gear, victims of a classic rookie blunder? We deserved to die.

"Forget dying," Sue says. "What about my Juneberry pancakes?" She brought pancake mix for breakfast.

"Yeah," Bobby says. "Hell, we have to have some misery, or else this isn't a real trip."

Groping through the snow outside, I find my shoes filled with snow. Then slowly, painfully, we get ourselves organized, fetch shoes and vests and camera parts. Soon we begin emerging into the howling wind, one by one, to jam things at random into our packs, cook pots scummed with marinara sauce, dirty coffee cups, frozen underwear. Bobby suggests leaving the empty Dewar's bottle, which he calls a "summit register," but I take it anyway.

Then we're trudging off across the icy rocks, climbing toward Harney Peak in pain and mortification, cursing and laughing by turns—because we have to go up again to get down. Bobby is in the lead, calling back at me to be heard above the shrieking wind: "Hey, you've got to come ice climbing with me in Wyoming this winter!"

"Are you insane?" I ask.

. . .

Two days later the weather has cleared, and I return to the first boulder that Bobby put me on. I find that I can walk effortlessly up it. Has something changed in me, or has the rock simply decided to accept me?

I know something changed in me over my days in the Black Hills. I was taken by the haunting quality of the place, the crystal towers carelessly placed against the backdrop of these old forests, dark and strange, and the eternal twilight of their Hansel-and-Gretel world, and the blackness beneath the earth so intense that it could seem almost luminous. As I make my way out of the Black Hills, I know that I will find only one location off this trail: lost. And I feel the damp and drizzly November lifting in my soul.

AUTHOR'S NOTE

Bobby and I exchanged emails and decided that we would work together again. But that same year he moved to Nairobi to photograph in Africa. He had another sister, named Faith, there. In 2007, she was driving him to visit friends when a great chunk of concrete came through the windshield. He was severely injured and suffered traumatic brain injury. No fall from a rock face, no launching of a bicycle off a trail. No freezing to death on a mountain. He was moved from hospital to hospital in South Africa, New York, then Denver, and it seemed that he might recover as he returned to his hometown of Cody, Wyoming. Then in September 2009, he fell ill and died shortly thereafter. No one ever learned where the chunk of concrete had come from. He was thirty-six years old.

· 6 ·

The All-Seeing Eye

MY FATHER TAUGHT me how to use a camera and a darkroom when I was about eight years old. He was a scientist, and he loved things with lenses, such as cameras, microscopes, telescopes, and even magnifying glasses. ZEISS loupes. We always had a selection of cameras in the house that anyone who was interested could use, along with a few microscopes in various stages of collapse and eventually a big six-inch telescope that my father had made. Late at night I used to watch him as he sat hunched over the kitchen table, grinding the lens by hand with jeweler's rouge.

The medical school where he was a young professor had bought an electron microscope the year before. It had the most amazing lens in existence at the time, made of powerful magnets instead of glass. The magnetic lens focused a beam of electrons rather than photons. While a light microscope could magnify something up to two thousand times, the electron microscope could enlarge something two million times. Magnifying something two million times is a dazzling achievement. An aspirin tablet magnified two million times would be more than twelve miles in diameter. To me and my father, this concept was as exhilarating as being told that we were going to be able to see creatures walking on other planets in distant galaxies. Yet no one else at the medical school seemed remotely interested in this new wonder. It drove my father crazy. These were scientists: Where was their curiosity?

So he decided that he'd be the one to use the new scope. He applied for a grant to go to Harvard and learn electron microscopy. When we returned from Boston, we rushed to the lab. The gleaming Siemens scope from Germany had a room all to itself. It was tall, reaching to the ceiling (or so it seemed to me). It looked like a great steel espresso machine. A bundle of cables issued from its domed top, and dozens of knobs, lights, and switches adorned it. At the base was a thick glass window a few inches square, and above it was a binocular microscope for viewing images on a phosphorescent screen inside.

There in the darkness with the screen glowing green, my father showed me the inner workings of a cell for the first time. I was astonished to learn that what I'd thought of as an irreducible blob of jelly was actually filled with molecular machinery, pumps and shafts, bearings and conveyor belts, all working at something. There were creatures walking to and fro, bearing zeppelins of materials, and assembly lines putting together exotic creations like fantasy towers in a cityscape. My concept of protoplasm would not survive that revelation.

A few years later when my father had finished grinding the lens for his telescope and finally had it assembled in the kitchen, we went out into the backyard on a frosty winter night. Stan Getz played jazz saxophone in the background. After what seemed like endless adjustments of the tripod and twiddling of knobs, he beckoned me to look. The image swam into view, and suddenly it was as if I'd fallen into a pool of light. As my eye adjusted to the brilliance of the surface, I saw that the moon was not the simple and vaguely white ball that I was used to seeing in the night sky. It was a devastated landscape in which a monumental battle must have taken place, a busy tapestry of bomb bursts and defiles, mountains and barren arroyos, an unimaginably complex design, the ancient record of countless violent events.

In between those two extremes of scale was the small magic box that I could hold in my hand to capture at will an instant in time that would never occur again, no matter how many galaxies came and went in the universe. My father, born in 1921, was a member of the first generation in which anyone could have a camera small enough to carry around. My own generation became the most well-documented group of people in the history of the world. And the members of my children's generation are literally growing up viewing the world through a lens or on a luminous screen.

At a recent family wedding, as the bride and groom arrived at the altar, all the people in the crowd, as if by a secret signal, raised to their faces a device for capturing what was about to occur—a camera, a phone, a video recorder. Even the children took photos with their phones. And I thought: Oh no. They're missing the moment. They must be planning to catch their own lives on the postseason reruns, because nobody's seeing this couple get married.

But I understood the lure of the lens. When I was very little, perhaps only three, one snowy winter day in Saint Louis, my grandmother showed me her stereopticon. She slid a transparency into it and then let me hold it to my eyes against the light of a window. An entire three-dimensional world came to shimmering life. I could smell the flowers and feel the sun on my face, the grass between my toes. I understood the lure of the lens: if you look through it long enough, you can vanish into it.

The lens could reveal the hidden truth in our world, but it could also deceive. Whole books have been devoted to the question of whether the reflection in the mysterious shiny orb in the painting *Allegory of the Catholic Faith* (ca. 1670) by Johannes Vermeer is actually a concave mirror that he used to project the images he painted onto the canvas, giving his paintings their dazzling realism. The fact that most of Vermeer's paintings are quite small lends credence to the idea that he used a so-called "burning mirror," which can project only small images. The British painter David Hockney convincingly demonstrated that Jean Ingres, the nineteenth-century French neoclassical painter, used a camera lucida to make his work both fluid and lifelike. We may have to come to a new understanding of visual art since the early Renaissance. Surely it is the grand upwelling of passion and talent that historians tell us it is. But at various times throughout history, it has also been a passionate love affair with the lens. Maybe it was really the earliest form of photography. And in fact, some scholars argue that photography "hijacked" the lens and led artists to turn away from realism toward more impressionistic and abstract forms. After all, if you were an artist painting nudes, how could you compete with, well . . . *Playboy*?

I was the articles editor of *Playboy* magazine in the 1970s and saw for myself the transformational power of a Schneider lens in the hands of a master like Pompeo Posar. The great wooden Deardorff camera could take a rather small, shy, and ordinary-looking teenager, project her onto an eight-by-ten sheet of Kodachrome film, and turn her into a mysterious ten-foot-tall celestial goddess with rays of light shooting off of her as if she were in Botticelli's *The Birth of Venus*.

We have so many different kinds of lenses today, I'm not quite sure we understand yet what the implications are for the future. Ever since Buzz Aldrin set foot on the moon and returned with photographs of our blue planet, we have been reinventing what it means to view ourselves and our world through a lens. That image of the earth, floating like a single living cell in the cold blackness of space, contributed more to the environmental movement than any legislation or polemic could have done. And it opened up a new world of lenses through which to view ourselves and our universe. The exotic lenses of the Hubble Space Telescope, for example, have given us the ability to look at objects whose light began traveling toward us thirteen billion years ago, not long after the moment when our universe was born.

There are even lenses that are made by nature rather than by people. The Hubble scientists used the gravitational field of a very large cluster of galaxies known as Abell 1689 to focus the light from thirteen billion years ago so that Hubble could detect it.

Today, the internet is a vast lens of infinite scope. And programs such as Google Earth, through which anyone with a computer screen—another type of lens—can fly up the Nile River from Khartoum or descend into the Australian outback, are changing the way we regard one of our most primary senses: the ability to see. We have become an all-seeing eye.

In every major city of the world now—and soon in every minor city— cameras are mounted in public places and on the dashboards and even on the chests of police officers, recording everything we do. When American Airlines Flight 587 crashed into Belle Harbor, New York, in November of 2001, a camera at a tollbooth snapped a picture of the event, which otherwise would have passed without any visual record. Lenses are now so cheap and small and competent that we can scatter them like seeds of corn.

But a lens is more than just a way of viewing and manipulating our interior and exterior worlds. A lens embodies one of the deepest mysteries in the universe: How does light know where to go? That may seem like a trivial question, but it's not. If you've ever placed a spoon in a glass of water and seen the way it appears to be broken, you have witnessed this mystery. The light travels from its source to its destination at one speed as it moves through the air. But when it hits the water, it slows down. To compensate for its slower speed, it changes the angle at which it travels just enough that it takes the least amount of time to get where it's going. Any other path would take longer. But how does it find that perfect path? No one knows.

Since light travels slower through glass than through air, it's possible to fashion a lens by making the glass thick in the middle and thin at the edges. Light traveling from all angles then passes through just the right amount of glass to slow it down so that all the light rays arrive at your eye at the same instant, resulting in a clear, focused image.

Because of that, a lens can be thought of as a time-shifting device. But it is a time-shifting device in many other ways as well. The Hubble Space Telescope can look back to the beginning of the universe, shifting our view across billions of years. But even an ordinary camera can take us back decades, and Vermeer's lens projected his images centuries into the future.

In that sense the lens is an extension of our memory and language. (The marvelous American photographer Sally Mann said that photography robs us of our memory, because all of our memories become memories of photographs.) Memory has been around as long as creatures have been around. It stores images of past circumstances and experiences to compare with the present to devise a strategy for survival. In humans, memory took on vastly more complex forms that included not only comparing past and present but also imagining a future that did not yet exist. When symbolic language came along—especially written language and art—it gave us an unprecedented ability to project the past into a future that could span countless generations. The great variety of lenses through which we now view our world has extended that ability further than ever before, giving us a view that ranges in scale from the cosmos down to the subatomic structures that lie beneath the surface of our solid-seeming world. No wonder my father was fascinated by them.

I now have a house of my own. It is littered with cameras and microscopes and clever devices for viewing the heavens. And with them, I've been teaching my children and grandchildren the wonder and mystery of the world of lenses.

· 7 ·

The Blowdown

THESE FORESTS STRETCH from central Minnesota to the Canadian line, and then they keep on going, all the way to Hudson Bay and across toward Alaska. On a map, the million-acre Boundary Waters Canoe Area Wilderness (BWCAW), between Lake Superior and Canada, looks like a postage stamp against the vast field of green that is the Superior National Forest, which blends unbroken into the George Washington State Forest and the Chippewa National Forest and does not pause at any of those imaginary boundaries on its way west.

When I first came up here in the early nineties, I was taken by the haunting quality of these woods, so different from the ones I'd seen below Superior or even out west. This is the largest boreal forest on the continent, heavy old pine, fir, balsam, spruce, maple, birch, cedar, and aspen, hung with ancient streamers of silver moss, towering out of a maddening understory of deadfall, brush, and vines. Wild rose, leatherleaf, and thorn apple grow in crazy tangles amid thistle and lady's slipper. Fungal villages populate the woody rot as fallen trees are sucked back into the earth like cotton candy going into a child's mouth. Hiking in from the trailhead, we lost sight of the road after ten or fifteen steps in a wall of willow as high as our heads. Then we were in the eternal twilight of this mythic world, the blackness almost luminous at times.

The forest is actually a northern jungle. Its darkness steals the sky and leaves you in a chaotic bushland churning with life and destruction. Where any light comes, it comes in great pillars and slim shafts, illuminating a mist that looks and smells like decay mixed with the incense of a cathedral. The scent of clove and myrrh mixes with the aroma of dying leaves. Sometimes, too, that radiant dark escapes the forest and overspreads the open land, and only when the wind comes to ripple the water and set the aspens dancing at its edge do you recognize that you're seeing a deep black lake alive with fish. The lakes here go on endlessly, from the east to the west where the glaciers went. They are pressed so close together that you can paddle and portage from Thunder Bay to the Little Fork River and Muskeg Bay. In the 1700s, voyageurs crossed them on their way from Montreal to the Pacific, covering some three thousand miles.

If you come from the city, one of the glories of this place is the quiet. At the edge of a lake, I heard the pebbles rattle as even the smallest waves withdrew. When a breeze came up, the aspen leaves clattered like coins. I heard a bear sneeze in the forest. And one day as I sat in a canoe trying for a walleye, a moose crashed out of the forest trailed by her calf and swam across the lake not fifty feet in front of me. They climbed the far bank and melted into the darkness. Then it was silent. So silent that when a crow flew overhead, his wings cut the air with a sound like someone ripping long bolts of silk. Fire is the enemy of this quiet, this cool darkness, and one day it will bring the noise and sunlight down to the forest floor for the first time in centuries.

· · ·

On July 4, 1999, the temperature here hovered around a hundred degrees, as it had for days. A cold front had descended into southern Canada from over the arctic pack ice. When that cold, fast-moving air met the steamy hot air north of Lake Superior, it was like throwing water into hot grease: it exploded into the stratosphere, creating what meteorologists call a "mesoscale convective complex." Far larger than a thunderstorm, more powerful than a supercell, it pulled winds down from twenty thousand feet or more and began working its way from South Dakota to the northeast, knocking down power lines, felling trees, sucking up thirteen hundred acres of the Chippewa National Forest, and expelling inundating rains that damaged nine thousand acres of lakeshore as it moved across Minnesota.

As the heat from the land fed the storm complex, it built in intensity, and by the time it reached the Boundary Waters, it was putting out sustained, straight-line winds estimated as high as a hundred miles an hour. For twenty minutes the storm locked on to the land here and flattened an area of nearly half a million acres. Then it was gone to the east, and the quiet descended once again. Almost immediately, the locals began referring to this event as the Blowdown.

The wildland firefighters who protect the Boundary Waters had long referred to the area as the "asbestos forest," because it was resistant to large fires.

The reason it wouldn't burn explosively was its lack of tinder or what they call one-hour fuels, as well as the absence of people to set fires. One-hour fuels dry out quickly. One hour after the end of any rainfall, they are dry enough to burn. Suddenly, in little more than a quarter of an hour, the forest had been transformed. Pine needles and small branches, dead and drying, littered the forest floor, and the so-called "fuel load"—the amount of fuel available to burn—went from between five and twenty tons per acre to between fifty and one hundred tons per acre. A forest that was unlikely to burn became a forest with the highest fuel load in North America and a probability of burning—perhaps catastrophically—that was put at nearly 100 percent. The fuel load was so high, the risk of uncontrollable fire in extremely harsh and remote terrain so great, that there were no computer models capable of testing what might happen.

The closest historical model was 128 years old from the area that encloses the Green Bay in Wisconsin. Logging, railroad building, and generally careless use of the land had left not only a huge fuel load on the forest floor but also numerous small fires burning unattended in the summer of 1871. Loggers burned slash, railroad crews cleared land for the Chicago and Northwestern line with fire and ax, and travelers routinely walked away from their fires without bothering to put them out. Everyone assumed that the rains would come, as they always had. That summer and fall they didn't.

It was dry and hot, and small fires scuttled along beneath the forest canopy like strange creatures on the ocean floor, consuming whatever was readily combustible. When any wind came up, they burst up into the tree limbs, and in September a crown fire exploded, setting loose thousands of birds across the town of Peshtigo near the Michigan line. A crown fire burns hot and travels rapidly through the tops of the trees. Ahead of it, whole trees, superheated by the flame front, exploded. But people were used to fire and smoke in the fall, and they stayed and stayed, waiting for rain.

Catastrophes are built out of the small pieces of our lives that we leave lying around unnoticed. The clouds came in, and it looked like rain, but all they got was wind. The front and the rain it carried were still in the Dakotas. For several days the wind blew and blew, but no rain came. The small fires began to consolidate.

Fire and weather are wicked sisters, born of the same blood: heat and air. They always travel together, aiding each other, bringing gifts and making mischief. Weather brings rain and makes the forest grow. When it grows too much, fire clears it, and then the rain makes it grow again. And sometimes, when a cold front approaches a big dry forest with a source of ignition inside of it, the world explodes, and the forest simply ceases to exist. If the fire is hot enough to burn through the root system, the forest never grows back.

Weather makes fire and fire makes weather, and the winds created by the Peshtigo fire ripped full-grown maple trees out of the ground by the roots and sent them aloft as firebrands, torching more forest up to three miles away. Papers from the town were found as far away as Canada and Michigan.

There is no clear line between conflagration and deflagration, between fire and explosion. The difference is the speed with which the flame front progresses. Stephen J. Pyne, author of *Fire in America*, writes, "In heavy fuels and under favorable conditions, the coalescence, which begins with the upper convective columns, occurs rapidly. The resulting holocaust is a synergistic phenomenon of extreme burning known as mass fire." Peter M. Leschak, author of *Ghosts of the Fireground*, refers to the fire at Peshtigo as "a kind of rolling explosion." And since it consumed 1,280,000 acres of forest in about four hours, that would appear to be accurate. (Across the lake in Michigan, fire consumed 2.5 million more acres the same day, October 8, 1871. The Chicago Fire, which happened to begin on the same day, got all the headlines.)

Only after the Peshtigo fire had done its damage—whole towns burned to ashes and up to twenty-five hundred people killed—did the rains come at last. If conditions were the same in the blowdown today, this Minnesota forest could burn from Lake Superior to well across the Canadian line in the time it took those rains to arrive. In the firefighter's art, the term "conflagration" is used to refer to a mass fire that is on the move. (A firestorm is stationary.) A conflagration produces its own wind in what some firefighters call a "fire tornado." It is a ballet of energy between sky and forest and can push hot columns of gas to fifty thousand feet. When they cool, the down-rushing tornadic winds explode outward in every direction in an expanding dome of fire. As the fire uses up all the available oxygen, the superheated fuels send great amoebic masses of unburned gas aloft, where they explode as soon as they reach fresh air. Horizontal vortices develop from those gases and reach out to torch trees and cause preheated structures to burst instantly into flame. During the Peshtigo fire, wagons in open fields caught fire far from any source of ignition. A mother was seen running down the street, her hair streaming back, skirts flying, clutching her baby. She burst into flames as she made for the safety of the river, which flowed through the center of town.

Fires of such intensity are not unknown in this region. The Little Sioux fire in the Boundary Waters Canoe Area Wilderness—the asbestos forest— burned nine thousand acres in six hours in 1971 without the unusual fuel load.

Making matters worse is the fact that there is only one escape road in the most densely populated area, the Gunflint Trail, and it's a cul-de-sac at its northern end, which is surrounded by the very forest that people would be trying to escape. The only way out is south, through nearly sixty miles of forest to the town of Grand Marais on Lake Superior. It brings to mind the fire at Paradise, California, which killed at least forty-two people who simply could not get out.

Ellen Bogardus-Szymaniak, who is the fire behavior expert with the Superior National Forest, said, "The potential for large, explosive fires has not diminished. But what we've done is made it so we can *slow* the fire from exiting the wilderness. And that's all we've ever wanted to do anyway." Although it's been a wet year in Minnesota, she said, "We still have very high intensities, and the blowdown will ignite even in very, very damp, wet conditions. It's like a big woodpile."

After the Blowdown, the fire district at Grand Marais, on the southern edge of the forest, was reinforced with more people and equipment as summer turned to fall, both prime seasons for wildland fires. The Minnesota Interagency Fire Center in Grand Rapids staged chainsaws, protective clothing, radios, tools, and other firefighting equipment in caches from Ely east to the Gunflint Trail. Various agencies contributed to leasing a helicopter, which carried a two-thousand-gallon water bucket, and air tankers that could scoop fourteen hundred gallons from the surface of a lake in one eight-second pass. They hacked helipads out of the forest and acquired four new fire engines.

They understood that if conditions were right, if a so-called "plume-dominated" fire similar to the Peshtigo fire were to begin, there would not be enough equipment or enough manpower. Once it happened—if it happened—the only strategy would be to try to move the people, who occupy about six hundred cabins, resorts, and homes in the area, down the Gunflint Trail before the fire overran it and cut them off. If the fire were to burn south to Lake Superior, even that might not work.

. . .

My wife Debbie and I stayed on the edge of the blowdown in a cabin that had been built by hand on Flour Lake. The lake was enclosed on all sides by the wilderness. Our first night, we sat by the water and watched Mars tow the full moon in an arc above the palisades. A front came in, and clouds hurried high to the northeast, cold and gray and tumbling, illuminated from below by the low-angled light of the rising moon. A loon cried all night long.

In the early morning, a black beaver with a white nose came to sit as still as a statue on a stump outside our window. A quarter mile across the lake a great, dark humpbacked hill rose from the silver water with a green that made me think of the dinosaurs that would have lived here before the glaciers cut these lakes out of Precambrian bedrock. Farther east, beyond the rising palisades that cleaved clean to the bottom of the lake, was the paler green of the sunlit forest. I could see three miles down the lake to where the misty rampart of the wilderness stood against the white sky. The day grew windy and white, so white that where water met sky, there was no line to show which was which.

After hiking and paddling in the undamaged forest farther south, we went to see the worst of the blowdown on a day when the sign at Station Number One of the Gunflint Trail Volunteer Fire Department read: "Fire Danger— EXTREME." As we headed up a small dirt road, a healthy-looking gray timber wolf trotted ahead of the car for a hundred yards and then loped off into the trees. Farther on, we stopped for a bald eagle, which appeared to be sharing some roadkill with a conspiracy of ravens. (The raven, largest songbird in North America and as smart as a dog, was also made nearly extinct by logging.)

We went in at the Kekekabic Trailhead. The trail ran up a steep, rocky slope to a ridgeline heading straight west along a gully. Half a mile in, we began to see the scope of the destruction. Thick evergreens had been snapped in half lengthwise and lay on their sides. Some trees had been torqued so rapidly and with such force that they had simply exploded into a messy kindling shrapnel. Stands of young aspens pointed the way the storm had gone. Their fibers had been permanently stretched by the wind so that they stood bent in the shape of Cs, some all the way to the ground. We passed whole areas where the trees had been blown in half, their crowns and upper stories gone. They stood in odd, jagged ranks, as if a cathedral had had its roof blown off and lay open to the sky. Everywhere were great piles of mature trees and even old-growth cedar and pine, turned into jackstraws and stacked in towering heaps, some of them spring-loaded like drawn bows. A two-foot-thick tree trunk stores a tremendous amount of energy when it's spring-loaded, and if it is cut or breaks, it rebounds with the force of a bomb going off. Not easy or safe for crews to clear.

Aside from the trail on which we hiked and a few others like it, the forest ran uninterrupted for hundreds of miles, and the shattered trees made the land impassable. Some trees had been uprooted, leaving root balls ten or more feet across erupted out of the earth, their fingers clutching huge rocks in a final spasm. Walking through there may have been hazardous, but I couldn't imagine what it had been like for the crews who'd had to clear this yard-wide trail.

Leschak was on one of those crews. He found a note stuck to a twelve-foot-wide cedar root wad. It read, "Welcome to Hell" and was signed, "Voyageurs Nat. Park Crew." He'd come from two hundred miles away.

We followed the trail through perhaps another mile of destruction. On the north side, the land angled sharply upward, iron red and black and rocky, piled high with blown down trees too dense to scramble through without a power saw. To the south, the terrain dropped away to rise again in cliffs, and down there we saw more of the same—great middens of burst and fractured trees. Some people think it's ugly, a sad thing that needs cleaning up. I think it's beautiful, a great wonder where nature leaves her signature. We're not used to seeing such clear evidence of her power. A Niagara of wind came through here, hard as water, and tore a hole in this forest measuring half a million acres.

An hour and a half in, the gulch below became swampy as the trail turned downhill. The cliffs to the south dropped away, and we descended a natural staircase of great boulders. A creek, crackling like fire, drained into a field of tall yellow-green grass with oxbow waterways gleaming through it. Swaying in the wind, the grass formed French curves and arches. In the waterways, lily pads rode the wind-freaked surfaces in pale purple and silver-green formations. The few scattered cattails appeared so intensely green and brown against those pastels that they looked as if they'd been painted there.

We found a flat, mossy rock and sat and ate sandwiches. We could hear the wind long before it reached us. There was no other noise. For perhaps a full minute, we heard it coming, deciding to come, preparing to come. It began as a far-off, rushing whisper and grew steadily until the trees three hundred yards away began to rustle and sway. At last we saw it descend from the crowns to bend the grass in long, undulating waves, changing all the colors from yellow to green to silver and brown and back again. And then it was gone. But one day it hadn't gone. It had just kept on building, and nature had had a game of pickup sticks with this forest. Soon trees had been exploding, flying through the air, pitchpoling through the forest, tearing one another apart. The cannonade of sound lasted twenty minutes, and twenty-five million trees went down.

On a day like this the fire will come. The report called *Fuels Risk Assessment* from fall 1999 says it will come. So does the six-pound volume entitled *Final Environmental Impact Statement: Boundary Waters Canoe Area Wilderness Fuel Treatment* from 2001. On a day like this, then, when the wind is ten to twenty knots, with gusts to thirty from the southwest, it will come. Then the cold front will arrive, the wind will switch directions ninety degrees, and the fire will appear as a gleaming wall, roaring and towering 150 feet above the tops of these trees, and it will sweep across this bog in seconds and take the grass and water with it.

Fire is good for forests. But catastrophic mass fires can burn down through root systems to bedrock and change an entire ecosystem. The Peshtigo fire destroyed not only an old-growth forest but also the ecosystem of microorganisms beneath it in the soil. That fire ensured that the forest would not grow back. The land was cleared completely. Grasses grew. Immigrants from Europe moved in to start dairy farms on the newly arable land.

· · ·

Here is why this forest still stands: In 1924, Ernest Oberholtzer, a prodigious explorer who lived here, learned that the local paper-mill baron, Edward Backus, was planning to build seven hydroelectric dams that would destroy a large area, including what we now know as the Superior National Forest, Voyageurs National Park, Quetico Provincial Park, and the Boundary Waters Canoe Area Wilderness. It was the legacy of the beaver: people were coming to cut down this forest to make paper.

Oberholtzer fought Backus all the way to the White House over the next few years. The concept of lands that couldn't be used for anything was an alien notion at the time. Oberholtzer's victory in Congress in 1930 marked the first time legislators had voted to preserve any federal land as completely wild. It is because of Oberholtzer that these woods retain their strange and mystical character. "Holtzer" means "timber man."

· · ·

In the years since the Blowdown, fire agencies have gradually worked—through prescribed burns and logging—to isolate the Boundary Waters Canoe Area Wilderness, where most of the trees were felled, from the larger area of the Superior National Forest and in particular from the Gunflint Trail.

Between two thousand and four thousand people come here in the summer, many of them to canoe and camp in the wilderness, days away from civilization, and I wondered what would happen to them if a fire started.

In fact, a fire did start inside the Boundary Waters wilderness area in the summer of 2011. It smoldered in a bog for days before anyone even noticed. Begun with a lightning strike, it was merely an ember. Then the wind kicked up, and humidity dropped to 18 percent. The fire burst into the crowns of the trees and grew from a quarter of an acre to 130 acres. As in Peshtigo, the people in the area expected at least two inches of rain and 30 percent humidity at that time of year. But they were headed into the driest autumn in 140 years. Firefighters began burning forest ahead of the fire to try to contain it. But winds kicked up again and blew the fire up to 4,500 acres. By the second week in September, crown fires were running toward Insula Lake. Late on the morning of September 12, firefighters were hiking in to warn campers to get out. The fire that is now known as the Pagami Creek Fire blew up and overran six of the eight wilderness rangers. Wildland firefighters are required to carry fire shelters. They are made of aluminum foil and woven silica cloth, which reflect heat and trap air inside for the firefighters to breathe. They are also lined with fiberglass for insulation. The six firefighters survived. But that afternoon, the wind shifted again, and the fire ran six additional miles to the east. It then turned and ran ten more miles northwest and escaped the BWCAW. The Pagami Creek Fire covered 93,000 acres by September 13 and burned on into October.

Ellen Bogardus-Szymaniak, the fire expert, told me that the only way to get rid of the danger of explosive fire is to wait until all this burns. "I'm feeling much better about most of the Gunflint Trail. If we do get a fire, and it's ripping for the boundary, we'll be able to slow it down enough to get folks out of the way. We're not going to stop it, but I think we'll be able to evacuate everybody."

I asked her what they'd do about the people far out in the wilderness, where fires were most likely to burn. She said they'd try to fly over and warn them somehow, "depending on the weather. But before they go out," she added, "they'll just have to understand that they're on their own. You smell smoke, you see smoke, you have ash falling on you, it's not a good time to go walking in the woods to see what's going on."

· 8 ·

ValuJet Crash

IN THE ANNALS of transportation history, such a flight would not have rated more than a log entry:

Left Miami 1:00 p.m.
Arrived Atlanta 2:55 p.m.

But before sundown, the go-teams, tethered by their pagers to calamity, were converging on a spot in the swamp where ValuJet Flight 592 had failed in its attempt to return to Miami after broadcasting a Mayday emergency to air traffic controllers.

The plane had departed on a scheduled flight but minutes later had reported smoke, bad smoke, first in the cabin, then in the cockpit. The white ship with a sky-blue tail had turned back toward the field. Controllers in a darkened radar room watched the plane on the screen and heard the voice of the captain, a woman named Candalyn Kubeck: "We're on fire! We're on fire!" Then they watched as the plane's neat identifying data block dropped from their scopes.

It was a hot and sunny day with a sky the color of polished chrome and cumulus clouds like herds of sheep. A man sat in his bass boat, fishing near Canal L67-A beside a levee. He was a private pilot and had been watching the northbound jets when he saw something amazing—a large jetliner turned on edge, one wing pointing at the ground. The fisherman knew it was a big jetliner and would accurately describe it to police as having two engines on the fuse-lage, none on the wings. Coming more or less straight down in knife-edge flight from seventy-five hundred feet, a sweptwing DC-9, capable of flight at nearly Mach 1, will gather speed quickly. Later its terminal speed would be estimated at 352 miles an hour. The fisherman watched in disbelief as the plane flung itself headlong into the Everglades not a mile from where he stood in his bass boat.

The explosion was tremendous. A black cloud obscured the chromium sun. There was a gap in time, a silent, searing moment before the concussion reached him and threw him back. He understood that this glittering craft with many, many human lives on board had just cast itself onto the naked rind of the earth, where it had burst and scattered and disintegrated. An immense dragon of smoke and matter blossomed on the flat, hot horizon. It bloomed and spread and then settled again, heavy with the oil of life and commerce. Smoke drifted slowly as the waves of water on their return to the swamp rolled out in curling, mirrored ripples and tilted his boat gently back and to like the weight on a pendulum.

The fisherman, his heart hammering like mad, picked himself up and reached for his phone. When he stammered that an airliner had gone down in the swamp, the dispatch officer in the Broward County Sheriff's Office was forced to ask, "This is not a hoax, you say?" Now the ripples would spread outward, taking in wildlife, families, towns, Indian tribes, and businesses and shaking the government officials who oversaw the business of airline travel, even ending some careers. But through it all, ValuJet would continue, eventually changing its name to AirTran to conceal its past from travelers in search of a deal.

For several minutes, helicopters and squad cars, boats and airplanes, and even people on foot on the levee searched without finding any trace of a wreck. The radio chatter carried the same message over and over: there was no plane. And if there had been a plane, there were no survivors. It appeared that an airliner full of people had been swallowed whole by the swamp.

By and by, a rescue pilot saw from his helicopter what may have been scraps of paper floating on the surface of the swamp, and there, look: where in every direction nothing but lily pads and saw grass stretched away in flat monotony, there was a sort of Rorschach inkblot. Everyone would see something different: a teardrop, a candle flame, a silhouette like those in Hiroshima after the first atomic bomb—a child, arms akimbo, flashed out of existence one sunny afternoon and stamped forever on a clock tower wall like a pressed flower. That beckoning shadow in the middle of five thousand square miles of wilderness moved people like a sign in the heavens. And people came from everywhere.

A Metro-Dade policewoman told a reporter, "This is Dade County. If it's going to get weird, it's going to get weird here."

· · ·

By nightfall it was impossible to avoid the impression that a circus had come to town, what with police and fire and rescue vehicles spinning their party lights on the Tamiami Trail. The helicopters rippled man-high waves of saw grass. The go-team members from the National Transportation Safety Board (NTSB) marched around looking like astronauts in their blue jumpsuits and Ray-Bans. TV trucks with their satellite dishes spawned scrub-cheeked newscasters, who looked like dissipated Ken and Barbie dolls. And all the while, discreet little medical examiner's vans went in and out of the deeper swamp across the top of the levee.

The police staging area was at the intersection of Canal L67-A and the Tamiami Trail, one of only two highways that run straight through the swamp past such curiosities as Indians who wrestle alligators and "Frog City," once a community, once a restaurant, and finally a business—just a man and his wife, really, who used to sit around a big bloody tub of frogs, stripping off their skins with pliers to sell the carcasses to restaurants. In this part of the Everglades, it is not unusual to find people sitting by the side of the road, drinking beer, relaxing on an exploded couch, as if they were in their living room watching TV. Now suddenly disaster had cobbled together this new and festive city beside the road.

By morning great white tents had bloomed like overnight mushrooms, stenciled with mysterious legends and crypto-military names, over which American flags drooped in the windless heat. Men with radios and guns bicycled in and out on knobby tires. There was the departure and arrival of helicopters, and the air was filled with the smell of kerosene from their turbines. A levee stretched out to within three hundred yards of the crash site, but the rough drive took an hour, so most workers went back and forth by helicopter and boat. Salvation Army trucks dispensed free food and drinks and a lot of bottled water through steamy ninety-degree afternoons.

A sign was posted in the area: "Everglades Wildlife Management Area— Please Help Keep Your Area Clean." But trash and cables were strewn everywhere, and yellow police line tape added a gala touch amid scores of squad cars, dozens of trucks, RVs, and vans. A yellow Metro-Dade fire truck bore a bumper sticker that read, "The Dudes of Hazard." Already the trappings of tragedy had been laid over the event to begin the long process of concealment. A wreath on a wire stand had been jammed into the mud by the water's edge, festooned with a white ribbon imprinted with "ValuJet Flight 592." So effective and seductive is the concept of tragedy that few would ever know (or even want to know) the criminal negligence that had gone into creating the slaughter.

The rocky roadside site abutted a shifting curtain of green and brown grass and cattails, where a sudden breeze could change the color of the landscape in undulating waves. Dragonflies hung in the air. Wild bay threw off an aromatic spoor. Cypress, palm, and live oak punctuated the sameness of this wilderness, which ran unbroken for a hundred miles to the north. Lily pads grew in flowering profusion, and mangrove formed dense undergrowth. Alligators would come up to the encampment to beg like dogs, their sad red eyes drooping, their stinking, prehistoric mouths hanging open, until someone would throw in a corned beef sandwich, whereupon the alligator would close its mouth with a wet slap and appear to dissolve back into the black water. There was nothing else to film, so TV crews set up and filmed the alligators. It would serve as "B-roll" for their broadcasts.

The US Air Force arrived. The Army Corps of Engineers arrived. The US Navy sent in special salvage teams. There was sonar, radar, loran, GPS, and every kind of communication device known. BellSouth put up a mobile phone booth, and local calls were free. Some of the experts considered sinking caissons and diking off the swamp and draining it to get at the airplane. But local engineers, old-timers, informed them of the power of this swamp and its underlying base of Loxahatchee peat. "You think you can beat this swamp, you got another think comin'," one of them said.

"I don't hold any hope we'll find any recoverable, large parts of people," Joseph Davis, a retired medical examiner, said at a press briefing. He was skeptical about ever identifying most victims. A Metro-Dade police lieutenant said, "You're dealing with a very big site and thousands of parts." He meant body parts, not airplane parts.

The father of one victim said, "It's hard for me to accept that over a weekend trip his life is terminated and they can't even find him," expressing a fundamental lament: that a trusted airline had caused him to vanish forever from the face of the earth, leaving not even a scrap to bury or a watch or ring to keep as a memento.

Cameramen had set up lean-tos of plastic tarp on aluminum poles and kept their cameras pointed up the canal, a waterway about as wide as the two-lane Tamiami Trail. You could tell the power of the station by the quality of its shelter. CNN had a beautiful white tent such as might be used for a backyard garden party, and its talking heads were known to exaggerate wildly when reporting the day's events.

Some days whole families of curious tourists or locals would come and set up picnics and sit with us, their children squeaking with joy as they kicked a ball or threw a Frisbee, while in the background the rescue workers carried stretchers to unmarked vans and then sprayed Clorox on their rubber boots to decontaminate them.

Canal L67-A led north, diminishing in silver-gray reflections to the crash site eight miles distant. Now and then boats would come back with gray body bags, and we could see them loading the rubber cerements onto stretchers and then into ambulances. The bags were never very full. They hung limp. I was talking to one TV producer with my back to the waterway when, in the middle of a sentence, she shouted, "Body bag!" then stormed off to her cameraman, shouting, "Goddamn it! I can't believe we missed it. Where's our fabulous crew?"

. . .

There had been some thought of triage at first, and lots of body bags had been marshaled, while the radio frequencies had carried messages alerting local hospitals to expect a large number of major injuries. But there was no triage. There were no wounded. Most of the body bags went unused. We sat around, increasingly mystified that the proud ship, packed full of friends and family and driven by the most sophisticated navigation and transportation technology ever devised, could simply disappear without a trace.

Well, there were traces. They had pinned it down to a particular area of swamp, and once they looked more closely, they could fly over it and see that carrion-bird shape, like one of those enormous ancient designs that are found stenciled on the sides of mountains in Peru. They saw a crater in the mud, a welling up of the muck, made in those first moments when the fisherman in his bass boat felt the waves. It was a concavity such as we might expect to see if a meteor hit the earth. The workers quickly gave it a name: the Pit.

At first as the airboats crisscrossed the Pit without finding anything, there was a pause in the search, because quite literally, no one knew what to do next. A plane had never vanished quite like that. Men began wading through but soon found that the jet fuel was burning their skin. Now the area around the Pit was being searched by men in rubber waders with masks and goggles and Tyvek suits, which they wore with the notion that the whole swamp had become this sort of fecal soup of 110 exploded bowels. There was concern at first that the roughly eight tons of fresh meat that had been thrown into the swamp by the crash would result in a feeding frenzy among all the ragged claws and snapping jaws that dredged this gumbo of growing things, and Dade County kept its trained snipers in place on the off chance that a beast might return to take down a rescue worker. But after a few days, word filtered out that the crash site was devoid of interested life-forms. In fact, it appeared to be devoid of most everything except buzzing flies and the heat and the lonely sound of a boat returning now and then with a disembodied human arm.

With nothing really solid to stand on, then, the searchers moved five abreast, working only twenty minutes at a time in the heat. Beyond the kerosene spilled by the crash, which burned the skin and eyes, heat exhaustion and dehydration were the primary dangers. Workers wore white Tyvek bodysuits under dark green waders such as fishermen wear. They wore bowlers and fedoras, panamas and crush hats—anything with a brim to keep the sun off the ears and face. With suspenders holding up their waders and their heads bowed, a net and hook in either hand, they looked like members of a lost tribe of Cajuns hunting dinner in the knee-deep mud.

The searchers would call out "Body part!" when they felt a piece of human flesh, and an airboat, which was following along behind, would move up to retrieve it. Each bit of flesh was bagged and tagged. Once on dry land, or what passed for dry land in the Everglades, those remains were removed, photographed, and put in a bag with a bar code label. The new bags were placed together in a larger body bag for removal to the medical examiner's office in Miami.

Monday, May 13, late afternoon. Two days after the crash, searchers found the flight-data recorder, one of the so-called black boxes. That happens to be a metaphor with an enigmatic meaning—the boxes are actually painted with orange stripes to make them easier to find. Searchers also removed seven body bags containing "hundreds of small pieces" of human flesh, some so small that it was impossible even to tell what part of the anatomy they had come from. The flight-data recorder turned out to be of the older type, which recorded only eleven flight parameters, not the hundred or so that the new instruments can track. The plane had been old and had had a history of mechanical troubles. ValuJet had purchased it from Turkish Airlines as a castoff, a "roach," as pilots call such a plane.

They had done it before. On a mild summer evening in Atlanta on June 8, 1995, ValuJet Flight 597 was barreling down Runway 27 Right on its takeoff roll. Everyone on board heard the loud bang as the right engine exploded, sending shrapnel into the cabin. One piece seriously injured the flight attendant in the rear jump seat. Another severed the main fuel line. Jet fuel sprayed into the cabin, setting a flight attendant and others on fire.

Another flight attendant rushed to the cockpit to tell the captain. Having stopped the plane, the captain punched the mike button and ordered his fifty-seven passengers to evacuate, but his voice never reached them. The electrical power had had been cut. The NTSB had been after the airlines for two decades to provide the PA system with its own power supply, but the Federal Aviation Administration (FAA) "indicated that it had determined that the cost of compliance with such a rule would outweigh any identifiable safety benefits," according to the NTSB. The passengers were on their own.

As soon as a flight attendant opened the front exit door, smoke rolled in, filling the cabin up to the ceiling. Passengers are told to follow the strip of lights along the floor in an emergency. No one had turned them on.

With toxic smoke rising around her from the flaming cabin furnishings, the injured flight attendant in the back found herself unable to open the tail-cone exit. It wasn't because of her injuries. She'd never actually opened one. It wasn't required training.

Passengers rushed the exits, but the openings were not wide enough, and people jammed against them. The fire began to consume the plane. The overhead bins caught fire, and flaming debris began falling. Fire trucks were racing down the runway, their emergency lights revolving in the oncoming Georgia night. Within seconds, the entire Douglas DC-9 aircraft was destroyed. It is nothing short of a miracle that everyone got out, even a two-year-old child and the injured flight attendant.

Like ValuJet Flight 592, that DC-9 had been purchased from Türk Hava Yolları (THY), known in English as Turkish Airlines. The NTSB found that THY mechanics didn't understand English and ignored the usual instructions for detecting and treating fatigue cracks in critical engine components. A disk that holds the turbine fan blades had developed a 1.5-inch fatigue crack, which is gigantic in metallurgical terms. It was certainly big enough to have been detected if anyone had bothered to look. When it let loose, fragments of metal and whole fan blades shot out at supersonic speeds in an explosive disintegration. THY has a history of catastrophic failures. By failing to close a cargo door properly (the instructions were in English), it helped to send a DC-10 and 346 people to their deaths in a forest outside of Paris in 1974.

It might be comforting to tell ourselves that ValuJet was the world's worst airline, that it bought the airplanes that even Turkey didn't want. But the same thing could happen on any airline. It already has.

It happened to Midwest Express Flight 105, a DC-9, on September 6, 1985; to United Airlines Flight 232, a DC-10, on July 19, 1989; and to Delta Airlines

Flight 1288, an MD-88, on July 6, 1996. All three of those aircraft experienced catastrophic engine failures. All three were manufactured by McDonnell Douglas, one of the most famous names in American aviation. General Electric made and inspected the engines. All had critical flaws, which were easy to detect through ordinary engineering tests. These incidents and accidents were the background against which the FAA and ValuJet conspired to conceal dire flaws in the airline's operation, which led to the crash in the swamp.

· · ·

That Wednesday, investigators poring over records at ValuJet headquarters in Atlanta found a cargo manifest that listed oxygen generators as cargo on Flight 592. This jolted the investigators with a deep sense of dread and foreboding. They had seen it time and again. Those sodium chlorate "candles" are like hand grenades. You pull the pin, and sodium chlorate mixes with iron powder, producing oxygen and a lot of heat (as well as table salt and rust as by-products).

The candles are standard equipment on many airliners, used to supply emergency oxygen to passengers. They are lighter and cheaper than conventional bottles of compressed oxygen. But they're tricky to use and easy to set off accidentally. As anyone who took chemistry in high school ought to know, oxygen and a lot of heat will burn anything, even steel. In five separate incidents prior to the crash, chlorate candles had burst into flames. In some cases, they had nearly brought down other airplanes. One candle burst into flames on the *Mir* space station and nearly killed everyone on board.

I interviewed an NTSB lead investigator, Greg Feith, who had become something of a media star, since he was the only thing the TV crews could film. He was young, articulate, and good looking, and he had the bearing of an athlete. One female reporter had asked him during a briefing, "Greg, how do you feel getting all this attention? How does it feel to be the Mud Stud?" And Feith had ducked his head shyly and demurred, but the moniker had stuck.

Feith described a test he had performed to see how hot the candles could get when they were stacked together in a cardboard box, as they had been on this flight. They had reached a temperature of two thousand degrees. As soon as the investigators saw chlorate candles listed on the cargo manifest, they felt that kind of certainty that comes from long experience.

Ronald Reagan issued Executive Order 12,291, which requires the FAA to conduct a cost-benefit analysis before it can force airlines to enact any safety measure. The FAA first established the going price for a human life: $1.5 million at the time. It calculates how much it would cost *not* to improve safety by comparing fatalities (number of bodies times $1.5 million) with the actual cost of the safety improvement. Nothing has to be done if it's not cost-effective.

Today the FAA still allows chlorate candles to be used on airliners and flown as cargo. As you fly around the country, they fly around in your seat back or beneath your seat in the cargo hold.

. . .

That Friday after the stock market closed, with ValuJet's stock down nearly 30 percent, the airline announced that it would cut daily flights from 320 to 160 in the interest of safety. In fact, that was not quite the truth. The FAA had finally stepped in and made them do it. But the FAA had known for at least a year that ValuJet was just an airline looking for a place to crash. And the FAA had done nothing.

Saturday, as investigators looked deeper into ValuJet's records, the whole operation began to seem like a house of cards. ValuJet was the fastest-growing airline in US history, but it had an accident rate fourteen times worse than any other airline's. It bought below-standard airplanes, and its pilots were catch-as-catch-can. Six months before the crash, ValuJet had tried to get a Department of Defense contract to carry DOD personnel but had been turned down with a scathing report on its lax safety and maintenance and its chaotic management. In fact, ValuJet had no maintenance. It was all done by others in a haphazard outsourcing scheme to save money. During 1994, ValuJet made fifteen emergency landings. During 1995, it made fifty-seven. In the first half of 1996, the rate of emergency landings had exploded to one nearly every other day. Its fleet was falling apart. In fact, ValuJet did not have a director of maintenance, a crucial function at any airline, someone who knows at all times where each jet is and what its condition is. Even so, immediately after the crash, Department of Transportation Secretary Federico Peña, went on television and said, "I have flown ValuJet. ValuJet is a safe airline, as is our entire aviation system." But Peña knew nothing about aviation. He was a political appointee, the former mayor of Denver, and a friend of Bill Clinton's. Anyway, he wasn't quite telling the whole truth.

Anthony Broderick, FAA associate administrator for regulation and certification, said, "We found no significant safety deficiencies." He was simply lying. The FAA had found huge deficiencies in safety and had ignored them. Mary Schiavo, the maverick inspector general of the US Department of Transportation (DOT), had been writing a caustic column for Newsweek about that very subject when Flight 592 crashed.

Meanwhile, passengers continued to defy common sense and buy the tickets. And ValuJet continued to fly.

On Sunday, May 19, a searcher found burned seat-rails from the first-class cabin, more evidence of a fire in the cargo hold that had burned up through the floor. The grim, exhausting search continued with saw grass matted down from a week's work and white-clad men on airboats standing off some distance, observing with rifles, like prison trustees. An Air Force reservist employed in the search found a wallet with five new hundred-dollar bills in it. There was a lot of money scattered throughout the swamp. People were on vacation.

Meanwhile the Mass Disaster Identification Team, a group of South Florida dentists, gathered to try to identify people by dental records. Its first job was to collect dental records for all the victims on the passenger list and put the data into a computer. "Someone will bring us a tooth or maybe two teeth or part of a jaw, and we'll see if we can make a match," said Dr. William Silver, head of the team. But at that point no identifications had been made. There were only two other sure ways of identifying someone: by fingerprint or a tattoo.

That same day, an investigator, cleaning mud out of a burned tire, found part of an exploded sodium chlorate oxygen generator embedded in the rubber, further evidence of how the fire had started.

The political furor raged around this scene, moving out from Washington in ripples. Senator Trent Lott said, "They [the FAA] did not as aggressively pursue problems at ValuJet as they should have." FAA administrator David Hinson countered, "Our inspector workforce did exactly what they are supposed to do." Which turned out to be another calculated lie. By June, FAA spot checks of ValuJet planes were so alarming that he had to recant, saying "serious deficiencies" existed. "Yes," he added, "we bear some responsibilities in this case." Associate Administrator Broderick said, "There are a number of things that show ineffective control and procedures."

. . .

Ten days after the crash, the crucial cockpit voice recorder had not yet been found. But then a homicide detective named Jimenez stopped in the swamp, exhausted and covered with sweat, and said a prayer, asking God for help. A moment later he stepped on the crushed and punctured device in a few feet of water. It was quickly packed in an Igloo cooler filled with swamp water so that the tape inside would not dry out and crack. It was immediately shipped to Washington for analysis.

In Washington, Greg Feith and the others listened to the tape from the cockpit voice recorder and came to understand that the crew of Flight 592 never had a chance. The time between Captain Kubeck's first indication that anything was wrong and her total incapacitation was a matter of seconds. At twenty-nine minutes and twenty-three seconds into the tape, she said, "We got some electrical problem." At twenty-nine minutes and thrity-one seconds, the cockpit voice recorder captured the screams of passengers. Feith told me later, "Children were crying, it was terrible." At twenty-nine mintutes and thirty-five seconds, the captain herself was screaming, "We're on fire! We're on fire!" Then the screams from the children subsided as they were overcome and mercifully put to sleep by toxic fumes from burning cabin furnishings. Then Feith heard nothing but the sound of rushing air as the plane accelerated into the Everglades.

After a week and a half of searching, there were still few significant body parts to send to the medical examiner's office. The only entire victim was the so-called lap child. A woman had held her infant in her lap for takeoff, and that baby had been small and compact enough to be thrown clear in the disintegration. Everything else—everyone else—was bits of flesh. Thumbs. Arms. "Oh, there were one or two torsos," a fire department searcher told me, "but not much else. No heads. At least not yet. It's probably all down there. In the Pit." But it wasn't. It wasn't down there at all.

· · ·

In March, FAA inspectors had written a memo that expressed concern about "a significant decrease in experience level of new pilots being hired by ValuJet as well as other positions such as mechanics, dispatchers, etc." and "continuous changes of key management personnel."

I spoke to a pilot who had flown with the first officer of Flight 592, whose name was Richard Hazen. Hazen, not Captain Kubeck, had been flying the plane when it crashed. The pilot I spoke to said that Hazen had not been competent to fly large jet aircraft and that everyone who worked with him had known it. He said Hazen was so bad that "I would not leave the cockpit to go to the bathroom when Dick was at the controls." Hazen had no scan. That is to say, he fixed his gaze on a single instrument instead of moving it from place to place to keep tabs on every system, as a pilot is supposed to. "I warned him on a flight into the Bay Area that the controllers wanted us at 180 knots because the separation between planes was at a minimum. He gave me 180 knots, but he couldn't hold his altitude or heading. He just fixed on the airspeed. I found that by calling out each instrument, I could get him to look around, but when

I stopped, he stopped, too." Once, attempting to make a turn, Hazen rolled inadvertently into a dangerously steep sixty-degree bank because he was fixated on his heading. He did not notice how steep his turn had become until it was pointed out to him. Early on it was suggested that if Hazen was flying when the fire broke out, and the captain told him to turn back to the airfield, he could have flown into the swamp by making such an error, especially with the added stress and confusion of smoke in the cockpit and an emergency underway. Probably he was just overcome by smoke.

Whether or not Hazen's qualifications had any direct bearing on the ValuJet crash, they point to a rather loose system. If Hazen had gotten through, what else had ValuJet failed to notice? Evidently, quite a lot.

A pilot is ultimately responsible for his flight. Hazen and Captain Kubeck were obliged to read the cargo manifest and ensure that there was no hazardous material on board. That was their job. An NTSB official, however, said that the manifest may have simply read, "co-mat," meaning company materials, something belonging to the company. The crew may have accepted that and looked no further. They were on a tight schedule. They didn't have time to poke around.

· · ·

The hangar was quiet. The floor was spotless, illuminated by fluorescent lights high overhead among the steel rafters. The windows, even the little ones in the steel doors, had been sealed roughly by plastic sheeting, giving the outside light an eerie quality. The first thing we noticed when we entered the hangar at Tamiami Airport, a few miles from the crash site, was the smell. When one of the reporters asked why it smelled like a morgue, he was asked, "Why do you think it smells like a morgue?" It was typical of relations with the press at the site. I asked one official, being escorted by the FAA, what office he was with and was told, "I don't think that's any of your business." And he walked away. The pathological secretiveness of the FAA is one cause of its troubles. I once flew with a stunt pilot who had a sign in the back of his plane where the passenger could see it. It said:

Check List
Sit down.
Strap in.
Shut up.
Hold on.

Which seemed to sum up the philosophy of the FAA and the airlines when it comes to passengers on scheduled airliners.

The FAA had good reason for wanting to keep secrets. It had inspected ValuJet five thousand times in three years but had failed to file a single report against the airline. Everything was done through discreet, convivial agreements between Lewis Jordan, ValuJet's president, and FAA officials, who didn't want to upset the new airline in its astounding success.

On the floor of the hangar where investigators were reconstructing the jet, only 4 percent of the airplane had been found. The hammered and mutilated primer-green sculpture was laid out on red and green plastic tarps behind a yellow band of police crime-scene tape. There were heaps of wire as big as raspberry brambles. There were spherical fire bottles from the engines and scuba-looking oxygen bottles for the oxygen masks. (The DC-9 did not use the sodium chlorate candles in its own cabins. It had merely been transporting them.) Swamp grass still clung to those ragged parts. The sodden blue and white ring binders, big as telephone books, were flopped open to the emergency procedures the pilots would have used in their last moments. Orange life vests were scattered here and there. A couple of exploded yellow plastic escape slides lay crumped and muddy, and enormous tires had been chewed up like wads of black gum. Searchers had found an engine: it looked like a crushed beer keg. Landing gear struts had been disfigured by forces we could scarcely imagine.

Greg Feith showed reporters soot stains on a piece of metal, indicating that there had been a fire. This was not news, merely more evidence to feed the investigation and a hungry press.

From across the huge hangar, a somber group of men who looked like university professors watched us as we inspected the collected wreckage. Arms folded, they sat near a large ventilating fan at a makeshift table of plywood and cinder blocks, which held a microfilm reader and reels of film of images of the thousands of parts that go into making a McDonnell Douglas DC-9. They would find a part, painstakingly identify it, and put it in place until the jigsaw made some sort of sense. They would, that is, if they could find enough of the airplane to accomplish the task. The rest of the plane, we were told, was down in the Pit. "We have 90 percent of an airplane that's unaccountable," said an NTSB spokesman. "We believe we know where it is."

. . .

Gradually, clues were pieced together. A company named SabreTech was over-hauling a ValuJet plane at Miami and had removed the oxygen generators from the seat backs, where they were installed to provide oxygen to passengers in an emergency decompression. The canisters were tossed in boxes and set aside. No one knew what to do with them. Someone called ValuJet and was told, sure, send them back. If there had been a head of maintenance at ValuJet, he would have said, "Don't you know those things can burn?"

Three aircraft tires had been thrown on the floor of the cargo hold. The cardboard boxes containing the sodium chlorate candles had been tossed in on top of the tires. As in the other five incidents where chlorate candles had caused fires, the ones on ValuJet Flight 592 had been packed without safety caps or pins installed to prevent them from going off. One of the candles had been set off, probably by jostling as the plane taxied out to take off for Atlanta. The burning canister ignited other canisters, and the whole chain reaction probably reached nearly two thousand degrees, burning the tires and then sending smoke and flames up through the cabin floor beneath the feet of passengers.

The NTSB had been recommending that airlines install smoke detectors and sprinkler systems in cargo holds for decades. It is commonplace for there to be items in the cargo hold that are caustic, flammable, even explosive or radioactive. A simple smoke detector would have saved those on Flight 592. The fire probably started before takeoff, but in any event, the plane crashed after being aloft only six minutes. With a fire warning, the crew would have either evacuated on the ground or turned immediately back to Miami. According to a report from the House Committee on Transportation, the NTSB's recommen-dation for smoke detectors was "rejected by the FAA because they believed the gain in safety would not justify the cost of requiring all aircraft to install such systems."

As the days went by down in the Everglades, I was left with a lot of time to think and do some investigating of my own. One thing I discovered was that Transportation Secretary Federico Peña's statement in the wake of the crash that "I have flown ValuJet" had a compelling history. Peña had flown ValuJet in late February. How exactly had the transportation secretary happened to be flying ValuJet slightly more than two months before the crash?

DOT Inspector General Mary Schiavo had sent her investigators to the FAA on February 7 to say that she wanted ValuJet inspected for its pattern of crashes and near catastrophes. Only recently, a ValuJet plane had burned to cinders on the runway, while another had suffered collapsed gear on landing. The FAA field office in Atlanta had immediately informed ValuJet of what

Schiavo was doing. ValuJet sent a lobbyist to the chief of staff at DOT to quash the investigation. On February 16, the FAA's own inspectors wrote an internal memo urging that ValuJet be grounded. But the memo was hastily buried by higher officials. An FAA employee anonymously called Schiavo, who immediately subpoenaed the memo. The FAA denied that it existed. In its 1996 Strategic Plan, the FAA had cited ValuJet as a model for the new era of airline transportation, the discount airline, the growth company, which others should follow. How would it look if they grounded their own model airline?

Instead of grounding ValuJet, the FAA secretly made a gentleman's agreement with the president of the company, Lewis Jordan. The FAA would perform a "white glove" inspection in lieu of grounding. It was done in secret to avoid publicity. In fact, the FAA quietly told ValuJet not to buy any more planes without their permission, because "it appears that ValuJet does not have a structure in place to handle your rapid growth, and that you may have an organizational culture that is in conflict with operating to the highest possible degree of safety." The public was allowed to see none of those behind-the-scenes machinations and went on flying on the cheap ValuJet tickets. People buy airline tickets the way they buy gasoline. Since they know nothing about either, they go for the cheapest deal.

At the end of February, DOT Secretary Peña had a flight planned from Atlanta to Washington on Delta Airlines. He changed to ValuJet to support the airline and send a message to Jordan that he had nothing to worry about with Mary Schiavo. Peña was Schiavo's boss.

"On April 2, 1996," Schiavo wrote, "the FAA advised my office that there was no pattern to the ValuJet accidents and incidents." She did not know then that the FAA had already sent ValuJet a memo stating, "ValuJet is not meeting its duty to provide service with the highest possible degree of safety."

When Peña flew to the crash site almost immediately after the accident to announce that flying was safe—ValuJet was safe, everything was safe—he did not fly on ValuJet. He already knew what was wrong. After the crash, the FAA began spot checks of ValuJet and forced it to cut its flights from 320 to 160. Jordan made it seem as if it had been his decision, but it was the first step in the unraveling of the cover-up. It was well known among pilots that ValuJet flew roaches, and now the FAA was grounding plane after plane.

On June 16, the FAA was finally forced—by Schiavo, by public outcry, and by its own investigators, astounded at what they saw—to ground ValuJet's entire fleet.

Peña and FAA administrator David Hinson closed ranks, firing Associate

Administrator Anthony Broderick, who had been the point man with the press and was an easy scapegoat. David Hinson was a former senior vice president of McDonnell Douglas, which had manufactured the DC-9 that lay in pieces the Pit. He was a former executive at Midway Airlines. Mary Schiavo said, "There was no charitable way to characterize what they [Peña and Hinson] were doing—they were simply lying to the public about ValuJet's record."

· · ·

Early one morning the investigators went quietly out in an airboat before the search teams could disturb the mud and cloud the water. As they slipped silently along in the dawn, peering down into the dark water, they could see the trailing edge of the airplane wing wavering in the water, which had cleared as sediment settled through the night. And one of the investigators who knew said that he suddenly understood that all those people were down there, who had been reading a novel or holding a baby one moment and the next moment were shredded into chum and buried.

Navy divers were brought in, along with special ground-penetrating radar and custom-made inflatable dry diving suits and experts of every sort to puzzle about how one company had made such a mockery of technology through its careless and ignorant use of it. More than the airliner was at stake here, more than ValuJet's continued existence, more even than the 110 lives that had been lost. The way we understood our world was at stake. We had established a long-standing truce with the forces of nature. Science was our new religion, and the technology it had spawned had produced a whole new world and with it a new set of beliefs. Unlike religious cultures, which take fate for granted, we believed that science and technology had put us in control. These people, the Mud Stud and his cohorts, were taking charge of this swamp and in doing so were setting right a fundament postulate by which we all lived.

The plan that had evolved concerning the Pit was that ground-mapping radar, hung on the side of an airboat, would scan the spot and produce a picture of the main wreckage of the McDonnell Douglas DC-9 where it supposedly rested like a sunken Spanish galleon. Then divers, wearing the custom-made dry suits, would descend into the Pit and assess the best way to raise the wreck. The previous day, a fragment of the captain's flight bag had been found, buoying hopes that this was indeed the mother lode.

There had been a lot of speculation about exactly how deep the mud was in the Pit. It was known that the Everglades sat on a limestone shelf that ran up to Lake Okeechobee. The bottom depth varied from place to place. In some places it was quite deep, perhaps as much as twenty feet. In others it was shallow. In order to swallow an old-fashioned DC-9, though, it would have had to be pretty deep. Moreover, the mud was not simply mud but Loxahatchee peat, a tangle of roots, vines, weeds, and other plant material, which over thousands of years had partly decomposed and woven itself into what some firefighters described as a kind of natural fiberglass. When a helicopter had lifted one of the mashed-up engines, the pull required had been four thousand pounds. When the peat had finally let go, the engine had weighed only two thousand pounds. So there was concern about how, once workers were actually down in the Pit, they would raise something the size of a DC-9—even a badly crumpled one.

The only thing that no one expected was the thing that divers actually found. After ten days of waiting, everything was finally in place for the big dive. Paul Toy, a Metro-Dade Police diver, finally suited up and went down. Less than a quarter of the plane, by weight, had been recovered in bits and pieces by then. Not one adult victim had yet been identified from the bits of flesh brought back in bar-coded bags. So Toy was expecting to find a ruined aircraft hull housing a mass grave. He was tethered to another diver, who remained on the surface to help if Toy got in trouble down there. This was spooky stuff. Toy could get tangled in the miles of wire and never come back up. Nobody envied him his job.

Toy descended and remained down in the Pit for an hour and a half. What he found was both a relief and a shock. The plane had cut a crater eighteen inches deep and about fifteen feet in diameter in the limestone bedrock beneath eight feet of water, mud, and peat. But Toy said afterward, "There is no aircraft in the pit. There's no airplane left."

The airplane had flown at such a prodigious speed into a solid wall of limestone bedrock that it had simply disintegrated, and that black cloud seen by the only witness, the bass fisherman in Holiday Park, had actually been the entire plane, along with all its contents, as the swamp vomited it back into the air for one last flight. It had turned to not much more than vapor and dust. Then it had settled and vanished forever from the face of the earth.

• • •

If you've ever lost someone you dearly love, you know this moment: after exhausted sleep has found you in your grief, has come on in twisted emanations like smoke and released you for a time from the rigors of emotional pain, that moment when you finally wake and lie in peace because you have not yet remembered the terrible thing that has happened, have not yet emerged from sleep far enough that the pain can grip and tear at you again. Sometimes it's the only good moment of the whole day before the world comes crashing down again.

Valujet flew the families of the victims to Miami and put them up at the Crown Sterling Suites hotel. It was an odd choice. For one thing, it was under the departure path of the jets, located in close proximity to the airport, making it impossible to forget even for a moment exactly why they were all there. Stranger still was the place itself.

The interior was a hollow ten-story cylinder with glass elevators sliding silently up and down. New Orleans–style wrought iron railings curved around the floors in tiers all the way to the top, where an immense skylight sifted a celestial light down on the faux jungle at ground level. People at all levels up and down the inner stories came out of their rooms, ranked around as if in a panopticon, to stand at the rails and look down and out and away. Great fat Japanese carp swam in an artificial grotto below. A waterfall in the tropical jungle crashed too loudly. Pinioned ducks swam above the carp in the pond. A baby's cry echoed in the tremendous hollow cavern.

The impression of great height seemed most eerie, as if the place had been chosen as a reminder of a fall from great altitudes. And those who came to stand forlornly at the balconies were there to pay homage and symbolically to join their loved ones in the endless reaches of the sky, so effectively duplicated in the architecture of that eccentric basilica.

Going up in the glass elevators was all vertigo. And the people leaning on the railings, high and small, as if in the clouds, appeared as saints in a heavenly hierarchy. It all seemed designed to replicate the flight, the fall, the last rushing roar, the final swallow of water as the glorious, delicate ship reached for its own reflection in the black and oily swamp and then turned instantly to hot mist and smoke and particles too small ever to retrieve. The FAA still says that airlines are the safest way to travel. But death has the last word.

The families drifted in and out of the lobby, and a slope-shouldered priest in a Roman collar from the Catholic Community Services counseled a couple carrying a gift of yellow potted flowers. The man was tall and fit. He looked as if he drove a new car and lived in a sound suburb and played a fair game of tennis. He wore pressed khaki shorts and a belt and a golf shirt and good sport shoes. They all wore green ribbons given them by ValuJet that said "Flight 592," as if there were some sort of twisted pride in giving your son or your mother or your sister to the cause.

Because of the hotel's proximity to the airport (and its corporate rates), the airline crews stayed at the Crown Sterling Suites, too, and while the relatives were ranged around the lobby, pilots and flight attendants in uniform hurried through with wheeled luggage on their way to another flight, past the sad faces, the flowers clutched too tightly, the empty stares under a turning Casablanca fan. And wreathed in the sounds of this false Eden, these people, as if from alien tribes, gaped in wide-eyed solemnity at one another across the lobby with its French-tile floors under heavenly light.

A woman came out of the elevator weeping and greeted the priest. The man holding the yellow flowers hugged the weeping woman and then held her hand and continued to hold his potted flowers while they talked. "That plane was loaded with saints," he told her. "Your brother is a saint. My wife is a saint." And she wept some more, nodding in agreement.

I watched the families posed in little groups, frozen in tableaux that seemed minute against the vast jungle of the lobby, just as their relatives were forever frozen like victims of the eruption of Mount Vesuvius. I had tried more than once to imagine myself in that plane. I once heard a survivor of another crash say, "We held each other and said good-bye." Now I felt certain that down in that weedy world were two people who had been seated together by chance (as this man in his golf togs and this weeping woman were together by chance), strangers who, at the last moment, with the full realization of the end upon them, had embraced and now were caught down there as if in amber, exactly like these relatives, these strangers, who here embraced in the sound of rushing water in the cavern of light that was this place, this cathedral for their grief.

· 9 ·

Spring Opening

I WATCHED RUSS LANDT in a yellow plastic hard hat walk back and forth in the snow behind the yellow bulldozer with no gloves, his battered boots soaked through. He was showing Steve Garrow how to make the first cut—the "pioneer cut," as they call it—into virgin snow. On the fourth of June, the snow where we stood on Going-to-the-Sun Road in Glacier National Park, Montana, was twenty feet deep. And that was the least of it. Russ's broad, clean-shaven face was deeply tanned, and his big Germanic head sat nobly on his stocky frame as he nodded and observed, "Steve's a good driver." A high compliment from Russ, the only living human who really knows where the road is once it's buried in snow. If Garrow didn't hit it exactly right, he'd be sitting out there with nothing supporting that fifty-thousand-pound Caterpillar D-7 "Cat" but a big wet hundred-acre snowdrift.

One of the things that made Steve good was that he remained calm. He had run four-man patrol boats for the navy in Vietnam and was shot twice for his trouble, so on the great scale of experience, this was not particular stressful to him. "They sank our boat," he had told me. "I wouldn't give that experience up for anything." Each man up here had a story. Each one had shrugged off civilization and come a long, hard way to freeze in the middle of nowhere, doing exhausting and dangerous work for low pay and no benefits.

I watched Garrow push big tumbling slabs of dirty spring snow into the cirque below. They would launch down the chute, gathering speed, and then explode on the rocks in puffs of smoke.

In this world of GPS and smart bombs, it was difficult to imagine not being able to find an entire road. From a mile away, I could see it well enough on the huge mountain, a fine filament vanishing into the snowfield. But finding it up close with a plow blade had humbled many men and had killed some others. People still talk about the driver who went out a little too far one day in 1964. Twenty acres of snow let loose underneath him. The slab avalanche, as it's called, cut right down to bedrock, snatching away trees and gobbling the machine up in one bite. The dozer rolled "seven complete rolls," Russ said. He was right behind the Cat when it happened. "It made a sound just like a 30-06 rifle shot when it let loose," he told me. "I was only three or four feet away from where it broke loose. There was no time to warn him." The Cat had become airborne as it went down, vaulting, landing hard on the cab roof with a bone-crushing sound, then leaping again in torrents of snow. Like a child's toy, it had disappeared in huge white breakers. Then everything was silent, and they could hear the crashing of McDonald Creek far below.

Russ rushed down the hill and found an arm sticking out. "A miracle he was even alive," Russ said. The first words out of the driver's mouth were "Is the Cat hurt?"

Russ said he'd seen fifty-seven avalanches come down in a single morning on the spot where we stood talking. "Lots of time we lose ground and have to retreat. They airlift us to the Cats in helicopters so that we could work our way back down."

Each year, as the plowing draws to a close, the park hosts an event called Show Me Day, in which the public is allowed to view the operation. Families, bicyclists, and hikers are led up the mountain to watch. This year a few days after Show Me Day, the Haystack Creek chute cut loose with a slab avalanche so big that it took out the road's historic rock retaining wall and shot it down the valley like old coffee grounds. "We thought it was pretty safe up here," Jim Dorman, the supervisor, told me.

Every avalanche chute has a name. "We have to have a name for a place about every quarter mile," Russ told me, "just so people can know where they are, in case something happens." There's Waterworks, Grizzly Chute, Crystal Point, and No Stump, just to name a few. There used to be a stump at a place called Old Stump, but somebody decided to remove it, so after that, the same spot was called No Stump. Tractor Gulch is a chute where a tractor mysteriously went backward between two rocks and over the edge one weekend, demolishing itself in the process. No one ever figured out how it happened. Probably ghosts.

Avalanches aren't the only hazard. Coming up at the start of the day, another crew member, Steve Garrow's brother Sean, drove into a fifteen-foot crevasse. As the dozer tipped over the edge, snow exploded through the windows. "Then you're looking at two to four hours of cable pulling," Russ said.

"You're looking at a straight drop-off and not much room to maneuver. We've fallen into three holes this year and broken out seven windows already."

The west-side operation, where we were, was the main operation for spring opening. Each year, it involves four pieces of equipment, two Cats, a rotary snowplow, and a loader with a custom-made bucket called a Bindle bucket, because it was welded up in one of the park shops by a man named Bindle. The seven-man crew is composed of three watchers and four operators. A smaller crew worked clearing the road on the east side of the park, and both teams aimed to meet at the Big Drift, just east of the highest point in the road, the Logan Pass Visitor Center. Big Drift could be under eighty or even a hundred feet of snow at times, and when the pioneer dozer went out on it for the first time, he would be performing an aerial act worthy of any circus, like floating a battle tank on a soap bubble. He would be nowhere near the road's actual surface. If he came down wrong, say on the double yellow line, he could not go back up and start plowing again. From that first cut out to the cliff's edge was all the space they'd have for road until the snow melted. That means that if he cut too wide, then when the road opened to traffic, there might be only one lane in that precarious spot, and crew members would have to stay up there to direct traffic. There would be a big traffic jam, a lot of angry tourists. It was a big deal. The perfect pioneer cut was therefore next to the inside wall, so the Cats could push all the snow out over the cliff and open both lanes to traffic. But cut too close, and the Cat would tip out and roll you down the hill.

I asked Dorman: Why risk lives? Why go to all this trouble to move a little snow? (Well, okay, a lot of snow.) The answer, of course, is money. Two million people visit Glacier National Park each year, and most of them drive Going-to-the-Sun Road in July and August. Dorman said that the businesses in and around the park lose $1 million for every day that the road stays closed.

· · ·

Rick Smith told me, "Sure it's dangerous. But we'd go crazy if we thought about it every day." Rick hailed from southeastern Kentucky, and with his fierce blue eyes and a full mountain-man beard, he looked it. It was hard to get Rick to talk, but it was even harder to get him to stop. Like so many, Rick had been seduced by the unreal beauty of the place. Once he'd fallen under its spell, he was no good anywhere else. Most recently, he'd quit a $50,000-a-year long-haul trucking job to work this $12,000-a-year seasonal job.

Rick was on his honeymoon with his first wife in 1976 when they drove

Going-to-the-Sun Road the second day after opening. The crew was still cleaning the snow away, and he knew instinctively that this was the job he wanted. "I'm a man's man," Rick told me. "And I've always been an outsider." A few years later, Russ Landt appeared in a *National Geographic* story, which portrayed the crew as an elite cadre of daredevils operating on the wild edge of things. Rick heard hair-raising tales that only made the job seem more romantic, such as Dennis Holden's fall in 1974, which carried him six hundred feet down the mountain.

Russ was making the pioneer cut, and Holden was his watchman. Russ had shut off the Cat and was walking back toward Holden when the avalanche took Holden down. Another few steps and Russ would have gone with him. "He went under five times," Russ said. He watched as Holden submerged and surfaced over and over again. "He was textbook, swimming with the avalanche to stay up. Luckily, he was on top when it all stopped." Holden dusted himself off and went to see his daughter in the school play that same night.

"That clenched it," Rick told me after recounting the tale. "This is my element."

Rick liked being up there in the snow, moving it, conquering it. He didn't want it to end. "This place will harden you and temper you, or else it'll break you," he said. "But the worst day I've had up here, cold and wet and miserable, still beats the hell out of the best day I've had anywhere else."

Something draws them. They all said it in different ways. When Russ first came into the park, he worked trail. But he'd heard about the snow crew, and it held a fascination that he couldn't describe. They were the Green Berets of the park, risking their lives to open the road. "The crew stories drew me," Russ said. "The avalanches. No, not the avalanches really but seeing twelve avalanches *in one day*. Something big was happening up there, and I had to know what it was."

The problem now was that Russ was about to retire, and someone else had to learn where the road was before he moved on.

As we talked, the clouds had gradually eaten our shadows. I could smell the park, a deep piney scent, lifting to us on those clouds. It was the smell of an untouched forest, rich and heady, which seduced us all. The valley was plunged into twilight, and I looked up the hill and saw the yellow dozer dissolve in mist. Through the sudden whiteout, I heard Rick's voice. "We're not moving," he said.

Walking out through dozer tracks, I heard Rick call behind me, "You hear a swishing sound up there, you grab the bank." His idea was that if I held the inside wall, whatever came down might simply go over my head. A crewman grabbed the bank during an avalanche in 1953 and was buried for seven hours. He lived to tell about it. Two others were nearby but didn't make it from the road to the bank. One man was recovered at once. The other was found dead of a broken neck.

"We take avalanche training every year," Russ said. "But being buried alive is a difficult thing to plan for."

They feel compelled to talk about what you can do or shouldn't do to affect your chances of survival. It can sound like voodoo: Swim backward until the motion stops, then throw one arm over your face, and stick the other up in the air like you're waving.

. . .

There was an air of excitement when I showed up at six forty-five the next morning. Everyone was on alert because they were going to use explosives. The road office was a dim shack. Gray deck paint was peeling off the rough-cut floorboards. A hand-built table dominated the room under harsh fluorescent shop lights. Jim Dorman, the supervisor, sat talking with two Montana cowboys who'd come up to help. They wore crumpled cowboy hats, greasy vests, and threadbare jeans. One of them, Tim Sullivan, was the park's official mule packer, a job his father had held before him.

Dorman, from Victoria, Texas, had clear blue eyes and red hair that had begun to turn gray. He used to race motorcycles but quit in 1970. "I was doing a hundred twenty-six miles per hour on a dirt road at night between Francitas and San Felipe," he explained, "and there were range cattle everywhere. I had two little girls, and I was twenty-nine years old, and I started thinking: What the hell am I doing? I never rode again." It didn't surprise me that Dorman had ended up here. He works fires in the off-season "because it gives me the excitement I lost when I quit racing motorcycles."

He went on: "I think if they were to try to build this road today, they simply wouldn't be able to do it." He meant for legal reasons. In the summer of 1996, for example, a couple was driving through the day after the road opened when a flake of rock peeled away from the cliff, cut through the car, and severed the man's legs. His wife watched him bleed to death. "It devastated me," Dorman said.

I went out to the garage to watch Peter Steinkopf loading AMFO (ammonium nitrate and fuel oil) for the shot. They call him the Powder Man, though no one uses black powder anymore. The term is a holdover from the 1920s.

Peter was a big, studious-looking man who wore plastic specs and a full beard. The garage was an airless, Gothic place of bare boards. Huge tire chains hung on the walls. It stank of coal oil. Peter worked on the tailgate of a truck, using a grain scoop to measure the pellets into ziplock bags. I saw waxy cardboard cases of DuPont #18 dynamite and great spools of detonating cord in the bed of the truck. Peter showed me how to punch the sticks and thread the det. cord and complained about how strict government regulations had gotten concerning explosives. I wondered why everyone was so nervous about the use of explosives, a common enough construction tool, and he told me about a woman on ski patrol in Teton who had been setting off dynamite for avalanche control the year before.

It was a simple bundle of dynamite. You light the fuse and throw it. She held the charge between her knees for leverage and pulled the starter—a sheath that fits over the fuse, which generates a spark when pulled to ignite it. But there was a howling wind up there that day, not uncommon. Also, the sun was bright. When she pulled the starter, she wasn't sure the charge had lit. So she put it back between her knees and pulled the striker again. In the glare and the wind, she still wasn't sure. A third time she put the charge between her knees. And not one of the crew members I asked wanted to say exactly what happened after that. Except that the woman had lost her life.

Going up the mountain that day, Dorman gave me a yellow locator beacon called a Skadi, which I hung around my neck like a medallion. Rescue teams home in on them to find avalanche victims. We hiked past an eighteen-foot-high snow wall. The avalanche chute went up the mountain half a mile and kept on going out of sight. Dorman said, "Let's go. If this came down now, we'd be dead." It was difficult to imagine in such a peaceful scene with wild strawberries growing right through the snow and acres of watermelon snow down in the cirque and the sound of rushing water coming up from below.

The rotary plow came into view. A dozer in front pushed snow back toward it, and the plow shot it in a beautiful arc over the cliff. We climbed a steep wall of snow. We could see Steve Garrow working the pioneer dozer up ahead.

"This is intense," Dorman said. "It makes my heart pump watching him. He has a foot and a half and that's all. He could go over at any time." In addition, his men were working fifty-hour weeks, and they were all tired.

We stopped at a spot where we'd shoot the snow off the wall. Marshall Stewart came ambling up with an ice auger and his Stanley thermos as Peter arrived to prepare the explosives. The crew was naturally cautious. Peter drilled holes in the wall with the auger. Then he packed the explosives with handfuls of snow and moved on. The process took on an interminable, dirgelike solemnity.

I wandered off to explore in the snow and followed rabbit tracks until they ended abruptly in a ghostly snow angel. I asked Dorman what it was, and he said it was the imprint of an eagle's wings, where the bird had dropped invisibly from above and left with the animal in its claws. Plowing up here, he said, he sometimes felt like that rabbit. I felt the invisible specter hanging above, ready to take us.

I heard Peter on the radio. "Fire in the hole!" he yelled. "Fire in the hole!"

I scrambled over the ridge just in time to see the shot. The sound was so loud that I jumped. The earth leaped and shrugged off a quarter mile of snow. The shot ejected yellow cordite smoke into the air over the cirque and tumbled immense boulders of hardened snow. Thunder went echoing away, clear down the valley to Kalispell.

It began to rain. I was perched on a rock over the cirque. Debris was sliding down the chute, and the yellow smoke hung in the air for a while and then began to dissipate. It was a good shot. Somebody broke out a few candy bars. We were all laughing.

I met Russ at the Spruce Park Cafe in Coram, Montana, which he calls "my office."

"This is my last season on the snow," he said, sitting at the Formica counter, drinking coffee. His wide, sad face and watery blue eyes smiled at me. "In 1957 I headed to California to get a job and I stopped here. I still haven't been to California. Thirty-six years I've played the odds, and sooner or later the odds are going to catch up with me. When a slide comes down behind you, you've got to walk out. If they come down again while you're on the slide, then you have to run or hop, and I don't hop quite so good anymore. That's how you survive up there," Russ said, summing it up: "Sometimes your gut tells you don't do it, and you've got to listen."

· · ·

Early the next morning, I watched as a Cat lifted smoke to meet the clouds. The backup screamer echoed off the dark cliffs. Behind the rotary plow, an arc of fluid snow spumed into the canyon, and when it stopped to turn, the trails of snow powder hung in the air and slowly drifted down like the remnants of a great silent firework.

The pioneer dozer pushed a mountain of snow its own size and nudged it into great avalanches over the edge and into the cirque where dirty snow gathered in rolls and ridges. With each stroke the dozer climbed up the pile of its own making and seemed to rear up on its hind leg and pounce and fall. Two eagles fled across the cirque at our level and eyed us curiously as they winged past and wheeled and turned.

The pioneer dozer was a beautiful piece of steel sculpture. The bucket was thirteen feet across and welded expertly in three sections, which were angled to make it concave. At start-up, it roared and clattered and spit clouds of dense smoke, and the exhaust port, black with soot, flapped loosely, and the hammering of the engine gradually smoothed and sped. It stank of fuel oil, but it was beautiful, all yellow and scarred like an old bear hide made of steel.

Jerry Burgess, the new park engineer, conferred with Dorman about plans to repair the North Fork Road, and the two men drew pictures in the snow with their fingers, like nomads drawing in the sand, as the sun angled up the morning.

We broke through to bare road between Rimrock and the visitor center, where the wind off the cirque scoured the pavement all winter and wouldn't leave snow sitting for long. I volunteered to help Jerry place stakes to mark this switchback section of road.

It was a true fact that no one except Russ knew where the road was. In this section, traditionally, pine poles were placed before the first snow to mark the edge of the road, and we could see them ahead in a chaotic zigzag over this arctic-looking landscape. But the previous fall Jerry had installed a locator wire along the edge to see if it might make finding the road easier, and now he walked along with an instrument and earphones, and wherever he punched a hole with his locator, I placed a stake with an orange flag on it.

We walked out of the groves of dwarf trees and inched along in huge snow-fields just short of the Big Drift, placing our stakes and listening to occasional radio chatter. Then we came around a curve and saw the visitor center.

It looked like gingerbread house by Frank Lloyd Wright. Snow reached the roof of the building and climbed part of the way up. We hiked across, encountering a stop sign at our knee level. We slid down a mountainous drift and into a dark snow cavern lit with blue sunlight. We found stone steps and climbed to discover the main entrance in a cave made by the overhanging roof and fifteen-foot drifts. The world was completely silent, completely cold.

Jerry checked the key code on the lock and then his ring of keys. He hadn't planned it this way, but he happened to have the right key. He turned the lock, and the door swung open. Jerry was the first man into the visitor center, which was something of a spring ritual—first man in buys the beer—because it signaled the end of plowing, since plows were coming from the other side and were meant to meet us there, at the highest point on Going-to-the-Sun Road.

I followed him in. There was something spooky and exhilarating about being up there, way up there, in the wilderness in this modernistic crystal palace. All the exhibits were covered with tarps. The whole building lay completely buried most of the year. Sun streamed in through the floor-to-ceiling windows. We looked at the landscape all around, and Jerry said, "Now would be the perfect time to see a grizzly bear."

We went looking around, and I found a wall clock set on a shelf. There was no electricity up there, so someone had neatly removed the battery when they'd closed in the fall and set it on the shelf beside the clock. "What time is it?" I asked Jerry. He looked at his watch and said, "One thirty." I put the battery in and set the clock.

We went outside and sat on the roof of the visitor center and watched the eastside crew come through the tunnel by Big Drift. Both crews were closing in. It was only a matter of days and of a few cases of dynamite. From up there we could see how insignificant it all was. We could see how miniscule was the effort to open this road or perhaps how amazing, to run a dozer along a banjo string, like a circus high-wire act.

We heard the eastside pioneer dozer operator on the radio. His voice seemed clear and close. We saw his plow pushing a huge mountain of snow—this black and noisy dot, this pixel in the great frame of Montana wilderness, smaller than a single star in the black sky, and suddenly the static broke with his tiny voice, and he said, "I can't get through this snowbank. It's never ending!" And we laughed. That's right. It's never ending. That statement suddenly seemed like the truest thing that either of us had ever heard, and we laughed and laughed up there on the roof. Soon the parking lot before us, under ten feet of snow, would be packed with cars. A serpent of Winnebagos would be inching across that thin ribbon of asphalt, absorbed in the landscape for a few short weeks, before these mountains made their weather once again, and the snow reclaimed it all.

· 10 ·

Johnny Winter

JOHNNY WINTER'S LONG pink fingers open and close as if trying to make a pattern in the air, a pattern that he can't get quite right. His hands float above his lap to the level of his face. Again, again, he makes the pattern, the luminescent fingers falling in twos and threes. A guitar lies untouched in his lap. He lets his head hang forward, lets his slender neck stick out. His long ice-white hair falls across his chest, which is bare except where covered by a small silver vest. The unearthly fingers, alien apparitions, move faster, and Johnny squints against the light, which hurts his eyes. He is composing music in his head, and it comes off the tips of his fingers.

No one is watching. The dressing room at Madison Square Garden is noisy with people in bizarre costumes—girls in see-through clothing with scaphoid breasts loose inside, bejeweled men in leather who jangle as they laugh and talk. They are eating and drinking, caught up in the state of being in the same room with Johnny, who sits like an emaciated idol, looking as if he's been living in a darkened cave beneath a flat rock and has slithered into this harsh light that is now assaulting his pink eyes. Johnny is pure albino, unarmed with the pigments that normally protect the skin and hair and eyes, as if some force in the universe annealed him with its lightning. He's hard to look at, almost as if he shines too bright. His beauty is metaphysical. He is a freak.

"Hey!" he hollers as if suddenly awakened. His voice cuts through the noise. "I've got to try that new guitar!" It's as if this idea has never occurred to him before. Try the new guitar. Somebody is upon him, snatching the Stratocaster from his lap and handing him the *new guitar*. With no amplifier, Johnny plays a barely audible sheet of sound, lightning streaming down the sky, bright fingers disappearing in a blur of motion. Johnny is listening to what he just wrote.

I used to play trumpet with Johnny in Houston. The last time I saw him before we were reunited in his dressing room was around 1968. At the time, he was not very well known outside the South, but to the people who worked with him, he was a star—a genius. Late one night, drinking Romilar CF cough syrup and riding in the front seat of a car with a beat poet named Peter Steele Byers and Johnny, I listened to him talk about his girlfriend: "Man, pussy is so wonderful. It's just so soft and—man!—you can just put your fingers in it and touch it, oh man!" He couldn't contain the very thought of how happy it made him. He stopped talking and grabbed his head as if it were going to explode. Things got to him that way. Life for Johnny was on constant overload, the light too bright, the volume too loud, the sensations always on the edge of pain and ecstasy at the same time. He was like that about music. And I sat there that night watching and listening to the only truly gentle musician I'd ever worked with and hoping that something good would happen to Johnny, something big and fine and stirring.

And it did. And I watched as he burned himself down with acid and grass and speed and then cocaine and heroin, riding that string right out to its end until he was pale as ashes in the glowing ember of himself. About that time, he was visiting Houston and stopped by to see my brother Gregory, who had played tenor saxophone with him. We had both payed with Johnny. It was at a little basement club on Fannin in Houston called the Act III. The stage was about the size of a double bed, and there were maybe a dozen tables. It was black-box-theater decor, and the cockroaches were the size of Cuban cigars. One of the musicians brought Wite-Out from an office supply store and painted "Eat At The Act Three" on the backs of a number of cockroaches.

That night, we went to a little apartment Johnny was keeping in Houston, and he laid open a medicine chest he carried with him. Inside were a paper of heroin, one of coke, some PCP, MDA, THC, LSD, weed, hash, ups, reds, and a few assorted devices for the administration of those potions.

"Welp," he said, "we can shoot some of this here smack, or we can snort some of this coke. But you can't have any of the MDA," he added with a big grin. "That's all mine." A bigger grin—he could hardly stand it. "I use that to fuck on!" And he grabbed himself and hugged himself as if he might bodily disintegrate just from the thought of how good it was going to be.

That was fairly near the end, we thought, we who played backup for Johnny. We who worshipped him. Johnny went off to a hospital, and we never expected to hear from him again. And the strange thing this night in the dressing room at the Garden is that he actually made it all the way back. He went to the edge and looked over, and where Hendrix and Joplin and countless others (Jim Morrison, Keith Moon . . .) fell right in and drowned, Johnny somehow managed to come back from the dead. The way he looks, all white and pink and stripped bare like a wax statue, you might think he was never really here to begin with, just a spirit passing through. Good-bye, porkpie hat. But here he is among us once again, ghost or saint, striking quiet lightning out of his soundless guitar and sipping bourbon and ginger ale, waiting to go on stage.

The Garden is an appropriate place for a man of his tastes and proclivities. The original Garden was designed by Stanford White, an architect who built homes for the rich of New York and the East Coast during the Gilded Age, a complex, brilliant, wild, driven, and desperately sexual man, who at the pinnacle of his career would design the Washington Square Arch at the bottom of Fifth Avenue in Manhattan, the Judson Memorial Church, New York University in the Bronx, and Madison Square Garden itself. Along with a sculptor, Augustus Saint-Gaudens, designer of the twenty-dollar gold "double eagle" for the United States Mint, he and several other men of the arts, founded the Sewer Club. The club occupied a rented room in a building on Washington Square Park. One member, the artist Thomas Dewing, described "scenes of mirth and physiological examination." The men could have sex or watch people having sex. It seems that there was scant distinction made, at least among some of them, as to which gender they chose for their partner or partners. White and Saint-Gaudens, who were very possibly lovers, later formed another sex club called the Morgue on West Fifty-Fifth Street. Like Johnny Winter's nights, theirs in the Gilded Age were long and excessively wild, with drinking, feasting, and shows or prizefights, all punctuated by interludes of sex in rooms and apartments they kept scattered all over town, including in the highest tower of Madison Square Garden, which Stanford and Gus had topped, much to the chagrin of New York society, with a giant statue of a naked teenage girl. Both Stanford and Gus were lovers of the teenage girls whose bodies were combined to create the statue. Johnny likes teenage girls. And they like him.

I leave the dressing room and go out to look at the audience. The Garden is filled to capacity. I want to look at people's faces, into their eyes, and all that comes into my mind is quaalude, Tuinal, Seconal, downers. It appears that you could go up and steal someone's appendix, and he wouldn't notice. And they are kids, fourteen, eighteen, twenty, reeling around the theater with their heart rates down to about forty. A real demented crowd. I can't figure out what draws that kind of people to Johnny, brilliant, white Johnny with that unearthly way of moving his fingers. I supposed deep down they can tell a kindred spirit when they see one. The difference is that the drugs never slow down Johnny's fingers the way they seem to slow down these kids.

I go back to the dressing room, contemplating the fact that the only thing between those kids and Johnny is a hollow metal door and a skinny guy who claims to have a third-degree black belt in karate. He wears a black kid glove on his right hand "for the psychological effect," he says with a soft Cajun accent. It reminds me of a man I know who is a slumlord. He carries a carpenter's claw hammer around with him all the time. When I asked why, he said, "I could carry a gun, but everybody down in the hood has a gun. They're not afraid of guns. They're afraid of crazy. And when I walk down the street at night talking to myself with this hammer in my hand, they cross the street to get away from me." This kid—except for the glove, you wouldn't even notice him until he walks Johnny to the stage. I go back out to watch.

Because he's albino, Johnny can't see very well to begin with. There's almost no pigment in the irises of his eyes. That pigment keeps you from being blinded just from opening your eyes in normal daylight. Going on stage is a psychedelic experience even without the drugs. Johnny's not blind. But what he sees is unlike anything you and I would ever see. What he experiences is like a hit of dimethyltryptamine. He lives in the center of one great white-hot, glittering rainbow flash. His world is on fire with light. People glow and shimmer in it like lens flares on a photograph. So when he steps out on stage under half a million candlepower of stage lights, he just gives up any attempt to see what's happening, and he plays, wailing into the void where other sounds, other musicians playing, are his only points of reference.

The downed-out kids haul up close to the stage and scream at him with love, with demented, slow-motion hysteria. From the upper balconies, bottles and cherry bombs and strings of Chinese firecrackers float down, some landing on the stage and detonating there. Johnny cranks up the volume and tries to outdo those sounds. He's unimpressed. They used to do a lot worse to us in Beaumont and Lafayette. I can see the crowd surging just as a very drunken man's body will do before he gets sick. Johnny's heat-death delirium screens it all out, and he keeps on playing. And maybe that's it. Maybe these embalmed kids come to hear and see Johnny because anything less intense would never penetrate their soporific haze. In a sleep that deep, it takes some heavy dreams to make contact. Maybe it takes a saint to get through to the dead.

· 11 ·

Space Station

I AM FLOATING down the length of the International Space Station some-where 250 miles above the North Atlantic, going about seventeen thousand miles an hour. If I tilt my head down as far as my space suit will allow, I can see the edge of my helmet and even my boots. As I jet around the exterior of the station, the misty earth below seems like a blue and living cell. Now Africa heaves into view toward the east. The Niger, like a great snake, undulates down its belly.

This is my first EVA, or extravehicular activity. The exterior of the space station, almost blinding in the airless sunlight, has golden handholds bolted all over it, each a glittering treasure of safety, labeled with numbers and letters to tell me where I am in the confusion of this mammoth structure. I can see the labels vividly in the blazing sunlight as I drift down toward the open cargo bay of the space shuttle. It's still docked there from our arrival on station, and the fifty-foot Canadarm (used for grappling satellites and pieces of the station) is folded up now, at rest.

Soon the space shuttle will close its doors, back away from us, and blast home in a fiery deorbit. We'll watch it burn in the night sky as it disappears into the blue. Night and day alternate every forty-five minutes here—a sunrise and sunset sixteen times during every normal Earth day.

Off to my right, I see another astronaut in his brilliant white space suit, working on something, perhaps a communications antenna. As he works, twisting a torque tool, he suddenly loses his grip, his tether fails him, and he is kicked off the station. I watch in horror as he goes tumbling head over heels toward a half-moon, which hangs in the black sky like a child's paper boat.

He's moving away fast. I see him reach for the controller of his SAFER (Simplified Aid for EVA Rescue) unit, which we all wear when working outside the station. It's a small tank of nitrogen to be used for jet propulsion. We have a minute's worth of fuel. By carefully controlling the jet, we're supposed to be able to maneuver back to the station. That's the theory. Now he punches a button with his big white-gloved finger, and the device automatically fires, calculating the force required to stop his rotation.

Gradually, his tumbling stops, but he's still drifting away. I breathe a sigh of relief, which I can hear in the headphones of my helmet. "Is he all right?" I ask. "So far so good," the controller says. "Let's see if he can get back."

I see the astronaut searching, trying to find us. I could yell and scream, but my disembodied voice over the voice link would do him no good—and he'd never hear me without it in this deadly vacuum of space.

He's still drifting farther and farther away from the safety of these golden handholds. He's completely disoriented, but he must act fast. There's no way to retrieve him. The shuttle is docked. Otherwise it might try a risky maneuver to pick him up. And the station can't move, not that fast, not that precisely. His only hope is his SAFER unit.

I see him turning this way and that, trying to find us in the sea of blackness. The black sky is all around him, sprent with stars, and the space station must appear like all the other tiny white dots. At last, I see his head jerk as he catches the lights of the station. Facing home now, he begins firing the nitrogen jets. I can hear the controller reading out the lost astronaut's speed, angle, and closure rate, as well as the amount of fuel he has left.

As the lost man makes his one and only attempt to get back safely, I drift around the station, mesmerized by the surreal and blinding light, the whiteness of the floating city, and the confounding complexity of all its details, from the giant solar arrays—gleaming articulated fields of onyx more than half an acre in size—to the high-frequency antennas, which rotate to track communication relay satellites far above our orbit. A robot arm moves along the main truss like an inchworm, clutching beams with a titanium grip. I've learned every system, yet even so, the whole remains incomprehensible, just as the whole experience of being up here does.

In my headset I listen to the controller talking to the lost astronaut. Each of us knows this might happen. Each of us accepts the risk. I hear the hiss of jets in the headphones as he maneuvers back toward us, and I watch the sun wink off his black face shield as he turns his head left and right to gauge his trajectory—no ILS, no GPS, this is a nonprecision maneuver—by guess and by god.

First he gets going too fast. He'll crash into the space station like a bug hitting a windshield. He has to slow himself down. But he overdoes it, stops altogether, and has to start again—all of this wasting precious fuel. He's down to 5 percent of the tank's supply when the controller directs him to make one last try. But the jets propel him off at the wrong angle, and he runs out of fuel. Now he'll drift along, and soon he'll run out of oxygen, too. And then he'll die. His batteries will probably last longer than his air, so we'll be able to converse with him the whole time. Maybe they'll get his wife and kids on the communications pass so that they can say good-bye.

I remove the virtual-reality headset that encloses my head and take off the white pack I'm wearing. Suddenly—shockingly—I find myself in a cluttered laboratory. Bundles of wires go everywhere across beat-up industrial carpeting beneath an old acoustic tile ceiling stained by leaking water. Boxes piled everywhere and bins of candy and pretzels, a wooden ladder against the wall, an orange traffic cone. A youthful trainer wearing a goatee plugged into a virtual-reality headset with a large white pack on his chest. That's the controller I was talking to. A metal cage with cables going out of a six-axis robot. Cabinets full of wire, a whole room full of Silicon Graphics computer bays, all off-the-shelf equipment put to new purpose. "Paint don't make it go," David Homan said of the cosmetic catastrophe around him. He is manager for virtual reality applications at Johnson Space Center. He studies me with a faint smile. "Pretty realistic," he says with evident pride. It was. My heart is in my throat. I'm sweating.

Homan is a thin, rumpled man in his forties, whose decades of work in computer graphics have culminated in this, one of the world's most sophisticated virtual reality labs. His main task now: to train astronauts for the dangerous task of assembling the International Space Station, which after countless delays and tens of billions of dollars spent, has finally begun to take shape in orbit. When completed (target date: 2004), the station will weigh 470 Earth tons and, at various times, house astronauts from sixteen nations, including Japan, Russia, France, and Brazil. It will span 356 feet, making it the largest man-made structure ever to orbit Earth, longer than *Saturn V*, which sent men to the moon. More than one hundred thousand people worldwide are now involved in building, designing, or supporting something having to do with the station. Assembling it in space will require more EVAs—spacewalks—than have ever been performed before in the history of space exploration.

The "astronaut" I was watching during my EVA was actually a technician who was testing the equipment. He now takes off his headset and pack, and the trainer—the controller who was trying to talk him back home, the young man with a goatee—smiles at him and says, "Well, you're dead. You want to try again?"

As they reset the computers, Homan shows me around the back lot of NASA where the gritty garage tinkerers make their magic. Each NASA center has a place where the dirty work is done. Earlier, I toured the NASA center at Huntsville, Alabama, a kind of hillbilly heaven, where they build and test various components of the space station. It is a vast tract of empty land, the site of a former army munitions plant and gunnery range, scattered with burned-out and used-up gizmos—rocket engines, actual rockets, tossed out whole in fields and rusting away among the weeds—and gigantic steel-and-concrete test stands with sluice canals for carrying millions of gallons of water to mitigate the enormous howling sheets of flame thrown off during a burn. From such humble beginnings come the showpieces that NASA shoots into space. They paint the things gleaming white, slap a big American flag on their sides, and roll them out for everyone to admire. Then they leap from the earth on tails of fire.

Going bald, Homan wears khakis and Top-Siders, steel spectacles, and a threadbare shirt with a fistful of pens stressing the pocket. He is fond of hitting subjects at an oblique angle. He explains to me that with all the in-space construction required to build the station, there's a real possibility of losing an astronaut and not being able to get him back. "My EVA experience is fairly limited, though," he adds. "But that was in college, and I didn't inhale."

. . .

When I met with Bob Cabana in November of last year, he was just about to take off to assemble the first pieces of the International Space Station in orbit around Earth. A marine colonel, Cabana would command the shuttle mission that would mark either the beginning of a glorious, cooperative new era in space or the greatest boondoggle in NASA history, depending on the person you questioned about it.

Small and boyish-looking, with salt-and-pepper hair, Cabana is a member of the elite group of the nation's top astronauts. I caught him on a break from training at Johnson, and we talked in a small conference room. He said that he had dreamed of space since childhood. He told me about the time after he returned from his first flight. In the middle of the night, he woke up and had to use the bathroom. It was dark, and he was disoriented. His first thought was simply to float off the bed and fly over to the bathroom. He had forgotten that he was no longer in zero g. His body told him it would work, but each time he pushed off, he just lay there like one of those practice dummies they use to teach medics CPR. He was pinned to the mattress, helpless.

After his second trip to space, the same thing happened. This time he intended to walk across the wall to the bathroom. Again, his muscles wouldn't work. Some ugly force was holding him down.

"The third time I came back from space," he said, "I woke up and thought, Shoot. I'm back on Earth again." For an astronaut, Earth is the penalty box.

Ordinarily very controlled, astronauts such as Cabana and Jerry Ross, Cabana's chief spacewalker for the first ISS mission, become animated when they talk about space. On Cabana's first flight, the training had been so deeply ingrained that he didn't look out the window until he was in orbit.

"I was just fixed on the instruments and on the tasks of monitoring that I had to perform," he said. The rocket sways up there before it lifts from the pad. The engines are thundering as liquid oxygen and liquid hydrogen run through the pumps at a rate fast enough to empty an average-size swimming pool in twenty seconds.

"You can feel it almost more than you can hear it," Ross said. The whole cockpit vibrates and shudders, and at first it is difficult to tell that you're moving. Then steadily the g-forces begin to build, until it feels like an elephant is sitting on your chest, and it's all you can do to take a breath. "It's only eight minutes, but it can seem like the longest eight minutes of your life."

An explosion rocks the superstructure, and sheets of flame pass across the windshield as the solid rockets separate. Day transforms to night as you leave the scattered light of the atmosphere, then comes a big kick when the shuttle separates from the massive external fuel tank. Astronauts say that it feels as if the ship has exploded. "You just can't help thinking about *Challenger*," Ross said. "I never go up without thinking about *Challenger*." On January 28, 1986, *Challenger* blew up seventy-three seconds into its flight, killing the crew of seven, including a civilian schoolteacher named Christa McAuliffe. She was thirty-seven.

When Cabana finally looked up from his instruments on that first flight into space, he realized that they were already in orbit. Seeing the earth below, the universe beyond, he knew that life would never be the same again. Each astronaut I've met has said the same thing. As Cabana and Ross talked about it, there was a look of pity in their eyes. For this was the pinnacle of experience, and they were looking at someone who would never have it.

• • •

For months before Cabana's mission, I went down to Houston to watch the guys train in the Neutral Buoyancy Lab, a swimming pool large enough to submerge elements of the space station. It's eighty feet from the roof of the building to the bottom of the blue water. Suspended above the surface are yellow cranes that can move up to ten tons of hardware at a time. It was nine in the morning, and the water was swarming with divers there to assist the astronauts.

Ross and another astronaut, James Newman, were hanging in their space suits, suspended from racks—it's the only way to get into them. They wore headphones and skullcaps, which made them look like monks. A woman fitted shoes onto Ross's feet, then a crane picked him and Newman up and dumped them into the water.

Under the surface, Newman and Ross practiced attaching communications antennas to the outside of a model of part of the space station. Walking around in space is one of the most dangerous parts of the job—holding on to those golden handholds, using torque tools that can spin you around like a top and kick you off into the void, as I'd seen in the Virtual Reality Lab. There's nothing virtual about it in space. It *is* reality. And while the astronauts are usually tethered for safety, they have to move around, clipping on and unclipping and then clipping again as they go. This is just the sort of repetitive behavior that can become automatic, leading to one unconsciously doing the wrong thing or doing things in the wrong order. NASA considers the risk of an accident due to the failure of a tether or while an astronaut is temporarily untethered to be significant.

In space, Newman and Ross can zoom from one place to another, but today, the divers must move them. Ross says, "Guys, will you beam me over to the other site now?" And the divers pick him up and move him to the next location. I hear him grumbling when he discovers that the elements he needs for the job are not there. It takes half an hour just to get this far—sitting underwater, trussed up in the suit—and he has nothing to do. He barks through the communications loop, "Four months from flight, and we've been working for over a year. We ought to have this stuff down by now. I'm starting to get ticked. We've got to get beyond this."

No one ventures a response. They know they've messed up. Indeed, there are a few problems with the space station that are still being worked out. For example, if the station flies at an altitude that points the solar arrays at the sun for maximum electrical power, then, as the astronauts' space station handbook says, this "results in the same side of the Station facing the Sun, while the other side faces the darkness of deep space. While [pieces of equipment] on one side of the Station may overheat, those on the other side may freeze. "

I was told that the problem was "being worked." That's NASAspeak for "We have no idea what to do about this."

. . .

The procedures for assembling the space station can be drilled to perfection in the pool, but there are some problems and risks that no one can fully control. One of the most significant issues is orbital debris. A lot of junk has accumulated in space. As satellites and old fuel tanks age and disintegrate, this adds even more debris. A new rocket is launched every four days, on average. Then there are meteoroids. NASA has a whole department, the Orbital Debris Program Office, devoted to space junk. Jeff Theall does the computer modeling there. "We had to determine what the threat was, what the most likely particles you're going to be hit with are, and what the probabilities of being hit with specific sizes are," he explained. There's so much junk up there from decades of shooting off rockets that the air force has a radar system for tracking the roughly nine thousand objects it can detect. But smaller objects cause trouble, too. The space shuttles' windows are so damaged by small particles of space debris that they have to be replaced after most flights. Debris is such a nuisance that the shuttle flies backward whenever it can.

If an object larger than ten centimeters were to hit the space station, the results would likely be catastrophic. But the probability of that is low, because the radar system can detect those objects. If something that large is on a collision course with the station, a docked Russian Progress spacecraft can fire its jets to lift the station two miles higher to evade the object. In addition, NASA has developed shields that protect occupied areas of the station from objects smaller than one centimeter, which are the majority of the particles in orbit.

"The primary danger," Theall told me, "is in objects that are too small to track and too large to shield against. Between two and ten centimeters, there is a danger." And there are more than a hundred thousand objects in that range.

The toughest shielding is made of Kevlar and Nextel blanket placed between two layers of aluminum. If, in a worst-case scenario, a particle of metal, for example, were to penetrate that shielding, the effects would be disastrous. The closing velocity between the space station and the object would be about ten kilometers a second. Upon impact, the object would turn to molten metal. As it exploded into the interior of the space station, the observers inside would be blinded instantly by a brilliant flash of light, rendering them helpless. Next, they would be burned by the tremendous heat generated by the molten material—the severity depending on the amount of splatter. And finally, the station would begin venting.

"If you take a hit in the back of a manned module," Theall said, "the air coming out could cause a thrust vector to spin the station like a top. It may spin it so fast that you'd break joints. Or so fast that docking mechanisms would release. Even if the crew were safe, they couldn't get out. More likely, crew members might suffocate because the module they are in gets hit and the air escapes before they can move and close the door. In talking about them, you start to visualize them. It makes your blood run cold."

At first glance, this dire scenario doesn't seem too likely. Theall calculates something called the assessed probability of no penetration (PNP), the chance that the station will *not* be pierced by some type of orbital debris over a ten-year period. NASA's sections of ISS have a 0.99 PNP rating, based on the American standard of shielding. Everyone in the sixteen-nation ISS coalition is adhering to a similar standard—except the Russians, who are going considerably lighter. Their service module in particular could be pierced by a speck as small as three millimeters. This makes being on the ISS like living in apartment building where only half the people have smoke detectors. Once the Russian vulnerability is incorporated into the calculations, the entire station's PNP suffers considerably. The chance of being penetrated jumps from one in a hundred to one in five. And that's factoring in Russia's plans to upgrade their level of protection, both before launch and with additional shielding to be added after the ISS has been in orbit for a few years. NASA has urged them to do this and will probably transport the extra protection in the shuttle. Before the improvements are made, the odds will be more than one in three that the station will be penetrated. And the best guess is that between one in three and one in four penetrations would be catastrophic—you'd lose either a member of the crew or the station itself.

"Their approach to risk is far different from ours," Theall said of the Russians. "They don't place as much importance on orbital debris as we do. They point to *Mir* and say it's flown thirteen years and has not been hit." *Mir* has been hit, at least by objects large enough to make dents that are visible on the inside walls of the quarters where the crew lives.

Theall nonetheless attempted to reassure me about the risks posed by orbital debris. While the odds of penetration seem high, particularly before the Russians improve their shielding, the station's overall safety rating seems good. He estimates that there is only a 5 percent chance of losing a member of the crew or the station. And NASA is working toward an even safer standard—a 2 percent chance of catastrophic failure.

Theall said that there are greater dangers than space junk: ionizing radiation, for one. "If there's a big solar flare—and odds are there will be while the ISS is up there—it could make the astronauts very sick," he said. He believes that the loss of human life during EVAs—the "lost in space" scenario—is the number-one hazard. And EVAs will make up the bulk of the work as the station is built.

The idea for a space station began before the Russians launched *Sputnik* in 1957. Back then, many engineers thought that the best way to explore space would be to establish a station and work outward from there. But President Kennedy needed a big public relations coup, and going to the moon seemed more heroic.

Just before Neil Armstrong's landing, NASA was working on a concept for a space station that would house a hundred people, a plan that was gradually whittled down to *Skylab*, an experiment involving three astronauts at a time. They occupied *Skylab* for six months during 1973 and 1974. Under Nixon, the idea of a space station was revived, and he approved the shuttle as a service vehicle for it. Under Reagan, development of a US space station (*Freedom*) was at last approved with a budget of $8 billion, and before long, the figure had swollen to $31 billion. By the time Bill Clinton became president, the space station employed twenty thousand people, and that first $8 billion was gone without a single, nut, bolt, antenna, or toilet having been launched.

One of the main reasons for drawing the Russians into the ISS program was that NASA had little experience with space stations, while the Russians had kept *Mir* occupied almost continuously since 1986. Our astronauts measure their experience by counting the hours they've spent in space. Cabana has about a thousand hours. Ross has about eleven hundred. Yuri Gidzenko, who will be among the first three people to live on the station, has nearly two hundred days in space. Sergei Krikalev, who went up with Cabana and Ross and who will join Gidzenko living on the station, measures his experience in years—one and a quarter and counting. (I got a look at him at a press conference, and he has a really far-out stare. His face barely moves when he talks.)

But experienced or not, the Russians didn't have the money for their piece of the station. By the time Cabana and crew took off in December of 1998, their launch was more than a year behind schedule because the US had had to bail the Russians out. Russia was warning NASA that while the rest of the station was being assembled, additional delays might occur in delivering its second component, the service module, which was to provide propulsion, communications, the distribution of power, and even living quarters. *Air & Space/ Smithsonian* magazine reported that Russia's "delays have already brought the largest international space project in history to the brink of political disaster," predicting that the partnership "might not survive" and "was already unraveling as the station's first pieces moved to the launchpad." More recently, the Russians announced that they would not be able to supply the six Progress spacecraft per year that would be required to prop up the station's orbit, which decays over time. (The word "orbit" at such a low altitude simply describes an object falling over a very long period of time.)

And those weren't the only troubles with Russia. On the night of February 23, 1997, a chemical oxygen generator aboard *Mir* burst into flames, threatening the lives of everyone on board. The fire even cut the crew off from one of the two Soyuz craft, their lifeboats for escape. *Mir* filled with smoke, and the sickening stench of the fire lingered for months afterward.

In June that same year, Vasily Tsibliyev was flying the Progress resupply vehicle by remote, attempting to dock it with *Mir*, when it slammed into the station, tearing a hole in its thin aluminum skin. As the station depressurized, Mike Foale, an American astronaut, rushed to the Soyuz to evacuate, only to find that the Russian cosmonauts wouldn't abandon ship. Foale found himself all alone, waiting for the Russians, knowing that the rule book called for immediate evacuation. The realization slowly sank in that they simply weren't going to do it. Here was the crux of the cultural gulf between the two nations: The cosmonauts would die heroes and be celebrated back home, bringing honor to their families. But for American astronauts, not only was dying bad form, but it could put an end to the whole program, not to mention their own careers. Astronauts didn't go for that dead-hero stuff. They much preferred success to failure.

After a mad scramble, in which the punctured module was sealed off, the crew realized that the collision had damaged one set of the solar arrays that supply electrical power. *Mir* slipped into a free drift, the remaining panels couldn't track the sun, and the batteries ran down, plunging them into darkness. Nothing worked. Even the toilet was electric.

That was not the end of their troubles. When the Progress clipped *Mir*, it had sent the Russian craft into a slow roll. Russia's mission control had no Apollo 13–style solution to the mounting vexations. In the end, it was the American astronaut who thought of using the Soyuz's rocket engines to stop the spin and reorient *Mir* toward the sun to restore power. The events gave NASA an unsettling preview of the difficulties that lay ahead when working with the Russians on the ISS. Indeed, the long-delayed Russian service module, a key element of the ISS, is closely modeled on *Mir*'s core block.

· · ·

Congress has tried to kill the space station more than once, but it just won't die. It mutates and reinvents itself—much like NASA. Today, the agency has redefined itself once more, with the International Space Station as its cornerstone. And NASA is hitting hard on the idea that the ISS is the future of mankind—in science, in exploration, in every way imaginable.

The reason that the space station (i.e., NASA) won't go away is its potent combination of bureaucratic might and missionary zeal. Because people of passion have their own kind of power, too: the power to persuade. The outward manifestation of this passion is their stuff. No one can deny it: NASA makes the coolest stuff. NASA is a cult of hardware, the great garage of America's homegrown tinkerers, those jack-of-all-trades types who knock together gadgets with the cast-off junk of others, forming the dream of the moment in cascading iterations and stillborn, crackpot trials and errors, until they come up with stuff so cool that the rest of the world simply can't ignore it any longer (as the Wright brothers, the ultimate crackpots, did).

One day at Kennedy Space Center, I met up with a retired engineer who had volunteered to escort journalists around. We went out to the launchpads on Merritt Island to see the rare sight of two birds at once: *Endeavour*, which Cabana would take up to start building the space station, on Pad A, and John Glenn's bird, *Discovery*, just to the north on Pad B. Because people had lost interest in the space station, NASA and others involved hoped that John Glenn's flight would attract public attention to *Endeavour*.

We made our way along the brackish bayous that cut through Kennedy like a spider web, through mangrove and pampas grass and yucca. Up close, the whole contraption that would launch the space station seemed old and dirty and far too complex to make any sense—as if some artist-cum-engineer had gone mad up there. But as I studied it, I perceived that within the seeming chaos was the small bird—the shuttle orbiter itself, in which Cabana, Ross, and Kirkalev would rise with the nucleus of the ISS—and all at once it appeared to me as a fetus in an iron placenta with Teflon blood vessels, gray, white, and yellow, running in a crazy pattern around it, and there seemed to dwell within that lunatic tangle a deep and inscrutable intelligence. No, the artist, the engineer—they weren't crazy at all. They had simply been driven by an incomprehensible passion to this godly vision.

One such visionary was Roy Tharpe, who grew up on Merritt Island in the shadow of rocketry and has worked at NASA ever since he got out of college. One day he was on a survey crew on Complex 34 when a Titan rocket was taking from Complex 20. Tharpe thought he was safe several miles away, twenty feet up on a scaffolding. But the rocket took off, lost its gimbals, "and suddenly I found myself nose to nose with a Titan missile," Tharpe told me. He jumped from the scaffolding, and the rocket thundered over his head and destroyed itself somewhere out in the salt marsh.

Energetic and curious, Tharpe was a tall man with bright blue eyes, a gentle smile, and a shock of white hair. On the shelf behind him in his office was a bust of Kennedy. Tharpe was now launch site manager for the ISS. The components of the station were assembled in this building—his building. They were assembled, tested, and proved. Then they were brought out to the launch-pad. The station had given Tharpe (and NASA) a new lease on life. For the first time in more than twenty years, he said, it was "every bit as exciting" to work here as it had been during Apollo. "I was rode hard and put up wet in Apollo," he said with a misty smile. "We partied hard, too. Apollo launch parties were a sign of the times."

In describing his work, Tharpe immediately fixed on passion as the driving force. "That burning fire has got to be in your gut," he said. And now more than ever he believed in the space station. "We didn't find diamonds on the moon, but we're going to make diamonds on the space station," he told me. "We're going to do unbelievable things in microgravity."

Ever since Apollo, the great debate about NASA—and about the space station—has been: Why do we need it? What is it for? NASA's answer is that the space station is an orbiting laboratory for doing the best kinds of scientific and medical research, and the visionaries of NASA believe that it is going to change not only the way we do that research but also the way we live. We can't deny that the space program has done so. Research begun at NASA has brought us better versions of everything from running shoes and Velcro to pacemakers, sunglasses, and a wide variety of electronic devices.

"It's about vision," Tharpe said, storming around the room, gesticulating. He called Dan Goldin "Superman, the most persistent person for human space flight. He is numero uno and has that fire in the belly," Tharpe said. "Superman, I tell you. He survived the uprising in Moscow while he was negotiating the space station. We were on the phone with him. We could hear the bullets."

On a TV monitor above Tharpe's head, I could see a live, closed-circuit image of Node 1, called *Unity*, which Cabana would take into space. It was finally real—Tharpe could walk down the hall and see the work progressing. And he could hardly contain his excitement.

I went down that hall to a gigantic hangar called the high bay, where they were doing the final tests on the node—the actual version of the model I'd seen Ross and Newman working on in the pool. In that enormous room, in the midst of a chaos of scaffolding and wire, men and women in blue hospital scrubs, hairnets, and particle masks were working all over the node, an alumi-num cylinder fifteen feet in diameter with six hatches used for docking other elements of the station. When an astronaut named Nancy Currie helped to grapple the two main pieces of the ISS together in orbit, she wouldn't even be able to see them. She would have to watch on a video monitor using the Space Vision System. She would bring one within six inches of the other, then Bob Cabana would fire the shuttle engines to dock the two components, just like docking with *Mir*. That is what astronauts are. They perform astonishing feats such as this one, the equivalent of bringing two apartment buildings together while blindfolded without breaking any windows.

Ten days before Cabana's flight, the Russians launched the Functional Cargo Block, called *Zarya*, a twenty-ton pressurized element. Once in orbit, *Zarya* extended its solar panels from an accordion fold a few inches wide to seventy feet tall, like the unfolding of a butterfly's wings as it hatches. During the process of assembly, *Zarya* provides power, propulsion, and communi-cation by way of the antennas that Ross was practicing attaching in the pool. Once the service module is up, *Zarya* will be powered down as larger solar arrays—some twenty-seven thousand square feet of them—are assembled and begin to function. Eight miles of wire are required just for the electrical power system.

"I don't think people realize how big this show is going to be," Tharpe told me. And indeed, without being in the middle of it, as we were then, it's difficult to grasp just how big it is. It's said to be the largest peacetime scientific and engineering project in history. The water system on the station will be so sophisticated that it will turn pure urine into drinking water. Along with other wastewater, that's what the astronauts will drink—their own urine. Trash will be collected into a Progress module, and when it's full, they'll send it back to Earth, allowing it to incinerate itself upon reentry into the atmosphere. Interestingly, the space station will have no central control panel or cockpit in the convention sense that an aircraft or a big ship has one. It will be run through small, portable IBM computers, which can be plugged into outlets placed all over the station.

Aside from the moon and Venus, the space station will be the brightest object in the night sky. Students on the ground will be able to take photographs from a camera mounted on the space station. They'll do it through the internet. The quality of the images will be the highest ever generated from a spacecraft. This is the ultimate cool stuff.

I discussed the spiritual nature of their work with Cabana and Ross. Ross said he thought that in the near future, I'd be talking to a crew that was on its way to Mars, but in the meantime, he hoped the science done on the space station would "help to reveal some of God's secrets to us for the benefit of all mankind." I asked him why he was doing this. He said, "I think God has a plan for me. I think God wants me to be here." I realized that at NASA, in the astronaut corps, they're all white male Christians. Even the blacks and the women are white male Christians.

Cabana said, "Time on orbit is extremely precious. It is very difficult to take time and just appreciate where you are. I always tell all the first-time fliers, 'You have to take some time up there to appreciate where you are and what a unique opportunity it is, how fortunate you are to have it, and how special it really is. And you have to just look out the window and make a memory in your mind. Don't take a picture of it, because you're going to be disappointed when you get home, because no picture is as good as what you see. And you kind of burn that into your brain and it's special.' And I've got one from each of my flights."

As we left, I told Cabana that I thought his was a good answer. He laughed and shrugged, saying, "I knew that's what you wanted to hear."

On my last day at Kennedy, I watched them load the node into a huge canister and seal it up. Then a giant door in the side of the building opened, and the canister rolled out to the launchpad. *Unity* was unloaded from it and placed aboard the shuttle. Hanging out with the astronauts, Tharpe and I watched the space station being assembled. He told me, "ISS, in terms of exploration, forms the basis of deep space by giving us a deep understanding of living in space. We revere our astronauts. We don't want them to die. The Gemini program was a stepping-stone to the moon. Rendezvous and docking—people forget about Gemini. ISS is our Gemini. It's mystifying to me to this day how technically competent we were to pull of the stuff we had to do to go to the moon. Now how do we muster that to go to Mars? Get NASA out of the day-to-day operations and engage the private sector. Eventually, industrial groups will run the space station. That's the key. Wait'll we find that first drug that'll cure cancer— the universities and pharmaceutical companies, they'll all want a ticket then."

Eleven days later, in December of 1998, Cabana, Ross, and Newman launched in an attempt to do in space what they had practiced in the pool. And everything went smoothly. After eight days of work, Cabana floated through the air lock and went inside the newly hatched titanium dragonfly to turn on the lights. The crew plugged in an IBM ThinkPad 760 computer, one of the basic control units for the space station. Ross even tested the SAFER system. He was tethered, of course.

After a few days, they all climbed back into the space shuttle, closed the cargo-bay doors, and lit the fires to come home. For the first time in years, the station was out of danger of being put on the scrap heap.

. . .

For years Dan Goldin has been telling everyone that we're going to Mars. I sat in his office in Washington one day as he waved his arms and pointed at a painting of Mars as he tramped up and down in his cowboy boots shouting, "That's where we're going! We're going to Mars!" He leaves the impression that Mars is just the next subway stop after the moon. At its closest, Mars is thirty-six million miles away, 150 times farther than the moon. For comparison, imagine flying in a balloon from Manhattan to Albany, a distance of about 140 miles. Now imagine flying the balloon all the way around the world. That has been done, but it took more than a hundred years to accomplish. The flight to Mars would be at least a six-month trip, and we don't know how to keep astronauts alive and healthy in space for that long.

On my last day at Johnson Space Center in Houston, the hot, high sun looks like a white hole in the sky, a hazy window to other worlds. I enter the small building where machines make identity badges. I have to return mine. The woman who takes mine wears a red button on her shirt that says, "Mars or Bust." I ask her what the button means. She pulls on it and looks at it as if she hasn't noticed it before. "I don't know," she says. "Just everybody wears one."

· 12 ·

The Cult of War

I HAVE NEVER killed anyone, but I've seen a lot of death. When I worked in a medical school, I saw many cadavers in various stages of dissection. One I recall looked like a man who'd been hit by a land mine. Vessels ran like wiring, pale and colorless, in every direction from the bone and muscle that had been wrenched back to expose bulging organs, which seemed to be fleeing the bonds of white tissue, frail as cobwebs under the dew of formaldehyde. And there was always something green, a fluid, a pus, a suppuration—no one ever seemed to know what it was, that green stuff coming out of the corpse.

It's the same green the army has chosen for everything. A truck pulled up near us, out by the forest at Fort Bragg, North Carolina, where we waited for the C-130 transport plane. The truck and the plane and even the forest seemed to be that color of death, and the trailer fixed on to the back of the truck was green, too, and the green officers wore green clothes as they unburdened the truck of its wooden crates of bombs and rockets, mines and bullets, missiles and flares, and laid everything out on the wet green grass.

"You lose my shit, and I'll hunt you to the ends of the earth," an officer from the Eighty-Second Airborne Division told someone. He wore a T-shirt and sipped coffee out of a thermos cup as he stood over his stores. The rounds were laid out on the grass by the airstrip as if for the Fourth of July, and men with clipboards were walking along the rows, counting them, writing, double-checking for accuracy.

One big area was set out for M16 cartridges, boxes and boxes of them in speed loaders. The M16 is the military version of the AR15 assault rifle. Next to those speed loaders was ammunition for the Squad Automatic Weapon, a machine gun known as SAW. Each belt held two hundred rounds. They were stacked in green metal ammo cases. I saw 40 mike-mike all in gay colors, nestled in wooden crates that lay open on the ground. The mike-mike-grenade round has the diameter of an old-fashioned silver dollar, squat and short and improbably colored. Blue ones are practice rounds, which leave a dye marker where they hit. Blue in the military is the color that signifies something for practice only: it is fake, unlike corpse green, which signifies what is real. Smoke grenades are green and yellow and red. Beside the crates of mike-mike were silver flares for illumination and signaling. Red means "Cease firing."

Squatting beside a wooden crate, a paratrooper was zipping open cardboard tubes, each a foot long and five inches in diameter. He'd pick one out of the wooden crate, zip the pull string, twist the cap to make sure it was loose, then put it on the ground. I picked one up and looked inside. It was one of the new mortar rounds, a little silver-finned rocket with a selectable fuse in its conical golden-colored nose. By flipping a switch, I could set it to detonate on impact, on proximity with the ground, or on a whim. These paratroopers would be firing the new mortar rounds for the first time on this mission. Until that night they had been firing mortar rounds from the Vietnam era.

I was impressed with how casually these soldiers handled these high explosives. Holding a mortar rocket next to my chest, I felt that I was carrying my own death like a baby. The soldier next to me was cradling the tubes against his stomach as he zipped open the paraffin seals. A few yards across the green grass, I saw a man sniffing a command-detonated claymore mine with a cigarette in his mouth. Although the cigarette was unlit, he looked crazy putting his face so close to so much death. One paratrooper ambled past with an armload of mortar rockets, bobbing and weaving and kind of jiving to a tune no one else could hear, saying, "I'm own 'splode on impack."

An officer was saying, "Claymore jumpers, listen up: keep it on your body. Check to see it's all there, tester and clacker." To anyone familiar with modern infantry warfare, the claymore mine is infamous, but no more so than the stand of grapeshot was in previous wars and times. In fact, the claymore *is* a stand of grapeshot brought up to date with modern materials. Its fiberglass shell is packed with plastic explosive in which are embedded seven hundred steel ball bearings. It is a rectangular device about six to ten inches long and an inch and a half thick, dull silver in color, curved from side to side, with pointed metal legs that fold down from underneath so that it may be stuck into the ground like a miniature drive-in movie screen. When it is fired, that load of grapeshot sprays out, and anyone within a 325-foot swath is reduced, as they say, to Hamburger Helper.

Pure night had fallen over the forest and the airfield. The high-intensity floodlights outlined the troops starkly where they lined up for the munitions they would pack on this jump.

"Do these mortar rounds fit in the butt pack, sir?"

"It's a stuff, but they'll fit."

Dozens of men now sat in groups on the ground clacking rounds into clips, putting rockets into butt packs, smoking cigarettes, talking. Between us and the first rising stars, the busy airfield was ablaze with lights and roaring airplanes. Out on the grass, an officer threw himself down with a cigarette between his teeth and began doing push-ups.

"I don't know how they expect us to fire all this," a big, gentle-looking jumper said, zipping speed loaders into M16 clips with a practiced hand, spacing them with red phosphorous tracer rounds.

"All right, jumpers!" an officer yelled. "When I call you, I want five at a time, no more, no less."

The jumpers began lining up, two by two, helping one another into their parachutes and packs. It is a little difficult to imagine what a paratrooper has to put on in order to accomplish a mission such as this one. First his load-bearing vest goes on, a webbing device that holds two canteens, butt pack (which may contain mortar rounds), ammo pouch, knife, flashlight, and so on. Then his thirty-five-pound parachute goes on his upper back, with straps over his shoulders, across his chest and stomach, and through his crotch. Then his reserve chute goes onto the strap across his chest, and below that is his ALICE (All-Purpose Lightweight Individual Carrying Equipment) pack (or rucksack), which can weigh thirty-five pounds or more. It is affixed to the front of his body upside down, so that the metal brace, which rests on his kidneys when he's walking, encompasses his belly when he's jumping. The bulk of the rucksack hangs down to his knees. If he is carrying anything extra, as some of the men are tonight (for example, the bases for mortar tubes, which are the size of card tables), the extra paraphernalia is attached outside the rucksack. Last he straps on his personal weapon, such as the M16, which is in a weapons case.

Thus encumbered, he is ready to be inspected to see if all the straps and lanyards, clips and hasps, have been done up right, to see if the parachute is still holding together, if this is all going to come unraveled like a skinless baseball in midair. Parachute riggers in red seed caps and green T-shirts scurry around the field making last-minute adjustments on the rigs. Each jumper in inspected from top to bottom, and then he waddles off to the grass, at this point thoroughly wet with dew, to collapse in a heap against the backdrop of the black forest and try to get comfortable while waiting for a C-130 to taxi out.

It is bad enough to be a pack animal, weighed down with 150 pounds of equipment, and it's bad enough to have to wait and wait, trying to get comfortable inside of all those biting straps in the wet grass with the night growing cold and the chiggers trying to crawl up into your crotch where no hand can reach. But the thought of jumping out of an airplane like that—well, it seems so extreme, so desperate, that it's difficult to imagine what threat could inspire a person even to consider it as a means of self-defense. As with the perverted genius of the claymore, one is forced to wonder where it came from. Was it a nightmare? Divine inspiration? Or is there truly evil in the world, and is this how it finds expression in the methods of warfare?

To say that war is an instinct does not satisfy. What instinct causes us to leap from an airplane? By what instinct do we walk through a wall of fire? Crawling into the coffin-like space of a Sheridan tank and devising strategies to prevent the 152-millimeter gun from taking off my kneecap during its recoil was hardly what I'd call an instinct. My only instinct in there was to get out before I died of fumes and claustrophobia. No, war today is not an instinct. It is a great deal of trouble overcoming the instinct of self-preservation. And I don't believe it could be done without something akin to a spiritual conversion.

Sometimes psychologists have used an unpleasant term to describe that transformation. They call it "brainwashing." The term is unpalatable because we've always used it against our enemies. But it's the only word we have for a stress-induced willingness to accept . . . well, just about anything. Even primitive tribes use it.

When the C-130 came, I got on and watched the paratroopers file in and get belted down. One story above the cargo hold, the air force pilots sat up out of the way in the dark cockpit with green glowing instruments while a hundred men in their amazing gear waddled up the cargo ramp and collapsed with a clatter of knives and rockets and automatic rifles onto the metal benches with the red web seats. I stood above them at one end, observing how they were wedged in—no one could move—and I felt the panic of claustrophobia rising within me.

But as soon as they were strapped in, they calmly took off their helmets, put their heads down—amid mortar tubes, giant mortar bases, personal weapon cases, spars and cables and conduit, the suffocating kerosene fumes, and the screaming Angelus of the engines—and they went straight to sleep.

· · ·

War cannot exist without an enemy. And so, through much of modern history, where enemies have been lacking, they have been invented to serve the purpose they always serve: to separate "us" from "them" so that we can make war. The Institute of Human Relations at Yale University published a book in 1943 called *A Social Psychology of War and Peace*. Its author, Mark May, in discussing the psychology of Nazi Germany, writes: "The primitive man attributes all fortunes and misfortunes to personal agents, living or dead, human or divine. He does not believe in *accidents*.... When a primitive society is persuaded that its troubles are caused by its early enemies, whoever they may be, it is well on its way toward aggressive war. The more intolerable its burdens and the greater its deprivations and sufferings, the greater will be its tendency to appease or to attack and destroy the causal agent."

In the case of Germany, May writes, "Hitler in *Mein Kampf* puts the blame entirely on the shoulders of the Jews and the Communists." Something like that can be said about the eight years of the Reagan administration, which put the blame for all the troubles of our nation on drug dealers and used the idea that our youth was being poisoned by drugs, combined with the already rampant fear of communism, as a way to rationalize spending ever-increasing amounts of money in Latin America, to incite racial stereotypes and a national hatred of Latin Americans, and to justify building up a military presence in the Caribbean in preparation for conducting warfare in Central America. The Eighty-Second Airborne Division, as well as tactical fighter units, have already been sent to Honduras "to conduct exercises" and to make a "show of strength." Since the United States has the largest budget in the world for military matters, there is hardly any need to show strength.

In other words, this story was simply a lie. The soldiers I trained with at Fort Bragg understood that they were going, eventually, to war in Latin America. They were already pretending to blow those little brown creeps to kingdom come. The stereotype—like that of the "gook" in Vietnam—was already formed. I was told that the Latin Americans they were going to fight were probably dealing drugs and that they were the source of all our troubles anyway.

But no matter what one despot or another does in any given theater of war—and no matter whether he is our despot or their despot—a central question always remains: Is war an act of will or an act of nature? Do we decide to go to war, or does war simply happen in the course of things, without our being able to stop it? Is war an upheaval of the species, as natural and neutral as a hurricane, or is it the work of evil minds?

The greatest military thinker of the modern world, Carl von Clausewitz, failed in a lifetime of revising the same work over and over again to find the answers to those questions. His critics are still arguing about what he was trying to say. His work is taught at West Point, and it is also studied by the enemies of West Point, including those who would prove that war is altogether wrong. Calling one side the evil empire and the other side good is fallacious because, as Emmerich de Vattel points out, war is not a fight of good against evil. The very concept of the state implies the right to wage war, and therefore all states are created equal. So, too, are all wars equally good and bad. And so, too, are both sides in every war. The only difference is who wins.

War throughout the ages has been the subtle turning of the wheel of paradox. Clausewitz's *On War* was unfinished at his death. Like Einstein's attempts to wrest a unified theory from the equations of the universe, all attempts to distill out of war a general theory have failed. In a fashion, Clausewitz wrote his book based on the man he most despised and most admired: Napoleon, who was the undisputed genius of the world in war but who wrote nothing down. It is said that Napoleon understood the elusive unified theory of war but took it to the grave with him. We are left with Clausewitz trying to understand Napoleon and all of us trying to understand Clausewitz.

Clausewitz's central problem is that he devoted his life to trying to make a logical structure out of something that can be made to seem logical only if you take yourself out of it and strip yourself of all moral and ethical responsibility to your fellow man. We force our children—and those soldiers I was watching practice for their own deaths and the deaths of others just like them were children—to fight and die because it's good business. War is a business, the best business on earth if you have no morals and if you don't care whose children you kill. Every time a bullet is fired, someone who is largely invisible to the public is made richer. Those innocents sitting uncomfortably in the C-130 practicing for death knew nothing of the real cause of war. They were parroting the propaganda. Most of these children would not even have heard of the companies they were making rich, such as United Technologies, L-3 Communications, Finmeccanica, the European Aeronautic Defense and Space Company, and BAE Systems. So war makes perfect sense if you are selling weapons. For the United States, which has the largest military-industrial complex in the world, that eventually led to perpetual war. And yet the suspicion lingers that there is even more to it that we have not quite comprehended.

· · ·

The anthropologist Tobias Schneebaum described living with a Stone Age tribe in South America for six months. The people were lovely, playful, affectionate. They took him in and gave him the status of a family member. And one night, with no warning, they all got up and started running through the forest. At their urging, Schneebaum went with them.

They ran and ran all through the night. Rain fell as they slogged through deep mud and across rushing rivers. They saw a nutria that would have provided good food but ignored it. Just before dawn, they came on a village of sleeping people not unlike themselves. Swiftly they entered the village and slaughtered all the men. In his book *Keep the River on Your Right*, Schneebaum describes the childlike glee with which they punctured the intestines of the victims with their spears, how they laughed as the gas escaped. They carried some of the bodies home, marching all day through the forest. That night, they made a feast of those they had slain.

Was it the march—the hunger and exhaustion and the rhythmic assault of muscles on earth and earth on bone—that induced the trancelike, hallucinatory state that turned peaceful, friendly individuals into killing machines? I believe that without the march, the killing would have been unthinkable. Besides, marching to kill your enemies means that they live far away from you. If you did the same thing too close to home, it would be murder.

Even Clausewitz recognized that, in this sense, war is more like art than anything else—a controlled transport of the mind and spirit. The truly great commander's state of mind, said Clausewitz, is the state of mind of a great artist at the moment of creation: his rules and skills are so fully absorbed that he is completely free, behaving by second nature, with ease of movement, relaxed at the most crucial moment, where all can emerge naturally, without effort, from that dark place of universal inspiration. Clausewitz writes, "War . . . is a wonderful trinity, composed of the original violence of its elements, of the play of probabilities and chance which make it a free activity of the soul, and of its subordinate nature as a political instrument, in which respect it belongs to the province of Reason." What Clausewitz leaves out is that war, like art, also contains an element of frenzy or ecstasy—in other words, it requires being out of one's senses, out of one's mind, in a state of temporary insanity, much as the artist or scientist is at the moment of creation or great discovery.

That makes war all the more inscrutable.

. . .

The drop zone (DZ) is an eerie place. Fort Bragg is all sand and pines and waterways that appear when it rains, then disappear again. The field is in a constant state of mock warfare, and you can never go very far without hearing the distant chattering of automatic weapons or the tin-gong sound of a big tube weapon, howitzer or mortar.

By eight on the evening of our assault, the moon had not yet risen, but the Big Dipper was up in the western sky, and a big orange planet burst halfway up beyond the southern tree line as I walked out onto what seemed like desert but had been the floor of an ocean ten million years before. The darkness was so complete that I could see nothing before me as I struggled through the sand. Then one of the stars in the southern sky resolved itself into an artificial light, and I walked toward it, knowing that it was a turn-in point and that I'd find people there.

Out on the vast expanse of sand in the clear air, I smelled his cigarette long before I saw him. By the time I saw him, I was almost on top of him. He was a young soldier, all wrapped in that dark green, waiting, shifting from foot to foot under the pale beacon stuck on a stalk in the sand. The jumpers would turn in their chutes to him, and he would log and count them. Then a truck would come around and take them back to be repacked. I asked him to confirm where and when the drop was going to happen, and he shrugged and pointed vaguely in the direction of the middle of the DZ, and I walked on, sinking in the sand with every step.

Eastward I saw a planet suddenly rise halfway up the sky. I had to watch it for a moment before I realized that I was looking at a flare. In another moment, automatic weapons ripped away, and then the heavy whoosh-thud of a howitzer peeled back the pretense of solitude for a moment before night closed once more around me. There is nothing quite like the sound of a howitzer—an enormous galvanized steel door being slammed, jamming the air all up into the valleys of those hills. Like surf, the waves of air come back when they've spent their energy out there.

Far in the distance I heard the faint mechanical hammering of aircraft engines that I knew so well from years of being around them. I looked north to find the red and green navigation lights moving toward us along a line parallel with the drop zone. I ran to get under it as it came on and on. I reached the middle of the DZ just as the C-130 drew overhead.

For some reason everything seemed to grow silent. The sky was light compared to the land, and against that shimmering, cold, feather-gray scrim, I saw the dark leviathan shape of the ship cross to the south. Without warning, a blossoming profusion of jellyfish sprayed out across the sky. Silently and swiftly they grew from black points in the sky to the swelling, round, living atoms of darkness, filling in the spaces between the stars.

The plane was gone, and truly there was no sound at all. As I stumbled on the ocean floor, watching scores of the creatures come down around me, I knew that one would surely drift down on top of me and engulf me in the trembling petals of its mushroom flesh. I could see, as they descended in the fluid of the air, that men were dangling from them. Within a hundred feet of the ground, each man pulled the release that dropped his rucksack to dangle on a fifteen-foot lanyard, and all around me I heard the snap-clatter-swishing of the packs as they dropped and the men prepared to land.

The first man hit with a crunch. I heard his "Oof!" and saw the gray jellyfish above him balloon and invert, dumping its bubble of air, then drift and fold and lie down quietly on the sand, as dead as an uprooted rag of seaweed. "Oh, God! I've got to piss!" the man hollered, and I heard the clanking of his gear as he tried to free himself of hasps and clips and webbing.

Then all around me men were landing—first the rucksack's crunch, then the man, hitting and rolling as best he could, encumbered as he was—and then the great weight of the parachute itself, the sea creature that had carried him there, dying in the dead sea air on the ten-million-year-old shore. They were all carrying live rounds, rockets, high explosives, claymores, grenades, and flares. I kept waiting for the explosion. It was just then that a jumper on DZ Sicily not far away was leaping to his death. I heard about it only later. But it happened while we were going out to play war that a man jumped into the path of another airplane. The propellers cut his shroud lines. He pulled his reserve chute but not soon enough to save himself. The jumpers go out at an altitude of only eight hundred feet. It does not leave much room for error.

After a jump into enemy territory, the paratroopers run for cover, regroup, and get on the march toward their objective as quickly as possible. On this night it was an enemy defensive position about seven clicks overland to the west. Sometimes, however, it takes time to get all those jumpers rounded up out of the sand and to separate out the injured ones. So before they go into the woods, there is a period of waiting. All the paratroopers stretched out on the sand in a low area of dunes and scrub cover. Some set up defensive positions with M16s and SAW tripod weapons. Others simply lay out, relieved of the burden of parachute and rigging, and went into a meditative trance. Some call it sleep.

Our platoon leader thought he might have broken his leg. "The goddamned jump was so well on target that I damned near landed on top of the

Humvee," he whispered, limping along. They had been aiming for the area where several vehicles were parked on the DZ. With no wind, they had hit what they were aiming for. In trying to maneuver to avoid landing on top of the High Mobility Multipurpose Wheeled Vehicle, which we used to call a jeep, the platoon leader had twisted his ankle. But he was a Ranger, and he was going on.

A transformation takes place when you move out into the night woods for combat. The men, animated before, seemed to blend into the earth. I had been talking to one, having an ordinary conversation, but when the absolute darkness of the forest fell on us, he wandered off and simply ceased to be. The night-fighter makeup, the camouflage battle dress, the way the men moved so quietly, made them all disappear.

The march was strenuous but not terribly so. It was simple: Put one foot in front of the other. Keep the man in front of you in sight but not too close. Don't bunch up. The enemy can take out a lot of men with one explosion.

The woods were a surreal thrill. My eyes played tricks on me. The road went one way, the men went the other. We crossed, then recrossed a stream. Star bearings gave way to a black canopy of trees. Sweat poured down my face and neck and back, but the air was cold. If we stopped for more than a minute, I began to freeze, and the men around me began to snore. They were like infants, constantly falling asleep.

Getting tactical, they call it, which means sneaking up on the enemy, camouflaging yourself, being quiet. It means that if anything strange happens, everyone stops and waits until it is all sorted out and they get a signal from up front. While waiting we were as quiet as possible, which for most of the men meant sleeping. After walking all night, I was able to manage it once or twice, though it was pretty unnatural for me just to sit down in wet clothes, freezing cold, wearing packs and packages, and fall asleep in pine needles. But I did it, and when I awoke, I saw the naked, deserted forest all around me and heard a silence such as I have never heard before and saw a blackness below and a full moon above through a hole in the trees, and I knew that they had walked off and left me out there alone in the middle of these seemingly endless miles of wilderness. (What a joke: Lost another reporter, har-har.)

I startled, sat up against the tree at my back, and heard a clank. My head spun left, and I clambered to my knees. Colonel Robert Lossius was on the other side of the tree from me, eating a piece of licorice. I wasn't alone at all. The men had simply turned into dark lumps on the forest floor. They looked like bushes or piles of dead leaves, but they were all still there, most of them asleep. I wondered what it would feel like to be their enemy and to stumble on them accidentally and then see all of this midnight earthen splendor rise up out of the forest floor to smite you.

Softly, I heard the whispering of the radioman somewhere ahead. We were moving out again. As we hustled out into a clearing, I could see that the moon had grown so bright looking at it was like looking through the PVS-7, the night-vision scope, which is to say that its light was like daylight but all tinged with a blue ethereal beauty, the restless energy of dreams.

We crossed a firebreak, went down an incline, and moved across an area of plants I could not even begin to identify, lost in sucking sands strewn with gritty meteorites, some of them as big as watermelons. It looked as if we were crossing the site of an ancient asteroid war, and we stopped for a few minutes, genuflecting, and I picked up a meteorite to see if I was hallucinating, but it was sharp and metallic and real. Out in the brush, I heard a noise, and I realized how much I hoped it was our own troops and not the enemy.

By the time we reached the first signs of human life, I was so tired that I didn't realize it was our troops. I nearly flipped meeting men with M16s pointed at us, men who were in a small clearing in the forest on white sand setting up mortar tubes on their big round ring bases. I came to understand only after we had passed them that they were our rear support team. And with that understanding, I came to realize that they'd be firing those silver-finned rockets with the selectable fuses and the golden-colored conical noses. They'd be firing them right over our heads to get at the enemy that we were attacking. I hoped they weren't as tired as we were.

I also understood that if we were stopping, we were about to attack. In the distance I began to hear automatic weapons firing. The tumbling M16 rounds made a snapping, zinging, buzz-bomb sound chewing through the pines. A big Apache helicopter thundered overhead, tracing a path back and forth. Unsure what this meant, I asked a soldier near me what he was doing. His weary, youthful face smiled at me through unearthly swirls of camo makeup, and he said softly, "He's killing people." And looking at his face, I recalled that before the attack on the village in Peru, Schneebaum and the natives had all painted themselves with jungle camouflage decorations.

The last hill was the hardest. That must be a rule of some sort, like Clausewitz's rule about never planning anything that depends on anything else. When we reached the bunker, drenched in sweat, so tired that we were seeing double, we found a couple of men in a trench eating MREs (meals ready to eat) and listening to radio static and watching the fortified enemy position dug into a low overgrown treeless area of weeds and bramble about half a click away. We were facing south. From the west another force, similar to ours, would attack. Then we'd close in, pinching the enemy between the two. Pretty standard stuff.

For the initial stage of the assault, the men with the SAWs, machine guns on tripods, threw themselves facedown on the ridgeline and set up their weapons. Soon the mortars began from behind us, and the offensive line opened up. We carried ear protection—little foam plugs—but I had dropped mine in the forest, so the wall of sound hit me and creased my skull between my eyes where a headache had been brewing for the last few hours. A white flare went up and illuminated the scene in its dancing candlelight, while red tracer rounds burned in steady lines from our position straight out into the sky.

Just ahead of our position, the land rose slightly. To avoid it, the men were shooting at the stars. Behind me the officers were screaming for them to get down, get their aim down, but no one was listening, and the ammunition was being harmlessly spent in the air. I watched one man direct his weapon straight down into the enemy position, but the machine-gun bullets would have had to chew their way through the soil embankment to get to their target. Instead they set the grass on fire around him, and he leaped away leaving his weapon idle in the flames.

Every once in a while, someone would get a straight bead on the enemy position, and the red tracers would ricochet as they skipped across the undergrowth, making weird right-angle turns upward. Some even made that ka-ching sound we've all learned to love from cartoon warfare.

As the flanking force moved in from the west, our firing team switched the stakes that supported the barrel and fired across at another angle. Out under the flare light and moonlight, I could see a couple of enemy vehicles—what might have been a truck and a tank—on the rise half a kilometer away.

The firing on our flank stopped, and we moved in for a better position, shifting south and west. I could see the men on a small bluff a hundred yards away setting up the DRAGON missiles. I heard more mortar rounds popping off overhead. Now the rounds were landing closer to the enemy vehicles, and we had moved in closer ourselves, so we were beginning to feel the effects of the high-explosive detonations, the quickening of the earth beneath our feet. It felt as if it turned slightly liquid with each explosion, the way the sand does at the edge of the surf.

I moved out into the brush with one of the claymore jumpers, helping him string out his electrical wire through the bushes. He would use the mine to defend against a possible enemy counterattack. The brown wire came off the plastic spool with the detonator already in place, and we stretched it out as far as it would go, and then he lay down on his stomach and stuck the metal legs into the sand and looked through the small gunsight on top to aim the mine the right way, making sure the side that said "Front Toward Enemy" was facing away from our position. He smelled the silver body of the mine and said, "Mmmm, I love the smell of a claymore." I got down on my belly beside him. I leaned in and touched my nose to the plastic body and inhaled. It smelled like cherries.

Then he slid the silver detonator into the threaded fitting on top, as if he were installing an electrical conduit for a porch light. He tightened the nut down. Then we got up off the ground and went back to our position, where he attached the clacker, as it's called, the switch that would detonate the mine. It was called "command detonated" because he would decide when to do it. It was simple, beautiful, deadly.

· · ·

The second attack came fast and furious, with both sides firing everything they had. People were throwing hand grenades, officers were shooting flares, every man was firing his personal weapon, men on their stomachs were sending the golden coils of ammo belts ripping through machine guns, and tracers were crisscrossing the sky. The sound was not so much a sound as a storm, like the winds of Armageddon. In front of me, a man was laughing and firing 40 mike-mike grenades as fast as he could load them. He pointed the weapon back at me and said, "Hey, reporter, you wanna fire some mike-mike?" I waved at him and started to crawl out from behind the boulder where I had taken cover. But an officer grabbed me by the backpack and pulled me back. I think it was Colonel Lossius. I think he was my guardian angel. But I didn't get to find out. Something else was about to happen, and it had my full attention before it even started.

A sound like a gong turned me back to where the DRAGONs had been set up. A sheet of flame ten feet long went back from them, and then I saw the missile, as big as a lamppost, gliding with its ghostly tail of fire, low across the grass and scrub. I was amazed at how slowly it seemed to move. As it went, it corrected its course with small bursts of white rocket fire out of the sides of its body, like a spitting snake, pop-pop-pop, and when it found its target—one of the vehicles I had seen—it destroyed it with a clash of metal that fractured the low clouds, a dull and toneless sound as big as the sky itself, the final closing of the final door.

I heard the claymore jumper beside me shouting, "Fire in the hole!" and I knew what was coming. I got down a little farther behind my boulder. My friend the boulder. Having helped the jumper lay the wire, I knew how close that land mine was, and although it was pointed the other way, the explosion could pick up rocks and trees and meteorites and fling them back at us. "Fire in the hole!" He repeated it three times. I saw the heads go down all along the line. The claymore commanded a lot of respect.

When it went off, I understood why. The boulder against which I was leaning—it must have weighed as much as an old Cadillac Eldorado—leaped as the earth heaved. They had told me not to look, but that's my job. I was momentarily blinded as the flash lit up the night. Trees were cut down by the swath of steel ball bearings. I don't even want to think about what happened to real people in Vietnam as they approached these diabolical devices.

Two more DRAGONs went off, spitting fire and angling slowly across the illuminated land, while mortar rounds kept crunching in ahead of us in clouds of sandy smoke. The enemy vehicles had vanished, and only the crackling of rifle and machine-gun fire remained. By and by a red flare went up—cease firing—and the men were left standing around, looking at the stores of cartridges they still had left. Some rich man had just gotten richer that night.

"What're we gonna do with this stuff?" the claymore jumper asked.

"I guess we'll just throw it in the bushes just like we always do," another soldier said, and they both laughed, high and weak, as if they were just spent, completely shot. It was as if, having spent their ammunition—both real and spiritual—they had suddenly snapped out of the trance into which the ritual of war had put them and were returned to their earthly keeps. But the sounds of war had cracked open the moon, and a weak light, like egg white, leaked down on us from above. The spell was broken in this broken light. Dawn was coming on.

• • •

Tolstoy asks:

> But what is war, and what is necessary for its success, and what are the laws of military society? The end and aim of war is murder; the weapons of war are espionage, and treachery and the encouragement of treachery, the ruin of the inhabitants, and pillage and robbery of their possession for the maintenance of the troops, deception and lies. . . . And yet this is the highest caste in society, respected by all. All rulers,

except the emperor of China, wear military uniforms, and the one who has killed the greatest number of men gets the greatest reward.

Like Immanuel Kant and many other thinkers, Tolstoy comes to the conclusion that war is evil in and of itself and that it is not possible to justify it under any circumstances. At the root of his objections are two main ones: The first is that those who fight and are killed in war, the common people, are the ones who benefit from it not at all. Again, recall that war is the world's most profitable business and those who reap the profit are an elite and invisible few. Certainly not the boys I walked with.

"The deluded ones are always the same eternally deluded," Tolstoy writes in *Patriotism and Christianity*, "foolish working-folk, those who, with horny hands, make all these ships, forts, arsenals, barracks, cannon, steamers, harbors, piers, palaces, halls, and places with triumphal arches . . . for whom, before they can look around, there will be . . . only a damp and empty field of battle, cold, hunger, and pain; before them a murderous enemy; behind, relentless officers preventing their escape; blood, wounds, putrefying bodies, and senseless, unnecessary death."

Tolstoy's second objection is to the notion of institutionalizing violence. In order for a state to wage war, the doing of violence to people must be an accepted method of achieving one's ends. It must become codified as a learned and learnable discipline. It must be taught by professors, and it must be continuously magnified, enlarged, improved on. In Aztec culture before it was destroyed by invading Europeans, the preparation and cooking of infant children for serving at feasts was such a discipline and was continuously magnified and improved on. And as with the meals served by Schneebaum's friends in Peru, I have no doubt that the dishes were delicious. Cortés and company were served such a meal.

For those interested in trying this dish, a suckling pig would probably suffice as a substitute for an actual human infant. Sear it over a hot wood fire until evenly browned, and then braise it in liquid with ancho peppers and spices. Serve with corn tortillas and vegetables such as squash.

So the very process of thinking through and refining violence against people causes a decay of what we value in civilization. To the extent that we become an institution of violence, we become more barbaric. That's why Tolstoy said, "Patriotism is slavery," for patriotism is the religious frenzy into which the masses are whipped in order to send them to war, while in peacetime it enslaves us all so that we must pay more and more dearly to maintain a constant readiness for war. If we are willing to send our children to be slaughtered for nothing, why not eat babies? In the great balance of justice and morality, is it better to kill your son or daughter at six months or at age eighteen? Because that's what war is.

To create the state ostensibly for the sake of the individual and then to degrade and destroy the individual for the sake of the state is an intolerable contradiction. Tolstoy's view was that it was no inadvertent contradiction at all but rather it was the hidden and true intention of all governments to ignore the individual and create states for the purpose of making war on other states.

In other words, we cannot do violence selectively. To do it to others, we must do it to ourselves. For every evil we confer on another, an equal evil is conferred on us. To murder my enemies, I must become a murderer. That is why Saint Paul said, "Bless them which persecute you: bless, and curse not.... Recompense to no man for evil."

The Epistle to the Romans was no idle chatter. Evil *is* dangerous stuff. It is like the claymore, which sprays rocks and fire back at us, or the jumper who thought he was jumping to practice killing but actually jumped to his own death. If there is an institutionalization of violence by the state for export (i.e., war), then the concomitant is always automatically the institutionalization of violence for internal use, which is called by another name: oppression.

W. B. Gallie, a professor of political science at Cambridge University and the author of the book *Philosophers of Peace and War*, writes about the lies that are necessary to conduct a war:

> But in all this falsity, the myth of the great heroic commander of genius stands head and shoulders above all other lies. . . . Tolstoy ascribes to Prince Andrei an attitude to Napoleon which must have been common to many of the ablest military men of the age: an admiration for his prowess and daring which came close to hero-worship, combined with a determination to cut him down to size in his role of national enemy. . . . Napoleon is presented, alternately, as something close to a criminal lunatic—a violent and unbridled megalomaniac dicing with hundreds and thousands of lives—and, on other pages, as a pitiable creature of circumstances or tool of fate. . . . But as a legend, as the embodiment of all the falsity of his own legend, he is presented as wholly evil. In this respect he is, in Tolstoy's belief, at one with all other allegedly great commanders.

One cannot help thinking of Eisenhower, Patton, MacArthur, and a score of others in our history books—or in even more recent times, of Reagan attacking Libya, Grenada, and Honduras, all backward, impoverished nations, and calling it honor and duty. Gallie concludes: "This suggests that most wars, and in particular great wars, have been wholly misunderstood by even the most intelligent of those who have taken part in them. And if this is so it must follow that questions of the use, the necessity, and still more the justification of wars have never been properly posed, still less satisfactorily answered."

· · ·

It was another night of combat, and at dusk we were driven on rust-red sand trails into the black pine forests, the vast wilderness of Fort Bragg. There was still enough light to make out the tents of camouflage netting covering deuce-and-a-half trucks, generators, equipment, and men scattered through the forest at the tactical operations center. We were going out this time to make an air-mobile assault against a missile installation, and when I arrived, everyone was making preparations to get in quick and get out fast.

When we heard the Black Hawk engines in the distance, men began lining up behind the chemlights at the edge of the clearing. I was to be in the third chalk, the third helicopter, and so I lined up behind a young captain and waited, watching the sky. I had been on a lot of helicopters in my life, but I was not prepared for what I saw. As the sound grew louder, the five modern, twelve-man, troop-carrying Black Hawks—long, lean, and lethal looking— materialized out of the moon-barren overcast and descended into the clearing. And their rotor blades began to scintillate with a dazzling, dancing fire.

The sound was deafening. The windblast tore at our clothing. Each of the rotor blades, as thick as a man and forty feet long, spinning at near-supersonic velocity, lit up like a Chinese fireworks display with a fantail of white and yellow cascading sparks. Each helicopter seemed to be topped by an immense spinning flint that cast its fiery light in every direction. I was gulping air, breathing so deep and fast that I was getting dizzy. I had no idea what I was seeing. But before I knew it, all the men had run away from me, apparently unaffected by the astonishing sight of the firebirds descending in our midst.

I forced myself to run after them and made my way beneath the whirling pinwheel of fire and into the open back door. I found a seat and belted myself in. I was crammed in with eleven other men with packs and weapons, and as the craft lifted away from the sand, the intensity of the rotor fire increased until it felt as if we were riding some strange and alien pyrotechnic creation to which the gods had lit the fuse. Only then did I notice that the door remained open because there were no doors to close.

As we lifted to just above the trees, the fire went out, and the rotors vanished from sight. The wind was cold and violent as we skimmed the treetops at 140 knots in formation around the impact zone while the howitzers fired, "prepping the area." When we descended into the white sand of the landing zone (LZ), that inexplicable scintillation lit up the rotors once more, and we leaped for the ground and ran away and dove into the tall grasses for cover from enemy fire. The insertion was quick, and the Black Hawks pulled up fast, blazing into the sky. I watched the fire disappear again and wondered what it could be.

All was quiet. I popped my head up and looked around: the field appeared deserted. But then, at a signal, dozens of men stood and began running toward the tree line, and I followed them through a ditch, over the landing zone, and into the forest, where we sat and waited in silence. After an hour, we moved out into the woods to walk all night, hidden and hiding and preparing to kill each time we heard something outside of our little circle of mutual protection.

When we were underway, I at once felt at ease, without a care in the world, and I certainly understood how I would rather do this than work in an office. I felt that I had a mission. I felt as if nothing could harm me. And after a helicopter ride like that, I felt a little like a god who had descended out of the sky on rotors of fire.

· · ·

War is considered a safeguard against the destruction of state units by others waging war. Nazi Germany and the outcome of World War II are the classic example used to illustrate that principle, which dates back to at least eighteenth-century Europe.

But that is a lie. The aim of war is war. And once we prepare for war, we must inevitably go and fight it. To say that we prepare for war to maintain peace is like saying that a young man and a beautiful woman make a fire and have a glass of wine, light candles and play Mozart, and then crawl naked into a warm bed together on a cold winter's night for the purpose of remaining celibate.

The trouble with all philosophies of war is that they regard war from the point of view of those waging it, not from that of those who are the victims of it—the people, the vast populations, who are killed, displaced, injured, or bereaved. Battlefields are not set aside in war as they are at Fort Bragg. To wage war is to wage war on people, in their homes. And to ignore the individual in any theory of warfare is to lose sight of the central effect of war on civilization.

War does not preserve civilization. It destroys it. And war does not ennoble men. It makes them dogs.

To choose war as a way of life simply because it is more fun and more interesting than other types of work is selfish and barbaric. But since most of the people who actually fight a war are far from selfish and barbaric, we must conclude that a state of mind is induced that allows them to act against what they know to be right. It is the state of mind that all cults must achieve in order to do their work.

The Airborne soldiers go through Ranger school, which lasts eight weeks and is a profound induction into the cult state of mind that warfare requires. The training starts at Fort Benning, Georgia, and winds up sometimes as far away as Utah. It is the most intense, demanding, and exhausting ritual training that the US Army has. Rangers tell me that after a week or two, the aspirant begins to hallucinate—how long it takes depends on the person. The ration is two MREs every three days. "Meals ready to eat" are the modern-day equivalent of the C rations of previous wars. In other words, the Airborne Ranger trainee is slowly being starved. It is not uncommon for a man to lose twenty or thirty pounds during the fifty-eight-day course.

He is also deprived of sleep, which is a well-known technique for mind control. Used by the North Koreans on American prisoners of war in the 1950s, sleep deprivation is used today by many religious cults. In addition to starvation and sleep deprivation, the Ranger aspirant is submitted to an escalating series of trials: forced marches, climbing sheer cliff faces dozens of stories high without ropes, being thrown into the middle of the snake- and alligator-infested swamps of Florida to find his way out. Fear of heights, fear of dark, fear of death, all combine to make one descend deeper and deeper into the self and to find whatever is there and to change it. To put it to sleep, some say. To wake it up, say others.

Robert Lossius, the colonel who took me along on a company assault one night, said that when he finished Ranger School, one of his buddies had sat down the next day and eaten seventeen sandwiches. Lossius himself ate so much chocolate cake that he got sick and threw up. He and some other new Rangers threw a beer party the next night. They invited all the new Rangers. But by the time the guests arrived, Colonel Lossius and his roommate had fallen asleep. The other Rangers knocked and knocked on the door, but no one answered. They peered in the window and saw Lossius and his roommate fast asleep, a keg of beer in the middle of the room in a galvanized tub of ice. Nothing they tried would wake the two sleeping Rangers.

The Airborne in general, and Ranger School especially, creates a cult. When two members of the Eighty-Second Airborne meet, the one of lower rank must say, "Rangers lead the way!" When you are out in the wilderness, wet and freezing, if you rub your Ranger tab, it will warm you up. That's what they say.

Warriors care about one another like members of a family, with a tenderness and attention to detail that goes beyond anything seen in normal groups, such as people at work. "Intimacy grows quickly out there," Conrad wrote in *Heart of Darkness*. The depth of our capacity for aggression is measured by the depth of our capacity for affection. If we did not care about our fellows, none of us would fight to protect the group. Soldiers are fighting not for country, not for freedom, not for justice. They are fighting for those around them. Soldiers who give their lives in battle give them for the soldiers beside them. Flag and country: that's all a *load*.

That primitive tribal element makes it possible to get rational people to go to war. And the quasi-religious processes of military training alter the thinking, the emotions, so that a warlike frenzy may be induced at the will of a commander.

Earlier in the evening, before the choppers came, I had been talking to a man sitting by a tree near the pickup zone trying to adjust his headgear to fit. He took off the headgear, and I could see that he was going bald. He was no kid. I asked him how long he had been in, and he told me had returned to the army after eleven years out in the world. He'd become manager of twenty-five Godfather's Pizza parlors in Texas. "I was making seventy thousand a year, putting ninety thousand miles a year on my car," he said. "I weighed two hundred fifty pounds, and I was miserable. I went to my doctor, and he told me that if I didn't change everything, I was going to die. But the only thing I knew was the pizza business and the army. 'Well,' the doctor said, 'give it a try.'

"When I went to the recruiter, he just laughed. 'You're going to have to lose eighty pounds,' he told me. He didn't think I'd do it, but for the next six months, I did nothing but work out and diet, and when I came back, he didn't recognize me."

Now he was sitting out in the sand at the fall of a cold, wet night, checking his night-vision scope and watching the troops line up at the chemlights taped to the trees. He was lean and fit, and he had found himself. He got up and shouldered his gear and looked around at me. "Well," he said. "Keep your head down." He smiled serenely and wandered off.

His story was not unique. I spoke to a man from inner-city Detroit who had been in twenty-three years. He wore black leather driving gloves with holes in them and had served two tours in Vietnam, forty months, out on special duty as a tracker, hunting down enemy leaders in deep jungle—pacification, it was called. Now he was forty and had five kids, and he told me, "My oldest is Airborne. Yeah, he's about to put his feet into the air any day now."

It may seem as if the army was his only way out of the ghetto, but one summer up in a battlefield laid out on 240 square miles of Wisconsin woods, I'd met another old man who'd been on the outside and come back in, and it was no ghetto he was escaping. He'd had a good executive job on LaSalle Street in Chicago. He'd had the car, the home, the money, the family—the works. He'd throw it all off for going back to war, even though it was only pretend war so far.

"It's not uncommon," a colonel told me.

"Why?" I asked.

"You just have to like the lifestyle," he said.

Before I left, I talked to a military policeman who told me about his father, who was a career air force aerial photographer. He'd turned up in Vietnam to go out on duty, and he remembered standing out on the landing strip loaded down with his M16, his photography gear, his pack and supplies, a .45 pistol, and flares and flashlights. When his Vietnamese counterpart had shown up, the man was wearing nothing but black pajamas.

"Where's your weapon?" the air force officer asked. "What are you going to do if we're shot down in enemy territory?"

"I'm going to bend over and plant rice," said the Vietnamese man. "What are you going to do?"

· 13 ·

Ballerina with a Gun

1 · THE BAMBOO ROOM

I took my mother to the doctor on a hot summer day in 2016. She had turned ninety-five that April. She had suddenly lost her hearing, and I thought she might have had a stroke. It turned out to be allergies, which had stopped up her Eustachian tubes, along with wax, which made it worse. As she was making her way slowly down the corridor of the professional building, she said, "I wish I could get Michael to do some of this." Michael, the third oldest of my brothers, was a doctor. (I was second, and Gregory was the oldest. Eventually there were seven of us, eight if you count the first one, who died.) Ever since my father had become a professor in a medical school, my mother had believed that doctors were the answer to everything. To my mother, the idea of having a doctor of her very own seemed the perfect secular answer to her Saint Louis Catholic family. In their tradition, the married couple was responsible for having as many children as possible. But in the spirit of tithing, the family was expected to give one boy to the priesthood. My mother's sister Mae had done that with catastrophic results for my cousin Dennis. Unfortunately for my mother, the moment her children were able to do so, they fled to locations just as far away from her as they were able to get. I was no exception, though I returned in 1969—not because of some noble wish to join my mother, but because I had several girlfriends in her general vicinity and because I suspected that my parents would feed and shelter me until I figured out what to do with my chaotic life.

"Michael's not here," I told her as we made our way out of the professional building and into the vast concrete parking structure.

"But you're so busy," she said.

"There's nobody else here, Mom. It's just you and me now."

She stopped and turned and looked at me and then proceeded to struggle on. I had offered her a wheelchair, but she preferred to walk. "You know," she said, "some people would have given you up for good. They just wanted to get rid of you." She let that hang in the air. "They would have thrown you away." I suppose a part of me wanted to know who those people were and what the mechanism of my disposal would have been. But I didn't have the courage to ask. What if she was talking about her own mother, Edna, who used to take me to a German bakery where plump and aromatic women in flour-dusted aprons made stollen that was a wonder for a three-year-old, thick with fondant and heavy with its burden of dried fruit and nuts? The women would say how cute I was and would hug me to their big bosoms, and I would inhale their sweet and sweaty elixir. They seemed to me so ripe and full and dusted with pollen, as if they, too, were densely packed with fruit.

Whoever had wanted to get rid of me, I had known that truth even as a child, before I had formed conscious memories. Children are deeply wise. They know what's going on. That day in 2016 was not the first time my mother had told me about my not being wanted. When I was in my sixties, she told me that when I was born less than a year after my older brother Gregory, people had advised her to get rid of me. She could have given me to the sisters at Saint Matthew's, or for that matter, she could have left me at the municipal dump in Saint Louis. I was born on a cold December night two years after the end of World War II. It would have been easy in those days. I would have vanished like a stone dropped into a well. Not a bird would have stirred in the trees. My disappearance would have become one of those family secrets that remain cloaked in a conspiracy of silence. Everyone senses the darkness that engulfs such a family. Even little children know, though they cannot say what they know.

When I was perhaps two years old, she found me standing in the bowl of the toilet, flushing and flushing with the water swirling at my feet, puzzled by the fact that I did not go down the drain. Thus would I rescue my mother from her fate. She also told me that at the age of four or so, I said, "Once you're born, you're stuck. You can't get out until you die."

My father earned his PhD in biophysics from Saint Louis University, and we moved to Texas, where he took up his postdoctoral position in Houston. People with Mexican surnames were not welcome there, and our family was no exception. I recalled the days of rage when the boys from St. Vincent de Paul school would chase me along the bayou to beat me after school, shouting, "Nigger!" and "Spic!" I learned to run fast. I learned to hide. I discovered a copse of bamboo that formed a spacious hollow enclosed by walls made of the smooth stalks, green and yellow, thick as my arms, a natural refuge from the asphyxiating petroleum heat of East Texas. The bare earth was cool. The tall stalks rubbed against one another in the breeze, making creaks and groans and fluting panpipe sounds. The lattice of leaves turned the harsh sunlight into an aromatic dusk. The wood itself was beautifully patterned in designs that made a secret script. I liked the fact that no one knew this place. I called it the bamboo room. Like my own unconscious, it was a world that belonged to me. At the age of eight or so, in the bamboo room, I first learned how to combine the deep art of dissociation and freezing with the hypnotic magic of language. I learned to make up stories there to escape torment from without and from within.

But the damage already done meant that other parts of my life veered this way and that in a fashion that baffled and frightened me. I watched myself perform as if I were a marionette on a string. By that time, I was in college with an apartment of my own. I was writing five or eight hours a day, and this perhaps unhealthy compulsion was nevertheless producing a body of work. I won writing contests. It seemed that I was accomplishing something that was promising. "You're so disciplined," people would say. But it wasn't discipline. It was obsessive self-soothing. It was my gateway to the seeking circuit. (You can see the seeking circuit at work when a cat is stalking prey, quietly, systematically, focused on its goal. You can see its opposite, the rage circuit, at work when you step on the cat's tail.) It's difficult to injure yourself typing on an electric typewriter, so no obstacle stood in the way of my obsessive writing. It took me out of my disordered self and put me in a state of flow that quieted the rage circuit. Yet the writing was not happy writing, nor was I a happy boy.

I sent some of my short stories to the *Paris Review*, and the editor wrote back:

> [The stories] arrived while I was floating around in the South Pacific. I wish I could be more enthusiastic about them. There is a sort of grim scatological and violent overtone to all of them which made it difficult for me to guage [sic] what your own attitude was: "Airplane Story" is a combination of wry humor and blood-chilling violence and I found that inconsistency bothersome; "Running Dog" has lovely lyric writing in it counterposed with violent acts; "A Very Bad Accident" is largely focused on a cripple. . . . I'm sorry. There is superb writing and textures so often, and I hope you'll continue to send us more.
>
> Best wishes,
> George Plimpton

A few years later, he put me on the masthead of the *Paris Review*, where I briefly kept company with William Styron, Peter Matthiessen, and Philip Roth, none of whom I ever met in the flesh. But I hung out at the Plimptons' apartment on the river on East Seventy-Second Street when George's infant daughter was in a playpen and he was playing Brahms for her on the stereo set.

My father was a wounded war hero who earned a PhD against all odds. He moved his growing family into a middle-class neighborhood across the street from the owner of the local Harley-Davidson dealership and also from an anesthesiologist and wedged between the county coroner and a building contractor who was throwing up housing developments just as fast as the laws of physics would allow. But my father by then had come to understand that a Mexican would never become a professor at Baylor Medical School in Houston, despite promises to the contrary. As a result of that realization, he had accepted a professorship at Northwestern University when I was in high school. I later joined the undergraduate student body and worked as an unpaid intern reading unsolicited manuscripts for *TriQuarterly*, the school's literary magazine. I had begun to see my work published in small magazines such as *Poetry* and the *Southern Review* and others whose names I have forgotten. The first time I saw my words and my name in print, I stood in awe of the mysterious process of which I had somehow become a part. I imagined that the letters had been engraved on the page in a sooty industrial building in downtown Chicago by men in inky aprons, sweltering in the terrible heat of the boilers that kept the towering machine, glistening black with oil, hammering away by day and night. Only much later in life did I, like authors before me, recognize the deeply troubling tone of my work, emanating unbidden from the distorted night shift that was my muse, that unconscious place in the brain where we process what is most urgent. The episode of my life that follows does not surprise me any longer, no more than the attraction between Antony and Cleopatra. But at the time, I found it completely baffling.

· · ·

2 · WHERE THE FOXES SAY GOOD NIGHT

I was working late one night, trying to review a pile of manuscripts that the editor of *TriQuarterly*, Charlie Newman, had told me to get rid of. I was sitting in the magazine's cluttered basement office in University Hall with its red leather couch and its World War II surplus desk, when a woman of great poise and beauty walked in. I had never seen her before. She was small, about five feet, with a face that had an exotic animal quality to it. She wore a full-length fur coat and red lipstick that popped in the flickering blue fluorescent light. Her black hair was smoothed back from her forehead and held by a tortoiseshell comb, from which it burst into a ponytail. With the hair pulled tight against her skull, the elongate shape of her head and her high cheekbones made her seem all the more vulpine. The way she carried herself with authority conveyed the impression that she was much taller than she was. And much older.

"I am Mrs. Newman," she announced in an accent that sounded Russian to my untrained ear. (She was Hungarian.) "Where isss Chah-lee?" She could not pronounce the r in her husband's name. Charlie Newman was a dissipated, gruff alcoholic in his thirties, who to my youthful eyes seemed as old as my father. Sinewy and cigar-chewing, he had a cinnamon beard trimmed close and wore steel spectacles that caught the light. I couldn't picture this spectral beauty attached to him.

I told her that I didn't know where Charlie was. She seemed to go slack. She collapsed onto the red leather sofa, which expelled a pneumatic exhalation and a musty odor. She sat with her hands in the pockets of her fur coat. Her knees fell apart, making a tent of her black skirt, and she heaved a great sigh as if she was exhausted. All at once, she looked like a doll that had been cast aside. At that moment I wanted nothing more than to rescue her.

Looking into the middle distance, she spoke softly. "He has a girlfriend, you know. Tula. His student."

I did not, in fact, know. I had no idea what to say. But as we began talking, I felt drawn to her in an eerie, almost frightening way. My gut told me that she was not merely attractive but also cunning and even dangerous, like Ecsedi Báthory Erzsébet, the notorious Hungarian countess who was supposed to have bathed in the blood of the children she murdered. The woman before me had a fierceness about her, and she laughed easily, tossing her head with defiant bitterness, her bright eyes sparkling. As she talked, my attraction to her began to build in an alarming, exciting way that I recognized as the feeling I experienced just before I launched off of the high-diving board. (I had no reason to dive at the university's pool. I was on no team. But some days I would simply climb and dive and climb and dive over and over again for hours until I could barely move. This activated my seeking circuit and induced a calming state of flow.)

Gradually, she began feeding me morsels of her story. Her name had been Ibolya Zöldi before she married Charlie. The Communists in Budapest had shot her father during the Hungarian Revolution in 1956. Ibolya had run with her mother and brother, but along the way her brother had been shot, too. She and her mother managed to make it to the border on foot. There they were allowed to enter Austria. Ibolya had been a promising ballerina in Budapest and was even more so once she was settled in Vienna. She was on the verge of becoming a star when Charlie swept into her life and spirited her away. At first she thought it was glorious, marrying a professor, a budding novelist, and being whisked away to America. But they moved into an upper-middle-class suburb, and she was left alone in a big house all day with nothing to do. She knew no one. Her English was not good. She opened a ballet school and taught snotty North Shore girls in a dim second-floor studio overlooking the roof of a light industrial building. Charlie soon lost interest in her. She began to suspect that he had other women.

A short time after Ibolya and I met, Charlie went out of town, and she invited me to her house for dinner one wintry night. I had a bad feeling about it, but I couldn't resist. The Newmans lived on a cobbled street in a wooded suburb named Wilmette. Charlie had an Italian hunting dog named Matias (Hungarian for Matthew). It was untrained, and whenever Charlie went out of town, Ibi locked Matias in Charlie's office, and the poor neglected animal tore everything to shreds in a rage of mammalian separation anxiety.

At some point I addressed her as "Mrs. Newman," which was how she had first introduced herself to me at *TriQuarterly*.

"Don't make me feel old," she said. "Call me Ibi."

Ibi and I drank vodka in front of a snapping fire, listening to Simon and Garfunkel. Her favorite song was "Cecilia," and she played it over and over, turning it up louder and louder as she drank, while the wind cried in the flue. She had made a peppery Hungarian goulash, and we ate it at the great polished dining table, which was set with candles, silver, and crystal goblets of expensive wine, of which Charlie had a cellar full.

To say that this was all completely new to me is a vast understatement. I had never eaten at a table set with silver or tasted a good wine. I remember the name Château Margaux on the label. I was not used to drinking vodka, certainly, and was far past drunk before we even got to the wine. But the alcohol had the effect of quieting my anxiety and any gut feelings that might have warned me about the peril I was in. In fact, I felt as if I'd somehow been transported to the palace of a princess in a fairy tale. After dinner, we lay on a silk Sarouk and sipped cognac in front of the fireplace. She rolled over and kissed me on the mouth and put her hand in my hair. I put my arm around her and pulled her to me, but she put her finger to my lips and said, "No. Not yet. I want to show you something." She stood unsteadily. I watched her weave a bit in place and then launch across the room toward a flame maple secretary. She opened it and drew something out. When she turned back to me, I saw that she held a silver revolver with a white handle. First I wondered if it was real. Then as she began to move toward me, I vaguely wondered if she planned to shoot me with it. But she managed to cross to where I lay propped on my elbow, and she collapsed to a cross-legged position on the floor, knees spread, as they had been that first night in the *TriQuarterly* office. She lifted the little pistol in her open palm and showed it to me. Charlie had given it to her, she said. She added that she planned to kill herself with it. The concept did not really register. Having come up through my own teenage fantasy world of Rimbaud and Dylan Thomas, Bob Dylan and Sylvia Plath, such a thing as suicide wasn't real to me. I'd never known anyone who'd committed suicide. It fell somewhere into the dim and misty space where such pursuits as war and polar exploration existed, far away and misunderstood. I thought perhaps we'd both do it. Wouldn't that be romantic?

Late that night I opened the front door to go home and found that the snow was blowing sideways across the lawns, the street a foot deep in it. Ibi pulled me back inside. She said, "You had better to stay." I learned that she and Charlie no longer slept in the same room. He slept in the big master bedroom with the dog. She slept in an unadorned room down the hall. It looked like a cell in a convent. A single bed took up half the floor space. Nothing hung on the walls.

I began visiting Ibi at every opportunity. When Charlie was in town, she would come to my apartment. I gave her a framed drawing by a friend of mine who was an artist. In quick and simple strokes, it depicted a man and woman lying together, holding each other. Ibi hung it above the twin bed in her cell. When she drank, she would speak endearments to me in German. She would unleash her ponytail so that her hair cascaded down her shoulders, and she'd rest her face against my chest, and sometimes she would weep. Her hands reminded me of Rodin's *Eve*. She called me Adonis. She drove home drunk in her Chevy convertible. It's a wonder she didn't get killed.

Late one night she had me design the urn in which she wanted her ashes to be buried. It was a kind of Chinese dragon carved out of wood with a lid that would allow her ashes to be put into the belly of the beast. I still have the drawing. The urn was never made.

Charlie's parents had given him their season tickets to the Lyric Opera of

Chicago, but he never went. Ibi took me to *Carmen*. I had never seen an opera before. We sat in one of the front rows, she in her jewels and fur, I in a cheap suit that my mother had bought me when I was still in high school. We had cocktails afterward at the Bow-'n-Arrow, an old art deco bar with a western theme. When I met her, I was twenty-three and she was thirty-two. But her sophistication and accent and demeanor made her seem far older.

That summer, Ibi insisted that I go with her and Charlie to his parents' country place in Michigan. I felt a thrill of alarm that whispered: Don't go, don't go! I asked her where it was. She smiled and ducked her head in that way she had, that vulnerable way that she showed me when she wasn't being fierce, when she wanted something. She shrugged and answered in German: "*Wo sich die Füchse gute Nacht sagen.*" Where the foxes say good night. She meant that it was out in the sticks somewhere. She didn't know where. She didn't care. Life had been carrying her here and there, willy-nilly, for years, and it was just one more place. When I hesitated about going, she turned fierce again and whispered to me, "I don't want to be alone with him out there." I felt the delicious fear sizzle through me once more. And I have to admit: the fear of her attracted me. And through the signals she was sending me in the stream, I knew that she needed to be rescued. Just like my mother. The stream. We are constantly and unconsciously taking information from the environment and from other creatures, a torrent of cues and signals that may not rise to the level of consciousness but that nevertheless register like love at first sight.

We took the ferry across Lake Michigan on a clear summer night and sat out under the stars drinking vodka out of Charlie's silver flask as the diesel engines sent a low strumming note through the steel hull of the ship. Matias ran around pestering people and then shat on the deck. Charlie scooped it up with the paper plate from which he'd eaten his dinner and tossed it overboard. We watched as the wind blew it back onto the lower deck. Screams from below.

· · ·

3 · BALLERINA WITH A GUN

Two houses nestled in the woods, one where Charlie's parents lived, down by the shore of Walloon Lake, and an A-frame where we stayed, concealed in the trees up the hill. Charlie made sure I knew that this was the same lake where Ernest Hemingway's family had owned a house. Windemere, as it was called, had recently been declared a National Historic Landmark. Hemingway had put the cottage in several of his short stories.

We got settled in the A-frame and then walked down to have cocktails and dinner with Charlie's parents. As we descended the hill through the forest, Charlie charged ahead, and Ibi pulled me aside. "You must move more slowly around Charlie's parents," she said. When I asked her why, she said, "Because rich people move more slowly." She was trying to tame the savage she had brought into her palace and to calm my Tourettic nervousness. (I had so many tics at that time that one cruel and cackling in-law nicknamed me Blinky.)

Charlie's parents, Joan and Charles, Sr., seemed pleasant enough, if somewhat boring. He had been the chief counsel for the *Chicago Tribune* in its heyday, but by then he was old and feeble. It was clear that the elder Newmans resented Ibi and thought her beneath their son. She was a refugee. Her English was not good. And they thought she lacked sophistication. The opposite of my view.

The cocktail hour dragged on for nearly two hours as Charlie and his father talked about the ski boat that lay murmuring against its rubber bumpers down at the dock. Charles, Sr., couldn't drive it any longer. It was for the kids. They spoke of the stock market and of Charlie's expected novel, *The Promisekeeper*, and of the Chicago Cubs, who had come in second in the National League East the previous year, 1969. Billy Williams had ninety-five runs batted in and twenty-one home runs for a batting average of .293.

When Charlie's mother made an effort at conversation with Ibi and asked about her dance studio, Ibi answered with as few words as possible. Things had not been going well at the ballet school.

The Newmans served wine with dinner and Armagnac afterward. Although we were already drunk, we stumbled back to the A-frame for a nightcap. It could get cold up there, even in the summer, so Charlie lit a fire. We sat in the living room, drinking by the fireplace. He flipped through an old *New Yorker* and said nothing, chewing on a dead cigar.

"Where's Ibi?" I asked.

"What?" He looked up, the round lenses of his eyeglasses flashing in their wire frames.

"Ibi. I haven't seen her in a while." He shrugged. "I'll go look," I said.

The main room was upstairs. I went downstairs to their bedroom, which had sliding glass doors that opened onto the wooded hillside. It looked as if someone had ransacked the room. The contents of their suitcases spilled out onto the bed and the floor. Ibi was not there. I slid open the door and walked out among the trees and into the cool night. I called Ibi's name, and the crickets that had been singing stopped all at once. Through the scent of pines, I caught the smell of her perfume, an aroma that I would never forget. L'Air du Temps.

I moved deeper into the forest and found her leaning against a tree. She didn't look at me at first. Her hair fell across her face. Then she moved her hand from behind her back, and I saw that she held the same pearl-handled .32-caliber revolver that she had shown me at her house. I snatched it from her. She raised her chin and met my eyes.

"What the hell is that thing doing here?" I asked.

Her hair was down. Her eyes were red and wild. "Charlie gave it to me. I brought it." She was slurring her words.

I unloaded it, putting the cartridges in my pocket and snapping the cylinder shut.

She laughed wickedly. "I can get more. You can't stop me."

I took her hand and led her through the woods and back into the bedroom. "Go to bed," I ordered. She smiled at me, a surly, knowing smile. I picked her up in my arms like a baby. She seemed much smaller when she was drunk. I carried her to the bed and covered her with a blanket. She didn't resist. It was cold in the room without a fire. I closed and locked the sliding doors and tried not to think of Charlie coming down there drunk and sleeping with her.

I climbed the stairs and laid the gun and cartridges on the table in front of him. "You gave that to her?" I asked. He just looked at me with a hangdog expression. "Hide it, will you?" And then I went to bed in the loft above. There we were, three lost souls in a cabin in the woods, helpless to understand what we were moving toward with our inexorable momentum. No one there to rescue us.

· · ·

4 · KINDRED SPIRITS

I was badly shaken by the incident with the pistol, and the voice of alarm had grown louder, even as the distorted inspiration of my unconscious tried to pull me back into her orbit. I kept hearing: She's just like you. But I had seen too much in the woods of Michigan. At home, I began pulling away from Ibi.

As summer turned to fall, Ibi had been calling me repeatedly, wanting to come to my apartment, and a tone of desperation had crept into her voice. I had no idea what to do. I was by then writing for a real magazine, and I felt relief when several assignments took me out of town. I didn't have to make excuses to Ibi about why I couldn't see her. Anyway, I had grown closer to Carolyn by that time. We had met in the English department the year before. She was arguably the prettiest girl on campus, but she was also not married, my age, and working on her PhD in English, so we were able to spend hours talking about literature. Moreover, she seemed wonderfully stable compared to Ibi. There were no guns, no sneaking around, no dramatic rescues.

I saw Ibi for the last time on an icy winter's day. I was walking along one of the main streets in town, crossing an intersection, as she came barreling down the road in her ivory and sky-blue two-tone 1965 Chevrolet Impala convertible. She had the top down, and the wind blew her hair around. She wore big sunglasses, and a yellow scarf flew out behind her as she lifted her right hand high in ceremonial greeting. She did not slow as she made the corner, and I stepped back and caught her wake as she roared down the lane. L'Air du Temps.

I drove Carolyn around in Eileen's sports car. Eileen had been my girlfriend for a couple of years but had warned me that we couldn't get serious, because I wasn't Jewish. Then when I met Carolyn, Eileen lent me her red Volvo P1800 roadster and urged me to pursue the tall, thin twenty-two-year-old with the straight and gleaming reddish-brown hair—long hair, long waist, long legs—and green eyes that fixed me in my finitude. She was writing her dissertation on food in Dickens. We talked about literature and food and politics late into the night. I wrote poems for her, and—better still—she saw them published in literary magazines. We were dazzled by life. We were beautiful. We were immortal. We were the perfect match of abused children recognizing each other in the stream.

I had rented a large apartment in a bad neighborhood not far from the lake. The living room was the size of a squash court and had ill-fitting casement windows, nearly floor to ceiling, that opened onto a view of a courtyard lawn and the sunset. But the landlord was stingy with the heat, and in the winter the wind screamed down from Canada over nearly four hundred miles of open pancake ice on Lake Michigan and right into my bedroom.

It was six o'clock in the morning, sometime in January of 1971. I would normally have been up already writing, but Carolyn and I were deep in sleep under a pile of Indian blankets. The phone was ringing. It was an old-fashioned Bell telephone with a rotary dial and a Western Electric double brass bell that sounded as if it belonged in a firehouse. I turned over and tried to ignore it. In those days, we had no answering machines, no voice mail. I may have gone back to sleep, but the phone kept ringing. At length, I gave up and bolted from the bed.

The office manager from *TriQuarterly*, Sue Kurman, was on the line. Her husband was an old-time radio journalist at WGN, and Sue had single-handedly kept the literary magazine running for years. She was practical, businesslike, and efficient, and I depended on her in more ways than one. In her spare time, she typed my novels.

As I picked up the phone, I was sputtering, shivering, croaking in that first attempt to speak after deep sleep, and it took me a while to get my mind around the fact that Sue was calling me at all. What sort of business could be so important that she had to call at six in the morning? Her voice sounded as bad as mine, and I thought I heard her say that she was at Charlie's house. His house? What was she doing at his house at this hour? Then, sensing my confusion, she simply blurted it out.

Ibi had waited in bed in her nunnery cell until she heard Charlie's key hit the lock upon his return from his girlfriend's apartment. Then she had shot herself in the right side of her chest with the pearl-handled .32-caliber revolver. At the sound of the shot, Charlie had begun running up the stairs. On his way up, he heard the second shot. Ibi had shot herself a second time for good measure. Charlie found her in a welter of blood. He fell upon her, trying to stanch the wounds with his hands. The air that he blew into Ibolya's mouth came bubbling out of the holes in her side. She was dead before the ambulance arrived.

I hung up the phone. I was sitting on the floor in shock when Carolyn came in, hugging herself, wrapped in a colorful blanket, asking, "What? What's wrong? What happened?" I was still numb a week later when Charlie came into the office and told me that he was leaving me in charge of the magazine. He was going out east for a while. The girlfriend, Tula, was going with him. Before Charlie left, we shared a tense scene at his house. I came to retrieve the framed drawing I had given Ibi. Charlie knew. Of course he knew. He sat stiffly in the living room by the fireplace before the silk Sarouk, where Ibi and I had drunk his vodka and listened to wild music and the whistling wind. He said, "You go get it. I don't want to go up there." And I did. Ibi's room was bare but for the framed drawing on the wall. The bed had been removed. The room gave no sign that she had ever existed. Not that she had lived. Not that she had died.

Charlie had been a lifelong drinker and existed in a self-soothing confusion of sexual frenzy. He eventually married five times. He couldn't get it right. He soon had his parents' money and ricocheted around the world, traveling to Hungary so many times that some of his friends began to think that he might be a spy. But he was researching his final novel, which seemed to contain both Ibi and the dog Matias and which Charlie in any event never finished. He hadn't published a book in more than twenty years when he dropped dead of a heart attack with the manuscript scattered all over his apartment in New York. The obituary in the *New York Times* said, "Mr. Newman's novels explore soullessness and atomization amid the ruined temple of postmodern life."

Charlie's nephew, his sister's son Ben Ryder Howe, found his uncle's final novel in boxes after his death and managed to piece together a publishable book. But even Howe, devoted as he was to his uncle, said of the book, "It's not a particularly nice vision—it's humanistic but in a perverse, misanthropic, and grotesque way, not to mention hostile to the type of educated reader who is likely to pick his novel up." He called Charlie "a great hater." And as someone who worked directly under him, I can testify that he was not a fun guy. Yet I felt for him. He seemed unreachably alone and desperate. And like me, he wrote obsessively. I believe in a way completely different from me and Ibi, Charlie and I were kindred spirits.

I continued to work at *TriQuarterly* for a time, going through the motions, but my heart wasn't in it. Some days I found myself just staring at the red leather sofa where Ibi had sat that first evening in her fur, looking so regal and fierce and unassailable. I saw her laughing in the flower garden at the Baha'i temple by the lake. I heard her voice reading Faulkner in German by candlelight: "*Lena sitzt am Straßenrand. Sie sieht, wie das Fuhrwerk über die Wegsteigung langsam näherrückt, und denkt: Ich komme aus Alabama: ein schönes Stück....*" I saw her hair exploding as she freed it from her comb and remembered the perfect power of her ballerina legs. Sometimes, quickened and still quivering, when she was about to put her clothes on to go home, she would stand in my room and go up on the big toe of one foot and point the other straight up at the ceiling, her feet tortured from point shoes. Caught like that, her Rodin fingers outstretched, her sex on display, she made a catastrophic portrait of beauty and waste.

The maddening thing was how little of her was left in the end. Charlie wasted no time in having her cremated, her ashes sent back to her surviving relatives in Hungary. I had nothing but a sheet of my typing paper on which she had written her name and a few phrases in German. "*Wo sich die Füchse gute Nacht sagen.*" I had a few photographs of her, at the zoo one day with me, water-skiing on those powerful legs on Walloon Lake that terrible summer. I still had her ivory-colored copy of *Licht im August*.

I suppose I could have stayed at *TriQuarterly* and continued to be an editor. It was a prestigious magazine. Charlie had taken the student literary magazine and turned it into an international success. I could have cranked out a PhD. I had already taught Charlie's class a couple of times. With our matching PhDs, Carolyn and I would have made a fabulous faculty couple. I would have grown a beard, worn the tweed, smoked a pipe, taught English, written some critical essays and some bad poems. And like the family secret of a disappearing baby, Ibi would have faded into mist and have never been mentioned again.

But the situation was just too weird. I was still an undergraduate, but I had a faculty identification card because of my job at *TriQuarterly*. When I ate in the faculty dining room, with my wild hair and my rock-and-roll clothes, surrounded by the pipe-smoking professors who eyed me warily, I felt audacious and ridiculous all at once. I realized how little I had in common with those academics. And I couldn't envision myself plodding onward, publishing E. M. Cioran, W. S. Merwin, Robert Coover, and Mark Strand for the rest of their lives if not mine. But Ibi's suicide—the reality of it—had shaken me up to such an extent that I knew I had to plunge into writing as a way of staying alive. Only many years later would I understand how Ibi and I had recognized each other in the stream as kindred spirits. I could have as easily been the one who committed suicide, like the toddler flushing himself down the toilet. I quit school. I left *TriQuarterly*. I devoted myself to the hypnagogic flow of writing every day.

At the time I had given up diving as my major serial obsession and had taken up pool, as in pocket billiards. The thunderbolt crack of the break, the quiet tap of the ball, the sizzle as it raced across the Belgian wool, the pleasant tick of its contact with another ball, the leap of the rebound off the rails, and then at last the satisfying pocket drop—even the yellow lighting on the green Simonis felt added to the soothing that I experienced when playing pool. I was so obsessed that I took my custom-made Craig Peterson pool cue on my honeymoon with Carolyn, which happened to be at a remote house in the jungle of Mexico, where *los indios*, my ancestors, had never heard of pocket billiards.

· 14 ·

The Chemistry of Fire

SITTING IN THE hospital with my wife, Debbie, and my former wife, Carolyn, I saw Carolyn's green eyes flash with a defiant confidence. But she also conveyed a subtle joy and determination in her task. She sat in a beige faux leather reclining lounge chair. An IV ran from a stainless-steel stand into her chest. That flashing look carried me back to the time when I first met her and she refused to go out with me or have lunch with me or even go for coffee with me until we had become properly acquainted.

Autumn 1969. At last Carolyn had agreed to a walk by the lake. We met at the park on a sunny day when a warm spell lured the monarchs down from their migration to Mexico. This was the chemistry of fire: We walked the parkland along Lake Michigan, marveling at the millions of blossoming wings hung about us in the naked trees. She was tall and thin with straight brown hair that fell to her waist—long waist, long legs—and those flashing green eyes that drew me in. She was working on her PhD in English. We talked about literature late into the night. We were in our early twenties, dazzled by life. We were beautiful. We were immortal. We were heedless, burning the days. Across town, Debbie had just met the man she wanted to marry.

· · ·

February 26, 2007. Evanston Hospital. My elder daughter, Elena, was ready with her Square Deal Marble Memo notebook. My younger daughter, Amelia, was away at college. Carolyn, their mother, sat between me and Dr. Rodriguez, a small dark man in a blue-gray lab coat, pockets bristling. Carolyn and I had been divorced for many years, and I considered it an honor that she had wanted me to lend support at this meeting. Debbie and I had been married for several years at that point. "Of course, you have to go," she had told me.

The doctor spoke. When I heard the words, I felt an electric current run through me. Ovarian cancer. My guts turned to liquid. I wanted to reach out and grab hold of Elena's hand, get on the phone, and fetch Amelia back home so that we could all huddle together. It seemed as if we'd just been told that our plane was going down. There was no place to hide. Elena's wedding to Simon was approaching in May. We had to think fast.

Within weeks the surgery was over, and we all began making the excursions to Highland Park Hospital for daylong rounds of chemotherapy. We became famous among the nurses. The girls—Elena and Amelia—would come with movies and music, and Debbie would bring tea for Carolyn. We would spread out in a noisy celebration as the hopeful poison drained into Carolyn's veins. Debbie recalled these sessions: "There was music and laughter, food and drinks. It was a joyous occasion. It was a party." That was Carolyn.

Once a nurse, preparing Carolyn for the day's infusion, looked at me and looked back at Carolyn and observed my wedding ring, her lack of one, and asked her, "So who is he?"

"Sometimes," said Carolyn, "a repentant ex-husband is much better than a real one."

· · ·

The girls and I took turns attending the meetings at Evanston Hospital with Carolyn and Dr. Rodriguez and his oncology nurse, Anne. Full-figured Anne with her pink and gleaming skin. Kind and pretty Anne, plumply radiating round her the sheer energy of life. She always focused the force of her concern on Carolyn and whisked her down the hall as if ushering her onto a stage. We took copious notes in our little notebooks. No detail of this menace would evade our powers of observation, as if we would fix it with our words and pin it down and revise fate itself. And indeed, the medicine worked. Right after her first round of chemotherapy, Carolyn took Debbie aside at a family dinner and said, sotto voce, "It's working. I'm in remission." And they embraced in tears.

Her first remission lasted twenty months, from March 2007 until November 2008. When the cancer returned, it was maddening. Her CA-125, the marker for ovarian cancer, was only 7.6, completely normal. CA-125 is a notoriously bad marker. It works for some people some of the time and not others. The cancer was there on the film.

On Christmas, with the sirens warning us to move our cars off the street during the winter snow emergency, guests arrived to find a great ten-point buck standing out in the blowing snow as still as a statue at the entrance to the tiny dead-end street on which Debbie and I live. Like a sign. We were all looking for signs. But signs of what?

. . .

Carolyn returned to treatment with carboplatin in 2009. Carboplatin is a kind of chemotherapy drug that contains the metal platinum, which is poisonous. Since cancer cells grow faster than normal cells, it kills them first. It takes longer to kill most normal cells, but the cells that grow hair and the lining of the intestine grow fast, so they are harmed along with the cancer cells. Genetic testing that spring had shown that Carolyn had a mutation of the BRCA2 gene that raises the risk for breast and ovarian cancer. She'd had breast cancer in 1989. That treatment had worked: the breast cancer never came back. Yet the fact that her uncle Bill had had breast cancer was a very bad sign. Breast cancer doesn't ordinarily appear in men unless they are from a genetic line strongly prone to cancer.

After her second round of chemotherapy, her ovarian cancer went into remission again. Her hair grew back, and she appeared the picture of health. Carolyn believed that she should have lived in post-Victorian times, perhaps as part of the Bloomsbury Group, as an intimate of Virginia Woolf and Lytton Strachey. She dressed the part. She was an expert seamstress. She designed and sewed many of her own clothes, including purses, hats, and accessories. She sometimes arrived at parties two hours late but always made a sweeping entry, dazzling her large and devoted circle of friends. She gave extravagant parties, especially when the girls were little, when she would throw them magical birthday parties imbued with the most outrageous fantasy. In college Carolyn had dated a professional actor named Johnny. The girls called him Mr. John Mohrlein. Carolyn recruited him to play the villain in a Nancy Drew mystery party. He stole all the presents, and the children had to find them. In a *Wizard of Oz* party, the children marched around the block on a yellow brick road that led to the ruby slippers, crushed under someone's garage door. Friends of Elena and Amelia still talk about those parties.

Now that Carolyn was back to her old self, she raced across the city and the nation and even the globe with Elena and Amelia. We gave parties and arranged outings that she might live every incandescent moment to its utmost intensity. Amelia, who had lived two years in Parma and spoke fluent Italian, took Carolyn to Italy in 2011. We had Christmases and chemo and birthdays and chemo, and Carolyn went ice skating weekly, the better to live in the whirling dizziness of the moment. An eight-year-old torpedoed her on the ice, and we then began taking her to therapy for her broken wrist and drove her places until she could drive herself again.

She wrote a note to us all, saying, "I told the doctor that I felt that I was standing over a deep chasm, walking on a tightrope covered in ice, with only cleats on my toes keeping my grip on the rope. And he said I had damn good cleats, damn good cleats!"

· · ·

December 2011. I drove Carolyn to the University of Chicago, where she enrolled in an experimental trial using a drug called Cytoxan. Carolyn's latest CT scan had come back with an interpretation that said, "No evidence of disease." Her CA-125 was nine, well within the normal range. I sent my progress report to the girls with notes that said, "We will find a way."

Our strategy of taking notes was clearly working. We were revising the future. One of Carolyn's notes from that period ended, "We take the success we have had so far, and, wrapped in a sheath of support and love, aim high for the future. Listening to Van Morrison now. . . . Crazy Love! c"

· · ·

I read that the speed of light is not really an absolute limit. But if you do manage to go faster than the speed of light, you begin to travel backward in time. I took that as an encouraging idea. It's what my youngest child, my son, Jonas, called a "do-over." Debbie always said that whenever she watched *Romeo and Juliet*, she hoped right up until the end that they wouldn't really die.

· · ·

October 2, 2012. Morning light, a slow coagulation. A drizzling rain. Carolyn had been feeling a fullness in her abdomen. Pressure on the right side since the summer. We went to see Dr. Rodriguez. Anne greeted us, rosy and taut within her scrubs. Dr. Rodriguez's exam was inconclusive. Anne drew blood. Over the five years of living with ovarian cancer, Carolyn had responded to carboplatin with long periods of remission and strength. Now, just a few weeks after her last round of chemo, Dr. Rodriguez thought there should be no cause for alarm. Perhaps the level of CA-125 from her blood work would tell us the answer. Perhaps not.

We had the answer the next day: her CA-125 had jumped from 9 to 348. The figure leapt off the page in lurid color as if her very blood had splashed there. The cancer had become resistant to platinum, and there were no good choices left. All the drugs that might help her now might also kill her.

. . .

I had a dream that we were all in Door County, Wisconsin, Debbie and Carolyn, the girls and their husbands (only they were still children), my mother (alive at ninety-one) and my father (dead since 2007), Jonas, and my six brothers, all of us on vacation together. Our family was whole, and Debbie had the family she'd always longed for. At age twenty-seven, her cervical cancer had taken that choice from her.

While Carolyn made piecrust in the rented cottage, I picked berries with all the children. Green meadows fell away around us, tumbling down to the lake, and bees were murmuring among the apples, which hung with heavy promise in the trees. The girls carried wicker baskets of red berries. Apprenticed to her mother, Florence Lorence, Carolyn had learned to make pies that were legendary in our family. No one could make a crust to match. The prayer card at Carolyn's memorial service would bear Randolph Rogers's sculpture *The Lost Pleiad* on one side and her recipe for piecrust on the other. We knew nothing of that in the dream, as we ate our pie among the pines by the black and gleaming lake, the girls, their mother, and I, Debbie and Jonas and the brothers, beneath the starry dome. I woke to the acute sense that danger was near.

. . .

I had been going more and more often, staying longer and longer at Carolyn's house. In part it was to give the girls some respite, to try to allow them to live their lives. Debbie was there at times, too, working quietly to make everything happen according to a reasonable plan. She took care of our grandson, Emmett, born in February 2012. She brought us lunch and made sure things went smoothly. She fulfilled her role as a strong and generous member of the team.

One evening she took me aside and said, "Go as early as you need to. It's the right thing to do. Alan did it for me when I was sick, and Margie let him do it. Now it's your turn to do it for Carolyn and my turn to give you my blessing. To do anything else would be stupid." She knew from experience.

Debbie and Alan were a couple for fourteen years. But that relationship eventually ended. Alan moved on to Margie. In the summer of 1996, Debbie was living on her own. She came down with something that looked like the flu. Bedridden, she began to lose weight. She couldn't work. She couldn't eat. Eventually, she couldn't stand. She lay in her apartment watching the leaves turn to fall colors. Her skin had turned a deep bronze, too. She shrank to a skeleton. The doctors were useless.

Alan was beside himself with worry. Here was a woman he had loved and lived with for a decade and a half. Yet he was in a new relationship with Margie that needed tending. He had no idea what to do.

Hearing of Debbie's condition, Margie told Alan, "You get over there and find out what's wrong. I'll be here when you get back." Alan rushed to Debbie's apartment. He picked her up like a baby and carried her to a hematological oncologist.

Dr. Olga Zuk took one look and said, "I think you have Addison's disease." The skeletal visage, the bronze skin. It was a classic presentation. Her immune system had turned against her and destroyed her adrenal glands. Dr. Zuk gave her a large dose of cortisone. About forty-eight hours later, Debbie was on her feet and hungry. Within the week she was gaining weight. Today you would never know that she had been days from death.

At that time, Debbie and I were still worlds apart, yet our orbits were flinging us closer and closer together. Many years later we would plot our paths through the neighborhoods of Chicago and discover how close we had come to meeting. We went to the same restaurants, coffee shops, and grocery stores. We had attended the same theaters, the art fairs along the lake. One year we were at the same Elton John concert. We both went to breakfast at a small café on Main Street in Evanston. We most likely saw each other. Indeed, our grandfathers—railroad men—had worked a few yards from each other at Union Station in Saint Louis. Our dry cleaning had hung on the same racks, like spirits waiting to be reanimated.

• • •

I began arriving at Carolyn's at six or seven in the morning. Sometimes a friend or one of the girls would be there. But often Carolyn was alone. We had discussed moving her into an apartment with no stairs. The girls had taken her to look at half a dozen apartments. But Carolyn would have to give up some of her stuff, some of her beloved library. We had all been working hard going through her things and preparing her for the smaller apartment. It was a race against the clock, and her needs changed by the week, often too quickly for us to keep up with. So during those long days in the changing light, I would go to a shelf and examine the books. I'd find one that I thought she might let go of and present it to her where she sat beneath a blanket on her maroon plush couch.

"Ruskin," she'd say, studying the buckram cover, turning the book in her handsome hands. "One has to keep some Ruskin. Put that one back." Viewing a popular science book called *Your Inner Fish*, she said, "You take that one. That's more your kind of book." And so a small pile of books would grow throughout the day, and as evening descended I'd carry them out to my car and drive to the library to give some of them away and keep the ones I wanted.

One morning I came in early, and she was not about. I called out but heard nothing. I climbed the stairs and found her sitting up in bed. Apart from being weak, she seemed all right. So I went downstairs and made her tea and toast and returned with her bed-sitting tray.

I went to the bookshelf and collected a stack of books. "Eliot you have to keep," she said. "Jane Austen. I won't read those anymore. Maybe the girls . . . Conrad. Yes, keep that. And Virginia Woolf." So went the morning. But when I suggested that we go down for lunch, I realized that she had not eaten her toast. Getting down the stairs was alarmingly difficult. She very nearly fell. I very nearly carried her. Later that week she gave me a deposit to put down on an apartment on a high floor overlooking the lake. "Look at the lake," she said. "Always look at the lake."

• • •

By Thanksgiving she was using a heating pad to ease the discomfort in her abdomen. She was having trouble eating. A brief experiment with a drug called Doxil failed, giving her a terrible rash on her hands and sores in her mouth and further destroying her appetite.

For months on end, Elena, Amelia, and I all had stomachaches. Our bodies were already mourning. Everyone around her had started to mourn as we reached out to her even as she faded before our eyes.

On our visits with Anne and Dr. Rodriguez, technicians began withdrawing fluid from Carolyn's abdomen. Within a few weeks, it began collecting so fast that we were at the hospital twice a week. The radiological oncologists installed a port to draw off the fluid at home by means of a great glass flask the size of a watermelon. I remember the shock and horror on Carolyn's face when one of the nurses referred to it as "the new normal." And yet I was amazed and humbled by Carolyn's good cheer. She never once complained or bemoaned her fate. We had begun to use a wheelchair for the long halls of the hospital. And each time I wheeled her out of the lab, she would raise her hand high in the air and wave at the staff and call out triumphantly, "Go down and look at the lake!"

. . .

December 9, 2012. Debbie and I joined with the girls in putting up Carolyn's Christmas tree. We got her the expensive kind.

. . .

December 13, 2012. On some flimsy pretense, Amelia's boyfriend, Terry, came to visit while Carolyn and Debbie and Elena and I were all together at our house. And in the grand old style that is so much his way, Terry asked Carolyn and me for our blessing. He intended to propose to Amelia the next day. And in the grand old style that is so much their way, Elena and Carolyn shrieked with delight. A date was set: November 9, 2013. The hunt for the dress was on.

. . .

Amelia and Terry gave a Christmas party. The diamond gleamed on her finger. Carolyn laughed as the people surged around her. All was bright and gay. It seemed that we might float forever on this tide of joy and affection with the snow softly falling in the muffled outer dark. Look at Elena, glowing with baby Emmett, not yet one year old. Look at Amelia, radiant with the promise of her coming wedding. Look at the laughing woman who brought these impossibly smart and lovely people into this sweet old world. Surely this was a sign of reprieve.

The girls had always spent Christmas morning at Carolyn's house, opening presents and eating the poppy seed cake of her Polish tradition. This year Christmas was at Elena and Simon's. Christmas morning, Debbie and I arrived to find Carolyn smiling—beaming, really—with a heating pad pressed to her stomach. Emmett scrambled through wrapping paper and climbed into empty boxes. Surely at any moment a message would arrive saying that all had been put right.

. . .

January and February were consumed with the dress. Carolyn and Debbie attended every expedition with Amelia to find the perfect one. Terry's parents gave an engagement party. Carolyn celebrated the fact that she felt well and the food tasted good. And yet there was something about the way she held herself, the way she only tentatively entered into conversation. There was an aura about her that conveyed an impression, difficult to pinpoint. She sat in a chair, and people came and went around her. It was as if she were a hologram, fading and shedding its light. She could sense it, too, I think. After she was gone, I found dozens of self-portraits she had taken, as if to illustrate the various sides of her personality. One in particular struck me later. Her head was tilted so that she had to look at the camera in a sidelong fashion. Her green eyes flashed with intense and alluring defiance. How well I remembered that look.

. . .

As tradition would have it, I was not allowed to see the dresses Amelia tried on, but I was allowed to drive Debbie out to the stores to meet Carolyn and Amelia and then sit and read at a café for several hours in far-flung places such as Highwood and Wheaton, Illinois. In 2006 Carolyn had made Elena's wedding dress out of hand-painted silk, which she steamed in her living room in a stovepipe invented for the purpose. But Amelia said, "I did not want to put that on her, and quite frankly I would not have had the patience to work with her for a year on it the way Elena did. It was nothing against her amazing craftsmanship, I just wanted to get it done." In the search for that dress, Carolyn seemed impossibly cheerful. Photos from those sessions show her grinning, laughing.

. . .

At our meetings with Dr. Rodriguez, Anne, ample and cheerful, began asking, "Are you throwing up? Are you throwing up?"

"No," Carolyn answered each time, a puzzled look on her face. But from the eager way Anne asked, I feared what was to come.

Dr. Rodriguez gently referred Carolyn to Michael Marschke, the palliative care physician. We went March 8, 2013. He was forty-five minutes late, which seemed a bit outrageous for someone who deals with people who have everything except time. As we sat in the waiting room, a young woman came in with an older woman. The younger one was impossibly thin. She walked unsteadily to a love seat and lay down on it, curled up in fetal position. And again I feared what was to come. Carolyn was already much thinner than she should have been.

When we were admitted at last, we were met by a man in his fifties, tall and rugged with salt-and-pepper hair, casually dressed. He introduced himself as "Dr. Mike." He asked Carolyn when she had received her diagnosis. She told him 2007.

"You've lived a long time," he said.

We were horrified. It was like a slap in the face. He said we should call for hospice services.

We went back to Rodriguez. Surely there'd been a mistake. Didn't all this mean that Carolyn had less than six months to live? What about our neighbor, Charlene, who'd had the same diagnosis, the same treatment, as Carolyn and was in complete remission? Why couldn't we choose that option instead? *There has been a terrible mistake.*

· · ·

Carolyn never regained enough strength to move to her apartment, which lay vacant, overlooking the blue-green lake. She, who always insisted that people get out of their phones and books and distractions and look at the marvelous lake, that freshwater sea, saw the lake but one more time on an outing on Lake Shore Drive.

We set up a single bed in her own dining room. A door opened onto the deck, and once the weather broke, we put out potted geraniums, pansies, ivy, begonias.

In memory it seems as if we were all there at her house all the time, though that must not be true. But one day we were all there, Elena, Amelia, Debbie, Emmett, and I. Jonas was only ten years old, so he wasn't there. Carolyn had a sewing room in her house that she called the Plaid Room because it had once been papered in plaid, though it no longer was. She had a large soft love seat in there, and Debbie found her seated in it as the girls sat nearby going through their mother's collection of tiny ceramic shoes. Debbie handed Carolyn a card with Vermeer's *Girl with a Red Hat* on the front. As Carolyn sat there, Debbie watched her read what she'd written.

On paper we have a complicated relationship. But in my heart I think of you as a dear friend. We've come a long way since we met, and I hope you feel the same. You have graciously shared two beautiful daughters with me and now a grandson. Without your compassionate soul, this powerful family would not exist. Thank you for all of your joy.

Carolyn looked up from the card, and the two women stared at each other for a long time before Debbie crossed the room to hug her, tears in both of their eyes. "Thank you," Carolyn said.

. . .

March had turned to April. In the mornings I would help Carolyn get to a chair so that she could look out at the flowers and the fern garden and watch the white-throated sparrows and warblers arrive from the south. The buildup and draining of fluid had continued to increase. Her CA-125 had gone mad, measuring in the thousands. She had begun throwing up regularly. She wasn't in pain, she said. It was just discomfort, exhaustion. At her last meeting with Dr. Rodriguez, she had said, "I'm tired of always feeling like shit." She was in a constant state of nausea.

One morning I arrived to find her sitting up in bed throwing up into a Tupperware bowl. I ran to the kitchen to get another. While I took one to the toilet to empty it, she threw up in the other. I took the full one and gave her a clean one, and she continued to throw up as I shuttled back and forth from bed to bath. I don't know how many times we did that. When it was over, I sat on the bed holding her so that she wouldn't fall over. I hadn't held her that way in many years. She was so thin. She lifted her chin and turned her head. Our eyes met.

"I love you," she said.

"I love you, too."

When I told Debbie what had happened, she said, "Of course. We all have a past. We're all adults here." Sometimes at night I wept, and then Debbie held me, too.

. . .

One of our former neighbors, a member of Carolyn's book club, came to visit. Roberta Glick was a renowned brain surgeon. It was a beautiful April day, and the doors of the house were open to the breeze and to the view of the flowerpots on the deck. After her visit, Roberta and I stood outside talking. As I walked her to her car, she said, "If Amelia wants her mother at her wedding, she'd better have it now."

"Now?"

"I mean this week or next. Yes. Now."

. . .

A friend of Amelia's from college had been engaged and planning a wedding but had eloped at the last minute. She sent Amelia her unused wedding dress by overnight express. The next day Amelia rushed to a tailor Carolyn knew well. The dress was ready in the morning. As word spread, Carolyn's friends gathered around. Christine, Carolyn's lifelong friend and former college roommate, asked Amelia, "What do you want on the cake?"

"All I could think of," Amelia said later, "was Snow White." To Christine she said, "I don't know. I don't know! *Bluebirds?*"

Father Chris at St. Vincent de Paul Church arranged the service. Terry's father, Tony, booked a restaurant for the reception. Christine's daughter Annie, who is Amelia's lifelong friend, ordered the flowers.

I took Amelia to a pawnshop to get the rings. When Elena married Simon, Carolyn had given her a tiny ceramic box with two tiny ceramic shoes inside. Carolyn and the girls had what they called the shoe gene, which made it physically impossible not to stop in front of a display window that had shoes in it, especially when in France or Italy. The tiny shoes she gave Elena were each an inch long. Carolyn gave her a note with the shoes telling her to always keep something that was just for herself. On Amelia's wedding day, Elena gave one of her shoes to Amelia. "I know she would have wanted to give Amelia something special," Elena said.

The day before, Amelia, Terry, and I held Carolyn over her kitchen sink and washed her hair. She was as frail as a doll yet smiling and determined. She would look her best for the wedding.

I was awed by Terry's bravery. A lesser man would have run screaming from the room.

April 21, 2013. Midday. Carolyn was taken on her last ride along Lake Michigan to St. Vincent de Paul Church to see her youngest daughter married. Our baby, who at four years old would rush onto the beach when we'd arrive in Door County for vacation and yell out, "Who wants to be my friend?"

Celestial light shone through stained glass of the church. Carolyn smiled, hand over her heart, and glanced heavenward as the soprano sang "Ave Maria."

. . .

April 22, 2013. Roberta gathered the book club at Carolyn's house. The group discussed *The Eustace Diamonds*, the third novel in the Palliser series by Anthony Trollope. I puttered around, bringing drinks and removing glasses. Carolyn had a small glass of juice in her hand, but she was too weak to hold it. It slipped from her fingers and splashed on the Tabriz rug that I had bought her as a gift one Christmas long ago. I rushed to soak up the juice with paper towels.

"Don't worry," Roberta said. And teasingly, to Carolyn, asked, "Do you have anything to add?"

"Plenty," Carolyn said, her voice barely audible. Then she launched into a complex and articulate legal discussion about the intricate plot involving expensive diamonds of mysterious origin. Her dignified whisper drew us all in toward her.

. . .

Emmett calls Debbie Gramma Deb. He knows her as a deeply loving grandmother and a delightfully good cook. In a way, Emmett has been the child she never had. Indeed, this family, with all its complications, has become the family Debbie longed for.

Now Elena has a second child whom Debbie and I dote on. I think back to Carolyn playing with Emmett and saying, "I just want him to remember me." Emmett calls Carolyn Grammy and is surrounded by reminders of her—the photos, of course, everywhere as in a shrine, but also Grammy's chair that she had reupholstered in dark green plush, and Grammy's bone-handled pocketknife that she gave me to keep for her (Emmett likes to hold it for long periods of time and knows not to try to open it). Grammy's rolling pin, with which she made her pies, hangs above a doorway in Elena and Simon's kitchen. Then there are the many recordings she made for Emmett of Beatrix Potter stories, such as *The Tale of the Pie and the Patty Pan* and, of course, *The Tailor of Gloucester*. So Elena works hard these days give Emmett and CC memories of Grammy. CC, whose name is actually Carolyn Claire, is four years old and very jealous that Emmett got to meet Grammy. Sometimes she cries and gets very upset about how unfair that is. "And I tell her," Elena told me, "that I'm upset, too, and that no one would be more upset than Grammy. And I feel a twinge." CC has recently said that she wants to drop the childish nickname and be called Carolyn.

Emmett listens, rapt, to her strong and tuneful voice as the tailor of Gloucester talks to his cat, Simpkin: "And oh, Simpkin, with the last penny of our fourpence buy me one penn'orth of cherry-coloured silk. But do not lose the last penny of the fourpence, Simpkin, or I am undone and worn to a thread-paper, for I have NO MORE TWIST."

When it ends, Emmett asks, "Is Grammy dead?"

She died the morning after the last meeting of her book club, in April, that cruelest of months. I was alone with her and could tell by her breathing that it was time. I called the girls to come quickly. Emmett, who had just turned fourteen months, was in Elena's arms when she came in. Seeing the situation, she called Simon. He came and took Emmett from Elena so that she could go sit with Carolyn. While Emmett and Simon played on the living room floor, Elena sat by Carolyn's bed holding her hand until Amelia got there. "It was clear that Mom was waiting for Amelia," Elena said later. "We held her hands, and Amelia described her shoes to Mom." They were ballet flats covered in golden sparkles.

I heard one of the girls say, "Oh, Mama. I love you so."

· · ·

The urn containing her ashes, a reddish wooden globe, was nestled in a richly colored wreath of flowers and displayed in St. Vincent de Paul Church in Chicago. There was a tremendous party, of course. Debbie carried the urn on her lap on the ride from the church to the Lincoln Park Conservatory, which Elena and Amelia had rented for the occasion. Debbie was shocked at how heavy Carolyn was and marveled at the mere fact that she held Carolyn in the end.

The Lincoln Park Conservatory, a great structure built of iron and glass in the high baroque of the 1890s, houses a mature tropical jungle. Along the winding paths among palms, fernery, orchids, and bromeliads, we danced as the music played and the slides flashed images of Carolyn's life from infancy on. The urn was on display in its wreath of flowers. Men in livery went among us, as Carolyn would have bade them do, offering delicious treats, champagne, and wine. Debbie and I danced to the "Tennessee Waltz."

Once when Carolyn's wrist was broken after the ice-skating accident, I was driving her to therapy. It was a long drive, and we talked of everything under the sun as we had when we were young and immortal. I said, "I write about survival. What advice would you give?"

She didn't hesitate. "Keep on dancing," she said.

When it was all over, I thanked Debbie for letting me do it, for lending me, so to speak, to the cause. With a woman less magnanimous than Debbie, the outcome could have been most unpleasant. Her bighearted response surprised me: "I didn't have to give it much thought," she said. "Alan was there when I was sick. And you were the love of her life, you know."

· · ·

Elena and Amelia had a bench placed in the park overlooking the lake. A small brass plaque on its back gave Carolyn's name and said, "Look at the lake!" At the time, the spot they wanted, before the old skating pond, was being renovated, so the city placed the bench a block south with the intention of moving it once the desired spot became available. But doing things the way the city does, they placed a second bench by the skating pond without ever removing the bench a block south. So now Carolyn has two benches saying, "Look at the lake!" And that is so fitting for her style.

· · ·

Amelia and Terry were already married when their planned wedding took place at the same church that November. The first wedding had taken place before a small crowd. This one drew a large crowd. The sky was somewhat cloudy, the weather brisk. The girls had had a special bouquet made that would be placed at the feet of the Virgin Mary in Carolyn's honor. As Amelia and Terry were crossing the vast nave with the flowers, a cloud moved away, and a shaft of sun fell through stained glass and followed the couple like a spotlight, suffusing the entire church with an otherworldly glow. Debbie leaned over and whispered to me, "It's Carolyn. She's here." And I felt humbled at the realization of how lucky I was to be allowed to watch all of these powerful women come to know one another, to love one another, and to find their strength as they embraced the rough and joyful reality of their lives.   ·

ACKNOWLEDGMENTS

Thanks to John Rasmus, my editor of thirty years. These essays would not exist without his talents and efforts.